MW00807156

For Rich

For One Week Only

The World of Exploitation Films

by Ric Meyers

Emery Books

Emery Books (emerybooks.com)/an imprint of Eirini Press
510 Long Hill Rd.
Guilford, CT 06437

Cover design: John P. Agostini
Book design: Denise L. Meyer

Library of Congress Control Number: 2010943378

ISBN: 978-0-9799989-3-5; epub: 978-0-9799989-7-3

Meyers, Richard Sam
I. For One Week Only.
　　　　Includes index.
1. Moving-pictures—Plots, themes, etc.
2. Sensationalism in motion pictures.
3. Sex in moving-pictures.
4.Violence in motion pictures.
5. Horror films.

DEDICATION

For Best Friends Past: David Cedarbaum, Stanley Goldfarb, Matt Blondin, Mark Lee, and Kevin Kelleher. With your help, I became the wretched character that I am. Can't thank you enough.

ACKNOWLEDGEMENTS

Too many thanks to even count must go to the three research assistants who made this, and the original edition of *For One Week Only,* possible.

Creative consultant, cheerleader, and support system Rick Sullivan was the publisher, editor, and head writer of the bi-weekly *Gore Gazette*, who opened his home and voluminous files.

Research assistants Jeff Wells (then the managing editor of the *Film Journal*) and Allen White (then an Atlanta film archivist with material going back to the 1930s) were priceless go-to guys.

An infinity of thanks also go to Jeff Rovin, who hired me to assistant edit *Movie Monsters* magazine, then asked me contribute to both *Famous Monsters of Filmland* and the *Weekly World News*, as well as write *The World of Fantasy Films* and *Great Science Fiction Films* books. He also deserves kudos for his exceptional library and his willingness to lend it out.

A firm handshake and a sudden, unexpected pat on the back goes to the crew at the once and future O'Quinn Studios, the original publisher of *Fangoria*, as well as my editorial mentors there, Howard Zimmerman, Ed Naha, and Bob Martin.

Thanks capable of counting must also go to movie producer Paul Gagne, the late great mystery author William L. DeAndrea, and comic artist Michael Zeck, who each magically appeared at integral moments with just the right fact, film, or word.

Then there's T. Joseph Coleman and the whole gang at Lux Digital Pictures, makers of the exceptional documentaries *Nightmares in Red White and Blue* and *American Grindhouse*, who have excellent timing.

Finally, thousands of thanks are due to cover designer John Agostini (with able assists from Matt, Mike, and the whole Raub family), artist Christopher K. Browne (who not only supplied a suitably gritty black and white illustration for the original edition, but a new, improved, full-color cartoon for this one), agent Steve Hartov, and publisher Denise Meyer.

As for the rest, you know who you are, and I saw what you did.

Table of Contents

INTRODUCTION

The way I heard it was: in 1983, a small textbook publisher decided to get into the mainstream market in a big way. Their tickets to ride? A lavish, full-color book on the making of the Oscar-winning movie *Gandhi* … and an energetic homage to the grindhouse movies of the sixties and seventies.

In Search of Gandhi was written by the film's director, Sir Richard Attenborough, and was as meticulously produced as the film itself. *For One Week Only: The World of Exploitation Films'* manuscript was slapped between two dull, unimaginative covers.

In Search of Gandhi was lovingly presented to bookstores on bended knee. Only thirty-three hundred copies of *For One Week Only* were printed.

For One Week Only sold out—accompanied by rave reviews from magazines as diverse as *People, Film Comment,* and even *The National Enquirer. In Search of Gandhi* tanked, taking the textbook publisher with it.

In the intervening decades, the information and illustrations in *For One Week Only* lay dormant, unsullied by any other publisher.…

Until now.

Welcome to the new edition of *For One Week Only.* Tenderly revised and repackaged, FOWO has risen, suitably, from the grave. Meet the new boss, same as the old boss. Because a funny thing happened on the way to this new edition; the genre I had come to praise was buried.

Back in 1983, when the first version was published, major movie studios were just dipping their toes into the bikini and piranha-infested waters of exploitation films. Now, more than twenty-five years later, it's been swallowed whole, leaving hardly a memory crumb behind.

Exploitation films were the price we pay for, essentially, living a lie. Once upon a time, many would like others to think that they were well-adjusted, considerate, intelligent people who would never enjoy—even revel in—the suffering of others.

However, throughout history, the most civilized sorts have otherwise entertained themselves in the most bestial of manners. Whether it was the Roman Coliseum, where Christians were fed to the lions and gladiators fought to the death, or France's Grand Guignol Theater, where realistic dramas of mass murder were enacted, everyone from the upper crust to the groundlings was left screaming for more.

It used to be that many received a guilty, sometimes secret, thrill out of witnessing savage action and titillating topics. It is quite possible that we all rankled against the self-imposed morals of our civilization. In this case, exploitation films performed a much-needed service; they allowed one to receive all of the perverted pleasure of looking at a car wreck without the guilt of knowing that the victims are real.

Not anymore. The major movie studios, who once spit on the very idea of making money off sex and slaughter, now bank on it. Once the coffers ka-chinged from the "body-count" marketing campaign created by Paramount Studios for the original 1980 *Friday the 13th* release, all bets were on.

Today, entire studios and TV networks depend on the "sleaze-as-usual" output of "reality" shows and slasher films. Even the most successful series revel in the carny sideshow atmosphere of disgraced politicians and fame-hungry celebutantes.

The entire industry this book was created to celebrate was wiped out by the establishment's embrace. There was no longer any need for marginalized grade Z movies once blood and boobs were being supplied by grade A powers-that-be.

But that doesn't mean these mulched monuments to mendacity should be ignored. This book, which was originally designed to venerate them, now serves to memorialize them. The films and filmmakers may be long gone, but they shouldn't be forgotten.

It is easy to find dreams and desires within the rank and file of exploitation filmmakers. Most, if not all, began their careers with the hope of making it in Hollywood, and tried to do the best they could with ludicrously limited time, money, and talent. It is hard, however, to find any honest care or legitimate concern in the packagers and distributors of these flicks.

Most of those folks were without shame, and, because of that, they accidentally conspired to create a cinema that can instill a sense of guilty freedom unparalleled elsewhere. There's a chasm between the imaginative joys to be found in *The Wizard of Oz* (1939) and *Satan's Sadists*, but there is joy in both nonetheless.

But enough rationalizing. The truth is that "exploit," according to the *Random House Dictionary*, means "to utilize, especially for profit" and "to use selfishly for one's own ends." Exploitation films were exactly that; movies that were distributed to make money. And the best way to do that was to either, one, make a great movie that thrills and entertains an audience, or two, find a way to tap into the basest desires within people … without getting arrested.

This book examines, trumpets, and sometimes condemns this difference. What follows is a comprehensive study of the "Golden Age of the Exploitation Film." No film is beneath consideration, but much care has been taken to make sure that the hundreds of movies discussed make up a representative group.

This is a guide—a frenetic tour, if you will—of a lost industry, pointing out the highest, lowest, sickest, funniest, and most twisted films ever foisted upon us. Enjoy them for their perverse entertainment value as well as their stunning advertising campaigns. For, as one of the greatest among them once wrote: "If you become bored, pretend it is real. If you become excited, pretend it is fake."

PREFACE

Caution: You are about to walk the line of cinematic sanity.

To maintain some semblance of order, *For One Week Only* concentrates on the American independent filmmaker and distributor. For this volume's purposes, exploitation films are defined as those films not distributed by a major studio. Some of these "major" movies could not be ignored, and weren't. But many others are missing with malice aforethought.

In addition, most of the foreign product is not included. Although that eliminates much of pioneering exploiter Mario Bava (*Black Sunday*, the lushly atmospheric 1961 story of the single day of every century that Satan roams the Earth), Dario Argento (termed a poor man's Mario Bava, whose 1976 release *Suspiria* featured a rain-shower of maggots falling on a ballet class), and Jesus Franco (a Mexican producer who made movies faster than tostadas [his films often look like re-fried beans as well]), it was deemed necessary considering the sheer amount of American exploitative output.

Of course, some are included on the weight of sheer audacity alone. How could any exploitation film book be complete without *House of Psychotic Women*? I mean really. At the same time, many fans may notice some of their favorite titles missing. The reason is that not only is the reader walking a thin line, the writer was also.

Some of the more famous movies must be included because of their effect on the entire industry. Others, as famed and beloved as they are (including most of the material of Roger Corman, American International, and Avco Embassy), are not because, simply, at this time, they are too well known.

The purpose of this book is to illuminate and inform about films almost no one knows about—not those many have heard of. If there was a choice between *The Pit and the Pendulum* and *Night of a Thousand Cats*, you can guess which one is included (you can read up on the pussycats' progress later in this book).

How did the others make the cut? Each title within was chosen because something about it illuminated some dark corner of the genre—be it via its title, content, style, creator, cast, crew, ad campaign, and even, ever so rarely, for the quality (or lack of same) of the film itself.

After much consideration, it was finally decided that the format of this book would be divided into three parts, covering the five major exploitation film genres: sex, drugs, rock 'n' roll; violence; and horror.

Each genre is examined in alphabetical order, after an introduction to the category—occasionally interrupted by sections entitled "Held Over By Popular Demand," which examine the contributions of a repeat cinematic offender.

So much for the ground rules. Like the moviemakers and films that follow, they exist only to be broken.

To avoid fainting, keep repeating: it's only a book … it's only a book … it's only a book…!

CHAPTER ONE
SEX, DRUGS, AND ROCK 'N' ROLL

The birth of the Twentieth Century saw the development of the motion picture camera and projector. Once the motion picture industry really got rolling in the 1910s, things went crazy. Filmmakers started making thrillers to their heart's content; sizzling little pictures filled with coarse action, dialog, and concepts. Prudes were so horrified that the same mentality that led to prohibition began to threaten Hollywood.

The burgeoning tinseltown protected itself with the "Motion Picture Production Code," instituted in 1930 and policed by its creator Will H. Hays, as well as the Breen Office (named for its first administrator Joseph Breen). Under its staunch, finger-wagging rules, things were pretty civilized for a while.

Sound showed up just as Wall Street fell over and played dead. The Depression was filled with bright, cheery visions to lighten the unemployeds' load, as well as bullet-ridden gangster sagas to serve as dark commiseration. By the 1940s, the major studios had a lock on the entire motion picture world. They owned everything—from the films themselves to the theaters in which they appeared. Each major studio had its own chain of cinemas to play with, making this the golden era of serious film-going.

Ah, but there's always the outlaws. Money was pouring into the theater coffers, and many less-than-scrupulous people wanted a piece of the action. The live burlesque theaters of the 1920s and 1930s became the movie "grindhouses" of the 1930s and 1940s. This was the "nudie circuit"—where real strippers were replaced with celluloid ones.

Untold numbers of sordid little films were endlessly played and replayed—the quality hardly better than a home movie. Many films were purchased from European distributors, where the moral attitude was freer (a very few actually featuring actresses who would become legitimate Hollywood stars). In the more reputable theaters, about the only recognizable exploitation films were "warning movies" which titillated the masses under the guise of a training film.

"Don't take drugs and don't have sex," these movies seemed to be saying, "or you'll wind up like this!" The most famous of these is *Reefer Madness*, directed by Louis Gasnier, and starring Dave O'Brien and Dorothy Short. It was made in 1936 and wound its way around the country for several years, ostensibly to influence people into outlawing the then legal marijuana cigarette.

"Marijuana," the ads ominously warned, "The Burning Weed With Its Roots In Hell!" Fashionably proclaiming it "America's Newest Narcotic Menace," the tragic tale of high school students Blanche, Bill, and Ralph gets underway. *Look* magazine synopsized the plot in 1938.

"(It) appraises the crime, debauchery, and tragedy caused by smoking. Sensual dancing and marijuana smoking make a weakling of Bill. Before realizing what he's doing, he becomes an addict of the habit-forming drug. He craves its strange, stimulating effect. Blanche commits suicide. Ralph is judged hopelessly insane. Bill's life is wrecked." Some fun, huh?

Lasting a perversion-packed 67 minutes, *Reefer Madness* was prickly propaganda at its best. Sensationalized, inaccurate to the point that the characters got hysterical while puffing great clouds of smoke, then ran around as if on speed and LSD combined, the film did its job. Straight-laced audiences were so horrified that the evil weed was banned.

It seemed as if the only way to get any exploitative excitement in those days was to make and see movies that trotted out titillation as education. The big break came in 1947, with the release of *Mom and Dad*—the first "birth movie." This film was so hot that theater owners were legally obliged to have sexually segregated screenings.

It, and many subsequent films, were nothing more than short movies—rarely longer than an hour—about life and love that would always culminate with an actual on-screen birth. This may have been the most shocking stuff for 1940s audiences, but it was enough to get the exploitation ball rolling.

It couldn't have happened at a more fortuitous time; 1947 was also the year network television really got rolling. Theaters would soon be hard pressed to hold onto their patrons. Finally, in 1948, the final blow to high-brow film-going was struck. The major studios agreed to abide by what is commonly referred to as the "Consent Decree"—by which a studio would no longer attempt to monopolize all three areas of the film business: production, distribution, and presentation.

The Consent Decree opened the exploitation Pandora's box. Fools and filmmakers rushed in where wise men feared to tread. They pored over the various rules and regulations that controlled the motion picture industry until they fell through a loophole. This led to 1950s "nudist camp" pictures.

Somehow the censors let movies about nudist camps slip by with nary a cut for much the same reasons the government didn't question religious practices. It was proven to the motion picture industry's satisfaction that nudists sincerely believed in what they were doing, so, standing on their first amendment rights, filmmakers shot over the camp walls to their audiences' content.

As the 1950s progressed, however, the theater owners found themselves in a quandary. Television viewing was up, movie attendance was down. They were losing money at the very least and losing their shirts at the very most. These "exhibitors," as they're called, were willing to show almost anything that would get people into their theaters.

In response, Hollywood began to inject more sex into their films than ever. The antics of Marilyn Monroe and, especially, Jayne Mansfield, put the coy puns and suggested recklessness of Jean Harlow and Mae West to shame. While the latter two talked about it, the former two had the bodies and the wardrobes to back it up.

Men who had made bundles on the nudist camp pictures saw the handwriting on the lavatory walls. The exploitation distributors knew that their inexpensive, ratty-looking little flicks couldn't hope to compete with the majors' slick product. If they wanted to keep working, they had little choice but to make a monumental decision.

"The only way we're going to survive," they seemed to say, "is to make movies that Hollywood either cannot, or will not, make." That reality was the crux of the entire exploitation film industry. And they would flourish as long as the studios refused to sink to their level.

★★★ HELD OVER BY POPULAR DEMAND ★★★
Russ Meyer

Russ Meyer broke the mold when the returns from his nudie pictures began to fall off in the early 1960s. Until then he was content to utilize his experience as a combat cameraman during World War II to photograph centerfolds for the fledgling *Playboy* magazine, as well as make skin flicks of his own that were alternately saucy and sordid.

When the profits began to lessen, he made the decision that would lead to his own minor empire. "I'll still show bodacious nudity," was the basic translation, "but I'll also have my buxom women kick, and be kicked, in the mouth. A lot."

One of the first great, and most influential, examples of his style was *Faster Pussycat! Kill! Kill!* (1966). The plot, put simply, goes like this: Varla (Tura Santana) is a heavy-duty lesbian who loves karate. Along with her favorite squeeze Rosie (Haji)—who is little more than a slave to Varla's whims—and somewhat decent friend Billie (Lori Williams), she goes out for what she foresees as a weekend of fast driving and debauchery. But the fun really starts when she challenges Tommy (Ray Barlow) to a game of automotive "chicken" (for the uninformed, that's where two cars charge each other head-on until one driver either chickens out or tries to survive the crash).

After Varla wins the contest, Tommy starts to complain, only to have his back broken by Varla's kick-ass ability. Leaving the cringing man on the ground, the trio kidnap his girlfriend Linda (Susan Bernard) and drag her to a nearby gas station run by an old, wheelchair-bound cripple (Stuart Lancaster) and his hulking, slow-witted son, subtly nicknamed Vegetable (Dennis Busch).

The fun never ends in a Meyer movie. Once there, Varla gets wind of the fact that the cripple might have some hidden money buried about, so she convinces Billie to seduce Vegetable in order to discover its whereabouts. Naturally, in a Meyer movie at any rate, he reacts to Billie's advances with full-fledged lust. A rape ensues, urged on by the cripple himself, who dropped by to become his son's cheering section.

Validly terrified by this experience, Billie attempts to run away, but Varla knifes her for this treachery. Rosie has the misfortune to discover the corpse and is, in turn, discovered by Veg as she's leaning over Billie's body with the bloody knife in her hand. Misunderstanding the situation, Vegetable kills the innocent Rosie.

Realizing that things aren't exactly going his way, the old man makes a wheel for it, trying to get to his house to grab his shotgun. Varla cuts him off by running him over with her car. Thankfully, Vegetable's older, handsome brother Kirk (Paul Trinka)—who, happily, is playing with a full deck—arrives to comfort Linda and battle Varla. Unfortunately, the karate kitten is more than a match for the man, leaving her demise up to Linda, who follows Varla's example by running her over with the old man's truck.

Meyer filmed this opus at a cost of forty-four thousand dollars—a relatively paltry sum. From the outset, the man knew what he was doing and did it with relish—not to mention ketchup. He followed this hit up with one sexy picture after another, some with loads of violence, others with just loads of pendulous bosoms. Most had a steady mixture of both.

That, in itself, was not what really cemented Meyer's reputation. Actually, he presented his crowd-pleasing mixture with fast-paced satiric style. The quicker he could move the picture along, and the more outrageous his plots and situations, seemingly the happier he and his audience were.

The laughter elicited by his broad characters (and I do mean broad) was the perfect antidote for any guilt any viewer might have about watching. It's little wonder, then, that Meyer's films were so consistently popular.

Faster Pussycat! Kill! Kill! is an example of Meyer's early work. *Up* (not to be confused, by any means, with Pixar's Oscar-winning 2009 animation of the same name) is an example of his later films. From the very beginning, the audience is told what it is in for. Francesca "Kitten" Natividad introduces herself as the "Greek Chorus" and promises a "cacophony of carnality" as the barely followable story of Adolf Hitler's modern-day murder is exposed.

Yes, he's changed his last name to Schwartz and indulges in all manner of bondage and sado-masochism, but it's still recognizably Adolf himself (Edward Schaaf) who has all sorts of sexual fun until he's killed by a piranha placed in his bathtub. The question now is "whodunit?"

Meyer certainly doesn't seem to care, and neither should the audience, as several subplots roar right along. Paul (Robert McLane) is having a homosexual affair with Adolf while his wife, Sweet Alice (Janet Wood), is doing the same with Gwendolyn the truck driver (Linda Sue Ragsdale). All these relationships are polarized when Margo Winchester (Raven de la Croix) shows up in town.

She calls herself an "interpretive dancer" (read: go-go girl) and is given a lift by town wolf Leonard Box (Larry Dean), who really wants to take her for a ride. Fighting off his strenuous advances with karate, she accidentally kills him, facilitating a deal with equally lustful Sheriff Johnson (Monte Bane). He won't tell about the murder if she does for the sheriff what Leonard wanted her to do to him.

Going to work in Paul and Alice's Restaurant (which is called Alice's Cafe so as to pun Arlo Guthrie's popular "Alice's Restaurant" song), she proves so successful that the owners decide to let her dance for the patrons. She is so good-looking that one of the eaters, a lumberjack named Rafe (Bob Schott), knocks out Paul, picks up Margo, Alice, and his ax, and runs right through the wall.

Sheriff Johnson follows with his own chainsaw and the two men send bloody hunks of each other over the edge of a cliff until both lie dead. Recuperating in the sheriff's shower, Margo is attacked by Alice, who reveals herself to be none other than Eva Braun, Jr. (nothing is impossible in a Russ Meyer movie). She admits to killing Adolf for perverting her husband.

No sooner does she confess than hubbie Paul shows up with a gun, threatening to kill them both for "not appreciating" him. It is then that Margo does some confessing of her own. Not only is she a dancer, but also a government agent. Paul and Alice are taken away by the authorities, but before the Greek Chorus can tell us the movie's moral, she is attacked by yet another lusty man.

Meyer's career is a good example of the conflicting adages: "nothing succeeds like success," and "familiarity breeds contempt." Welcomed with open arms, the critics began to take serious notice after the extremely high box office returns of *Vixen* (1968). Afterward, Twentieth Century Fox invited him onto their lot to make *Beyond the Valley of the Dolls* (1970) and *The Seven Minutes* (1971).

Twentieth should have known better, but there was method to Meyer's madness. Though he intrinsically knew that he was only truly great when he had the freedom to indulge his love of breasts and lunacy on a shoestring budget, he was happy to take the studio's money if they wanted to toss it at him.

On the one hand, the latter film, especially, was a mistake. Giving Russ an Irving Wallace novel to adapt—a potboiler with a straightforward plot and comparatively sane characters—was like selling the rights to the Bobbsey Twins to Hugh Hefner.

The former film, on the other hand, lessened the charms of his self-made movies by pouring on the cash. There's something glorious in cheap movies that only money can dispel. The same type of tacky film could be great at forty thousand and be just awful at forty million. Cheap subjects, it seems, thrive by cheap treatments. This will become painfully obvious in subsequent chapters.

Even so, *Beyond the Valley of the Dolls* remains a monument to high-class perversity, and takes on further significance as the first produced screenplay by Pulitzer Prize-winning film critic Roger Ebert, who has since gone on the record as loathing gratuitous violence. Something obviously happened between his brain and the screen, because this movie is filled with gruesome little tidbits (as were his subsequent collaborations with Meyer, including 1979's *Beyond the Valley of the Ultra-Vixens*, and allegedly, the aforementioned *Up*).

Happily, Meyer made millions selling his big-breasted, snappily-edited films to the home video market. Sadly, he died of pneumonia in 2004 after being diagnosed with Alzheimer's in 2000. Taking his story full circle, *Faster Pussycat! Kill! Kill!* was being primed for a remake in 2010.

THE ABDUCTORS (1972)
Produced by Ralph T. Desiderio
Directed and Written by Don Schain
Starring Cheri Caffaro, Richard Smedley, Jennifer Brooks, and William Crannell

"For Sale: Mistress In Bondage. Young, Beautiful, Innocent. Price: $100,000."
Imagine opening your morning newspaper and seeing that advertised on the movie page. But that's just what appeared on the poster for this —the third, and best (which isn't saying much), movie in what was known as the "Ginger" series—featuring Cheri Caffaro as the "female James Bond."

Three cheerleaders are waylaid on a back road by a bunch of white slavers. The girls are surrounded, ordered to strip to their underpants, and then bound and gagged. They are taken to the evil head of the ring (Patrick Wright), where they are shown what will happen to them if they do not cooperate. With a flourish, the villain reveals a kidnapped beauty contest winner spread-eagled in mid-air by leather cuffs on her wrists and ankles. This is designed to be shocking but is actually kind of quaint.

Scenes follow in which the quartet are poked, probed, and just generally abused until they get into the swing of things. All but the beauty contest winner finally go along with their captors' plans. Right after the cheerleaders have been turned into the willing, lascivious slaves of several businessmen, Ginger's boss (Richard Smedley) assigns her to crack the ring, utilizing the services of a beautiful brunette decoy (Jennifer Brooks).

Sure enough, in the best-edited scene in the entire film, the decoy is snatched out of the second-story window of a motel, transferred to the trunk of a car, and then to a helicopter while Ginger just generally hangs around, doing the best she can with the otherwise mediocre costuming, make-up, lighting, static camerawork, and tinny sound. The decoy's subjugation is lovingly delineated by the filmmakers until Ginger, as well, falls into the enemy's clutches. Using her feminine wiles, she escapes the kidnappers and emerges triumphant.

The Ginger series was based on a surefire conceit. Schain simply took *The Perils of Pauline* silent film adventures, combined them with the kinky thrills of the 1960s live-action British television series *The Avengers*, and mixed in some nudity. The budgets, locations, and scripts were workmanlike, but filmmaking capabilities of the crew were wildly erratic.

Some scenes, like the kidnapping of the decoy, were sharply filmed and edited, showing some snappy style. Most sequences, however, were awkward in the extreme, with several unnecessary seconds added to the beginning and end of every scene. One could occasionally see the actors waiting for the director say "action" or "cut."

While Cheri Caffaro herself could list many attributes, acting would not be among them. She could shake her bootie with the best of them, and was more than willing to display her physical charms, but the spell was almost always broken whenever she opened her mouth … and words came out.

THE AROUSERS (1972)
Produced by Tamara Asseyev
Directed and Written by Curtis Hanson
Starring Tab Hunter, Isabelle Jewell, and John Aprea

This is a nasty little film that is actually little more than another *Psycho* variation. But while Hitchcock's monumental 1960 film horrified with exceptional filmmaking ability and without gratuitous sensationalism, this movie — also called *The Sweet Kill*—was a prescient precursor to the slasher film. Its other major claim to fame at the time was that it was supposed to be matinee idol Tab Hunter's "comeback" movie.

After a career of mostly lightweight pictures (1963's *Operation Bikini* and 1964's *Ride the Wild Surf* among others), blond beach boy Hunter fell on middle age and hard times. According to reports, he may have seen this movie as his ticket out of the beach-blanket ghetto.

It certainly was a change of pace for him, but not for the veteran viewers of this sort of thing. Hunter played Eddie Collins, a physical education teacher with a mother fixation. After he helps two girls fix their car, he invites one (Kate McKeown) back to his place. Things proceed swimmingly until it's time for lovemaking.

As with most of these cinematic oedipal oafs, Eddie's fixation results in impotence, which the girl mistakes for rejection. She verbally lashes out at him, and he returns the favor by snapping her neck. This also succeeds in snapping his already stretched mind.

After hiding the dead girl in a sheet up in the attic, Eddie goes to a prostitute and acts out a recurring performance. The hooker plays dead on a table while wearing clothes that belonged to Eddie's mother. Eddie undresses her while masturbating. Some viewers enjoyed seeing the handsome hunk reduced to such displays, while others were left to admire and pity him at the same time.

From there, Eddie's life goes straight to hell. The very next day a student (Linda Leider) comes on to him in a deserted shower room. He kills her while yelling "slut." Meanwhile, the dead girl's friend (Cheri Latimer) has become so concerned that she convinces her boyfriend (John Aprea) to help search Eddie's place.

They find enough to convince them that Eddie needs professional help from either a doctor or a policeman, but he arrives home in time to see the pair leaving. He follows them home and murders the two. Well, it's dead people four and Eddie's mind nothing. His nuttiness is becoming so obvious that his kindly neighbor (Nadyne Turner) visits him at work, only to find a corpse in the shower.

Eddie adds another body to the hit list by making a pair of scissors part of his neighbor's anatomy. The film ends with Eddie huddled in the corner, obviously permanently agitated, as the camera moves in slowly for a close-up. *The Arousers* is just another good example of a bad movie … the kind of film that figures since Hitchcock did all of the explaining, all it had to do was ladle on the fake blood.

But in this case, the ladler was Curtis Hanson, who rode the exploitation film's wave into major studio fare, jumping from the glorified slasher film *The Hand that Rocks the Cradle* (1992) to the Oscar-winning *L.A. Confidential* (1997).

THE APPLE (1980)
Produced by Menahem Golan and Yoram Globus
Directed and Written by Menahem Golan
Starring Catherine Mary Stewart, George Gilmour, Vladek Sheybal, and Joss Ackland

We've had sex, we've had drugs, now it's time for rock 'n' roll. Of all the exploitation genres, rock is the least used, and therefore the least abused. The reason is that some sort of talent is necessary to write, perform, direct, and edit a musical of any kind, let alone a rock musical. That is certainly not the case with sex or drugs.

The exploitation rock musical started fairly inauspiciously. Producers would grab whatever rock group or performer that was affordable at the moment, and stick them into whatever script was at hand. Their attempts to pander to the teen audience were risky, to say the least, and often resulted in films that embarrassed old and young alike.

Bop Girl Goes Calypso was released in 1957. A painful United Artists mainstream mistake directed by Howard W. Koch (who went on to 1962's *The Manchurian Candidate* and 1968's *The Odd Couple*, among others), it featured such "popular and memorable" groups as The Goofers and Lord Flea. It told the heartburning story of songstress Judy Tyler's decision to forsake "bop" music for the rising star of calypso.

"Hip-roaring," said critics. "There's enough sound and fury here to win wide appeal from the teenage cats who dig their R-n-R (sic) with indiscriminate craziness."

Things improved mightily over the years, thanks to Elvis Presley and the Beatles (both in music and movie musicals), but exploitation rock films were still few and far between. It was up to an Israeli, Menahem (pronounced Ma-knock-hem) Golan—who had made several popular musicals in his native land—to mount the first independent science-fiction musical.

The year is 1994. The place is the Worldvision Song Contest. The people are Pandi (Grace Kennedy) and Dandi (Allan Love), who are singing the number one hit entitled "The Bim." Backstage, Boogalow (Vladek Sheybal) and his henchman Shake (Ray Shell) are scientifically gauging the reaction of the crowd. When sweet, innocent song-stylists from the Canadian backwoods, Alphie (George Gilmour) and Bibi (Catherine Mary Stewart), sing their "Universal Melody," however, Boogalow's equipment goes crazy.

He goes crazy in return, putting on a tape that drowns the sweet kids' song with prerecorded derision. There and then, he decides that their message of love is nostalgic and therefore dangerous. He and Shake prepare to "Biminize" the pair. Boogalow's wiles work on the more naive Bibi, who gladly accepts their attention, drinks, and drugs. Alphie, on the other hand, is a tower of virtue who refuses to sign with Boogalow's company.

Instead he sees a vision of futuristic hell with Boogalow as the Devil, Shake as the serpent, and all the world's evils as an apple offered to Bibi. To his horror, she accepts. Bibi becomes a Bim star and Alphie becomes a bum. He tries to rescue his girl, only to stumble into an orgy where he's drugged by Pandi. He then sees Bibi in bed with many different people, until he's beaten and bounced out by Booga-low's bodyguarding "Bulldogs."

If you think all this is a pretty lame attempt to copy *Yellow Submarine* (1968) in live action, just wait. Alphie is found the next morning sleeping on a park bench by the Old Hippie (Joss Ackland), who brings him to a cave where all the refugees from the 1960s live after being banned by the government.

After Pandi has a change of heart heralded in a song entitled "I Found Me," Bibi escapes Boogalow's clutches, marries Alphie, has a kid and lives with all of the hippies in the cave — but not happily ever after. Bim, Inc. and the "dreaded police" attack, maintaining that Bibi owes ten million dollars in broken contracts.

The worst has occurred, so what do the heroes do? Do they sing about the simple joys, charming all the cops into submission? Do they fight their way out? Does Pandi kill the entrepreneur and save the day? Get ready for this, now. No, the Old Hippie "waves his arms over his head and miraculously turns into Mr. Topps, confounding and astounding everyone," according to the film's official press releases.

"He takes Alphie and Bibi and all the Hippies away with him to a new planet, where he will start all over again. As they rise up to the other planet, Boogalow, Shake, Dandi and the police stand alone, trapped by their lust for power." Right. Sure. Isn't that a clever ending?

The Apple played worse on screen than it reads on paper. It only proved that independent filmmakers were just as susceptible to the rampant pretension that afflicted mainstream musical makers in the 1980s. *The Apple* joined the likes of the Village People's *Can't Stop the Music* (1980) and Robert Stigwood's *Sergeant Pepper's Lonely Hearts Club Band* (1978) as one of the most maudlin, cloying, brainless musicals ever semi-devised.

All these films aspired to the camp cult status of *Xanadu* (1980), but unlike the much superior half-hour animated *The Devil and Daniel Mouse* television special from Nelvana Animation in Canada (which had essentially the same plot), *The Apple* had unfathomable music, took itself seriously, and was pompous in the extreme. The one thing that exploitation films should not have is aspirations of grandeur. As Rick Sullivan would say in the *Gore Gazette*, *The Apple* is "a lobster … a real claw clacker."

THE BIG BIRD CAGE (1972)
Produced by Jane Schaffer
Directed and Written by Jack Hill
Starring Pam Grier, Anitra Ford, Candice Roman, Carol Speed, and Sid Haig

Ah, the W.I.P. flick.

Basically, the exploitation film can be divided into two types: those where people are abused and those where people are debased. In the first case, the main characters are pushed, and often brutalized, until they have no choice but to fight back or die. In the second case, the main characters are degraded until their whole life is rendered meaningless and they exist solely to be slaughtered. It's good to understand this distinction when discussing exploitation films in general, and "Women In Prison" films in particular (not to mention slasher films, but we'll get to those later).

Whatever they are called, these sort of movies are long-term successes, dating back to the likes of *Reform School Girl* (1960, co-produced by Samuel Z. Arkoff—a big name in exploitation circles) and United Artists' *Riot in a Juvenile Prison* (1960). There seems to be something wonderful about watching women at the mercy of all sorts of sadistic captors. It's not nice, but it's salable. So salable, in fact, that Schaffer and Hill were only repeating the prior success of *The Big Doll House* (1971).

In Hill's movies, women are essentially taking over what had been traditional male roles. If men were searched and beaten in prior prison pictures, the audience probably wouldn't think twice. But with women being strip-searched and tortured, it adds several dimensions to the clichéd plots. This sort of thing could be enjoyed by both chauvinist pigs and women's libbers. They could also be hated by both for the same reasons.

In *...Doll House*, attractive American Marni Collins (Judy Brown, a staple in prison pics) is locked in a banana republic's prison with a beautiful blond (Roberta Collins), a black ho' (Pam Grier, another exploitation staple), and a political prisoner (Pat Woodell), the mistress of a revolutionary. All are under the watchful breasts of weird woman warden Kathryn Loder and her sadistic supervisor Christiane Schmidtmer. After standard operating torture, the leading ladies escape, dynamiting the supervisor and leaving the warden's pet cobra to kill her. The republic's police and prison guards then gang up to kill all the escaping girls except Marni, who makes it to the end credits.

The Big Bird Cage is made from the same bars, only this time Anitra Ford (ex-*Price Is Right* model and star of *Invasion of the Bee Girls* [written by famed *Star Trek* movie director Nicholas Meyer]) is featured as a courtesan, who is jailed for knowing too much about a banana republic's government. The warden is a male this time, who has built what looks to be a "big bird cage" in the middle of the compound.

It's a grinding mill that seems fashioned from a Rube Goldberg blueprint, if Rube liked bloody workplace accidents. More bloody accidents are to come as a revolutionary (Sid Haig, who played "Harry the revolutionary" in the prior movie) attempts to infiltrate the compound in order to rescue his girlfriend (Pam Grier again, switching from the hooker to the mistress role).

This story is played for laughs as much as thrills, since the only reason Grier is in the prison is to recruit women who'll service the sexual needs of the other less-than-anxious revolutionaries. There's homosexuality of the male kind here as Haig is forced to act fey in order to become friendly with the other gay male guards. The result of all this is predictable escape mayhem—wherein everyone except the leading heroine, Anitra, gets croaked once more.

CAGED MEN PLUS ONE WOMAN (1972)
Produced by Avron M. Slutker
Directed by Edward J. Forsyth
Written by Jerry Thomas and Edward J. Forsyth
Starring Ross Stephanson, Maureen McGill, Don McQuarrie, and Abdulla the Butcher

Welcome to the great exploitation film fib. Every connoisseur of the genre knows it well. It's when a film title or poster or advertising campaign writes checks the actual movie can't cash. Back in the day, exploitation filmmakers weren't looking for the repeat viewer. Instead, they were the cinematic equivalent of the carnival side-show barker who would say anything to get you to buy a ticket.

This movie's title gives the impression that it is about an "innocent girl trapped in a men's jail," when, actually, it's an English import about a treacherous tease who tricks a poor schmuck into doing a crime for her. It is he who gets stuck in the cage for a few years. So, while the title doesn't outright lie, the viewer was fooled, the box office has your money, and everyone's happy, right? Actually, yes, because once the dupe is jailed, the picture doesn't disappoint. A guy is burned alive in his cell, a guard has a garden rake's prongs embedded in his spine, another prisoner is raped, and the bad girl is slashed to death for her trouble.

Herein lay the first law of exploitation film-going. The only job of independent distributors was to get you into the theater. From there, you're on your own. Once producers physically possessed a film print, they would use any means necessary, short of spending money, to wrest an admission fee from your pocket. If there is little love in exploitation filmmaking, likewise there is little honor.

Take, as a further example, *One Thousand Convicts and a Woman* (1971), yet another English import, directed by Ray Austin. Here the tease is a subtitle stating: "Story of a Nympho." That's accurate as far as it goes. It is only when one is in the theater that one discovers that while Alexandra Hay plays a warden's daughter who is hot to trot, the thousand men are more interested in safeguarding their paroles than sampling her wares.

This may make for more civilized viewing, but that hardly matters to someone who paid for some excitement. The fact of the matter is that the expectant viewer leaves the theater more frustrated and in a darker mood than he or she was upon entering.

The person eager to see the female version of the classic 1932 *I Am a Fugitive from a Chain Gang*, starring Paul Muni, got little satisfaction from *Chain Gang Women* (1971). Although American this time, the women of the title are farm girl victims of two escapees played by Michael Stems and Robert Lott in this Wes Bishop (producer, co-writer) and Lee Frost (director, co-writer) opus. They are saved and the chain gang men are killed by the farmer.

Each of these films was a pale plagiarism of the satisfying Roger Corman-produced women in prison pictures, as well as such slimy gems as *Girl on a Chain Gang* (1966), written, directed, and produced by Jerry Gross, who seemed to consider his name a divine calling. Although he will be seen again on later pages, this was his first movie, a real rip-snorter made in New York for seventeen thousand dollars.

The only ingredients he needed for success were actress Julie Ange, a sadistic warden played by William Watson, a valiant, noble, black prisoner played by R.K. Charles, and a plain prison dress several sizes too small for the shapely Ange.

"A Shocker!" the ads declared and then quoted one of the film's representative lines, "Any girl that good-looking just gotta be itching for action!" This was the kind of thing that endeared Jerry Gross to his audience for years to come.

CAGED VIRGINS (1973)
Produced by Les Films A. B. C.
Directed by Jean Rollin
Starring Marie Pierre Castel, Mireille D'Argent, Phillippe Caste, and Paul Bisciglia

This is one of the great exploitation titles of all time. It breaks almost every ground rule for appearing in this book, but like a leper at the door of Studio 54, there's no keeping it out. This is a shining example of the public's right to know.

This French vampire movie first appeared on these shores as *The Virgins and the Vampires*. That title thrilled very few, so the distribution company changed the name to *Crazed Vampire* in 1975, not realizing that the audience was more interested in breasts than beasts. Finally, when Boxoffice International, one of the least ashamed companies in the business, got their hands on it, they christened it with its final, mucho-marketable title.

No self-respecting trash lover was going to miss a movie called that, so more people than ever went to see the short (seventy-two minutes), cheap (less than one hundred thousand dollars), tawdry little tale of two rather unattractive French schoolgirls who accidentally kill a gendarme on New Year's Eve. To escape, they hide in a decrepit chateau that serves as a home for some ghouls, led by a vampire king.

Hypnotized into hanging around while their captors sleep during the day, the two mini-skirted heroines are then forced to lure unsuspecting victims into the castle. The top-billed of the two finds she cannot turn over her handsome prey, while the other sees her victim killed by the bloodsucking cult. After hiding her newly found lover in the huge chateau, the prettier one rejoins her companion just as the vampire is about to initiate them into the world of the undead. In other words, he's all set to drink their blood when he senses that she is no longer a virgin. Through his psychic powers he realizes that she had been "intact" just the night before, so her despoiler had to be nearby.

First, the prettier girl's friend is buried alive in an attempt to get the girl to tell the villains where her lover is. When that doesn't work, her chum is dug up and the vampire makes a show of setting them both free, but they are followed to the cemetery where her lover waits to fight for their slightly soiled virtue. Only after he beats the demons back does he leave the prettier girl for getting him involved in such shenanigans in the first place. Depressed, dejected, and defeated, the vampire decides that he's had it with humans. He enters his tomb and seals it off, allowing the two vixens to lead their own lives, for better or worse.

Admittedly, this is a pretty crummy viewing experience. Jean Rollin is one of the great hack European moviemakers. He started his career by providing thirty minutes of sex scenes to be spliced into an hour-long American film bought by a friend. That resulted in *The Vampire's Rape* (1967), made at a cost of five thousand dollars. *The Nude Vampire* (1970) came next, utilizing a seventy-thousand-dollar budget. Finally, there was *The Vampire's Thrill* (1973), a predecessor of the above-described film.

One big difference between *Caged Virgins* and the likes of *Chain Gang Women* is that the latter promised something it could have supplied but didn't. The former had a come-on title that made most knowledgeable viewers go just to see what it was all about. Almost no one expected to see caged virgins, and left the theater realizing that *Buried Virgin* wasn't as catchy a title. Those people might not be happy to know that Jean Rollin is still working. His *Fiancée of Dracula* came out in 2002.

THE DOLL SQUAD (1973)
Produced and Directed by Ted V. Mikels
Written by Jack Richesin, Pamela Eddy, and Ted V. Mikels
Starring Michael Ansara, Francine York, Anthony Eisley, and Tura Santana

This film is important for three reasons. One, it was seemingly the last gasp of T. V. Mikels, a man exploitation audiences had come to trust for outrageous entertainment. Two, it marked the return of Tura Santana, the heavy-hitting lesbian of *Faster Pussycat! Kill! Kill!* Three, it shows what happens when a small independent production company becomes too big for its britches.

Mikels had slowly been building up to *Doll Squad* after fourteen films made in a period of seven years. From *Strike Me Deadly* in 1965 to *Blood Orgy of the She Devils* in 1972, Mikels had maintained a good record of entertaining pictures. Finally though, he decided to try to hit the big time. That is almost always a fatal mistake. The lack of pretension and, most importantly, the vitality of the inexpensive quickies are almost always suffocated in the search for too high a goal.

Once the movie begins, some might fear they had stumbled into a showing of an alternate universe *Dr. No* (1963). Like that first James Bond movie, *Doll Squad* starts with the sabotage of a space launch. As in TV's *Charlie's Angels* (which this film predates by three years), Senator Stockwell (John Carter) and CIA Head Victor Connelly (Anthony Eisley) immediately call on the leader of the "Doll Squad"— a shapely independent operative named Sabrina Kincaid (Francine York).

She, in turn, calls on her karate operative Carol (Carol Terry) and pathologist Cherisse (Bret Zeller), only to be attacked by a pack of goons led by the evil Munson (Herb Robins). Sabrina escapes with her life by burning Munson with a hidden cigarette lighter, but the other girls are put out of action permanently. Now certain she is on the right track, Sabrina continues to investigate until secretary Nancy Malone (Lisa Garrett) commits suicide. Her death confirms Sabrina's suspicions, since the dead girl had been liaison to disgraced ex–CIA agent Eamon O'Reilly (played by continental Michael Ansara).

This looks like a job for the new Doll Squad! They are Sharon O'Connor (Leigh Christian), Elizabeth White (Judy McConnell), a girl known only as "Cat" (Sherri Vernon), and the ever-sultry Lavelle Sumara (Tura Santana). Together they locate O'Reilly's island headquarters and take off after him. Waiting for them are Joseph (William Bagdad), Rafael (Rafael Campos), and a set of twins: Dr. Cahayman (Gustave Unger) and Mr. Cahayman (Bertil Unger)—all under O'Reilly's thrall.

While this bunch holds the Doll Squad off, the disgraced CIA agent tells his international allies the plan at his desert hideout. Unless all the governments hand over the rule of the world to him, he will start another bubonic plague. Sabrina sets her team off to kill all the guards and plant dynamite charges while she sets off to face O'Reilly. On the way, she makes quick work of the scarred Munson and the drug-addled Rafael. When she finally meets her enemy face-to-face, it is revealed that they were once lovers.

Under the guise of a simple talk, the two desperately try to kill each other. Sabrina breaks the lovey-dovey spell by letting O'Reilly have it across the chops with a "mace-ring" and then finishes the job with a well-placed sword. The Doll Squad blow up Joseph, the fortress, and Dr. Cahayman when Sabrina gives the word. They destroy the remainder of the guards—led by Mr. Cahayman—with a bazooka before returning to safety and reporting success to Stockwell and Connelly.

Sounds great, doesn't it? But it wasn't. Once again, the poster proves better to look at than the finished movie. It has more action and better style. The actual film contains a great deal of posing by the girls, but precious few convincing sequences. It was hardly the blockbuster Mikels seemed to be hoping for. Apparently, plans were in the works for *The Return of the Doll Squad*, an "oblique blow for women's lib ... since it will involve two divergent doll squads, each in conflict against the other."

But it was not to be. While Geneni Films released the first *Doll Squad* in 1973, it was re-released by Feature Faire films in 1975, and again by Crown International pictures in 1980 under the title *Hustler Squad*. None made a dent in the public consciousness, but it is interesting to note that when *Charlie's Angels* hit the airwaves its lead operative was also named Sabrina.

Mikels, like Jean Rollin, continues to work. You'll see him again in this book, as well as on DVD shelves with such titles as *Mark of the Astro-Zombies* (2002) and *Demon Haunt* (2009).

★★★ HELD OVER BY POPULAR DEMAND: ★★★
Andy Milligan

This extraordinary filmmaker has more than twenty-five films to his credit, most made in the decade between 1963 and 1973. These include at least ten horror films but also at least a dozen sexploitation efforts. And not one is known to any civilized being outside grindhouses.

In fact, those who did know of him thought he was an Englishman, since many of his flicks took place in the U.K. and featured English-accented actors. At least three books list Milligan as British. This is not one of them. In fact, Andrew was a Staten Island resident who made most of his movies there before buying an Off-

Broadway theater. His Britishy period pieces extended from his love of costumes, inspired by his work in the garment industry. But then he bought his first sixteen millimeter camera and made his first movie.

The confusion is also maintained by fans of his gory horror efforts. There are no such problems for those who've seen any of his sexually oriented pictures. Those are as American as apple pie, prostitutes, and penicillin injections. Take, for example, *The Filthy Five* (1968), an early effort directed and photographed by Milligan.

Rita Roman (Anne Linden) is a washed-up actress and drug addict. She needs a fix bad so she can talk to her agent about a comeback in some sort of coherent fashion. In order to get the drugs, she is forced to make love to a pusher named Freakout (Larry Ree) because she has no money. Artificially calmed by the depressant, she is informed by her agent (Gerald Jacuzzo) that the networks have a new sitcom for her about an actress and a boxer.

To keep the series realistic, they've brought in a real washed-up pugilist, Johnny Longo (Matt Garth), who lives with, and is serviced by, prostitute Rose White (Jackie Colton). Well, it's hate at first sight for Rita, and Rose is petrified that Johnny's success will take him away from her, so the two women hit upon a clever plan. They stage an orgy at Rose's place, where they spike Johnny's drink with LSD. He gets so hopped up that he falls out a window, mangling both his legs. The word comes in: Johnny will be in a wheelchair for the rest of his life. That means Rita doesn't have to star with him and Rose has him on the dependent end.

Not exactly a fairy tale for our times, but Milligan was one of the first to inject wholesale profanity and casual use of hard drugs in his films. It didn't endear him to the mainstream, but it made money for the distributors—especially since Milligan rarely spent more than a week and fifteen thousand dollars on any picture.

His sex dramas allowed him to lavish gore galore on his horror films. He was one of the first to be completely shameless in its use. Two of his greatest-loved wretch fests were *Bloodthirsty Butchers* (1970) and *The Rats Are Coming, the Werewolves Are Here* (1971).

"Too Sensual To Miss If You're Curious," said the former's ingenious ad campaign. "Too Terrifying To See If You're Yellow!"—establishing the less-than-subliminal connection to the popular arthouse skin flick *I Am Curious Yellow* (1967). Producer William Mishkin was very cunning about that sort of thing.

As surprising as it might be for Broadway theatergoers, *Bloodthirsty Butchers* was a nascent film version of the Sweeny Todd story, with a few bloody embellishments. John Miranda played Sweeny, the demon barber of Fleet Street, who supplies choice human cuts for Mrs. Maggie Lovett (Jane Helay), the meatpie maker next store.

In this movie, however, Sweeny is given a run for his murderous money by

Tobias Ragg (Berwick Kaler), Mrs. Lovett's head butcher. While Todd is dispatching customer after customer, Ragg is hacking Lovett's husband, Sweeny's wife, and his own girlfriend to death. The competition finally becomes too much for the men to bear. They have a competition to see exactly who is the best butcher, resulting in both their deaths. Mrs. Lovett, in the meantime, is caught with her meatpies down by her salesgirl (Anabelle Wood), who has alerted the police.

What could serve as Milligan's "Odd Couple" picture was another inventive collaboration between director and producer. Milligan had finished a movie about a whole family of lycanthropes he envisioned calling *Curse of the Full Moon*. Unfortunately, the length of the finished film was only sixty-seven minutes, and Mishkin needed it to be at least eighty to have it well-distributed.

On the producer's suggestion, Milligan then shot more footage incorporating the subject of flesh-eating rats, since the mainstream horror rat movie *Willard* (1971) had done so well. The ninety-minute result was the mish-mashed *Rats Are Coming, Werewolves Are Here*—another sterling example of a "high concept" title.

"High concept" is defined as gleaning an entire film's story from one sentence. For example, *Werewolf in a Girl's Dormitory* (a 1963 Italian film directed by Richard Benson). After coming up with that title, actually making the movie is fairly redundant. In these cases, the pictures can never live up to the titles. Titles like these are often the last refuge of desperate producers. Usually the more extreme a title, the less entertaining the film. Audiences be warned.

But back to Milligan's movies. Having considered one of his first sensual extravaganzas, it is only fair to look at one of his last. *Fleshpot on 42nd Street* (1973) has the same endearing qualities that set the rest of his films apart. Namely, grainy sixteen millimeter filming, cheap production values, and self-deprecating dialogue.

Diana Lewis, a veteran of hardcore sex movies, stars as Dusty, a three-year veteran of prostitution who still looks as if she just stepped out of college. Her life is no preppy dream, however. Kicked out by her boyfriend because he's run out of dough, she hocks his television and obtains the price she wants by giving the pawnbroker something extra on the side (wink-wink, nudge-nudge).

Her transvestite friend, Cherry (Lynn Flanagan), comes to her rescue by offering living space in his apartment. Dusty repays his kindness by splitting all her hooking fees with him. Complications arise, among other things, when Dusty falls in love with a lawyer (Bob Walters) whom she picks up in a bar. Happily, he falls in love with her as well, promising that her past means nothing to him.

Even though Dusty fully intends to move out of Cherry's place and into Bob the lawyer's, she must honor a previous commitment to partake in an orgy. That turns out to be no fun at all, climaxed—in a manner of speaking—by the brutal beating of Cherry. Awash in a sea of perversion, Dusty sets out to find her lawyer love, only to discover that he's been run over by a car.

Poor Dusty's last chance at happiness is dashed by four steel-belted radials—a beloved, well-worn plot device immortalized by a classic *National Lampoon* article about "How to Write Good," which suggested every story end with the characters getting run over by a truck. Milligan followed suit here, as did Peter Traynor in 1977's *Death Game* and John Hough's *Dirty Mary, Crazy Larry* (1974), which featured magically appearing climatic vans and trains. Spoiler Alert.

Dusty, meanwhile, is forced to continue tricking on Forty-Second Street to survive. Andy Milligan did much the same, relocating to California and toiling on such pictures as *Carnage* (1984), *Weirdo* (1989), and *Monstrosity* (1989) before his death in 1991.

GALAXINA (1981)
Produced by Marilyn J. Tenser
Directed and Written by William Sachs
Starring Dorothy Stratten, Steven Macht, Avery Schreiber, and James David Hinton

William Sachs does his best work before word one of the script is written, and frame one of the movie is filmed. He was an exceptional idea man. Unfortunately, he was far from exceptional in terms of script and visual style. His pictures are exercises in audience frustration since almost anyone can see the promise inherent in his concepts, but at the same time they can also see his labored, unimaginative visualization of them.

This film concerns a thirty-first-century starship sent on a mission to recover the "Blue Star"—a gem that can harness the power of the universe—from a half-lizard/half-robot villain named Ordric (Ronald Knight) in a world of cannibals and futuristic bikers. On board the ship are Captain Butt (Avery Schreiber), space cowboy Buzz (James David Hinton), a black engineer with wings (Lionel Smith), a wizened Asian engineer who spouts truisms that make no sense (Tad Horino), Sgt. Thor (Steven Macht), and their voluptuous robot Galaxina (Dorothy Stratten).

The first third of the movie crawls along with introductions of the characters. A dinner scene is showcased in which it is discovered that Galaxina cannot speak and is programmed to electrically shock anyone who touches her. While she changes from her white body stocking to a French maid uniform to serve the humans, Captain Butt decides to eat an alien egg (for no understandable reason other than to waste time).

After a few minutes of Schreiber's comedy takes, a little alien creature pops out of his mouth and escapes into the bowels of the ship — not so neatly lampooning a similar scene in *Alien* (1980). Finally, the crew gets their orders after Thor risks electrocution to kiss Galaxina.

Knowing that the trip to retrieve the Blue Star will take them more than two decades, they have one last bash at an intergalactic brothel—a trip that serves to get Galaxina jealous. When the crew returns to enter their suspended animation chambers for the long voyage, the robot uses their down time to reprogram herself.

When the crew awakes, it is revealed that the little alien Schreiber gave life to thinks he is its mother. It has opened Butt's chamber right after take-off, making the Captain an old bearded man by the time they arrive at their destination. Thor, in the meantime, is amazed to find that Galaxina can talk and touch, and sports the niftiest low-cut sleeping gown ever seen.

The spaceship crash lands on the planet, giving everyone whiplash except the girl robot, who must now take on the villain herself. After entering a Western ghost town filled with human-eating aliens—including a Mr. Spock satire named Mr. Spot (David Cox)—she defeats the villain in a shoot-out, but is captured by a bunch of bikers who worship the god Harley Davidson.

Back at the ship, Thor heals his neck in an argument with Buzz, so they both race to Galaxina's rescue. Jumping on the motorcycle deity, they outrace the bikers and get back just in time to be captured by the resurrected robot villain. It is finally foiled by Butt's alien "son," but not before the ship's profanity-spewing, rock-eating alien prisoner ingests the Blue Star.

Done with style and verve, this all might have worked, but, instead, it was painfully disjointed, arbitrary, and dull. Sachs had all of the ingredients for an enjoyable outing, but just couldn't get it together. Even sadder, Dorothy Stratten—*Playboy's* Playmate of the Year—who almost saved the film on looks alone, was murdered by her estranged husband just before this movie was released. Tragically, violence is not only confined to the second chapter of this book.

HALLUCINATION GENERATION (1967)
Directed and Written by Edward Mann
Starring George Montgomery, Tom Baker, and Danny Stone

Reefer Madness may have helped get marijuana banned, but it also set the stage for many more maniacal anti-drug pictures. The most successful of these was Roger Corman's *The Trip* (1967), written by Jack Nicholson (yes, the Jack Nicholson) and starring Peter Fonda, Bruce Dern, and Susan Strasberg. Although, essentially, a straightforward delineation of one LSD trip, a prologue narration was tacked on to warn the audience about the adverse effects of the drug.

Some wonder why drug movies did not become as big as sex, violence, or horror films. Drugs seem to be a natural method with which to instigate horror, violence, and sex, but films concentrating on drug-taking still make up but a small minority of all exploitation product.

It seems obvious that sex, violence, and horror are preferred by the powers-that-be over drug-taking. Rarely does one see a narrated prologue warning about the adverse effects of prostitution, gunfights, or exorcisms. Only in drug movies is the moral almost always made absurdly clear.

Hallucination Generation was just one of the several films on the subject. Movies like *High* (1970), directed and written by Larry Kent, and *The Hooked Generation* (1968), produced and directed by William Grefe, belabored the same point. Here, George Montgomery, a fifty-one-year-old actor, whose career started in 1935 and spanned many entertaining westerns, starred as Eric, a bad guy who takes advantage of some disenchanted American teens living off the coast of Spain.

He convinces Denny (Tom Baker, though not to be confused with the Tom Baker who played the fourth Doctor Who) to help him rob an antiques dealer, but must feed Bill (Danny Stone) LSD to make him go along. In the process of the robbery, Denny kills the store owner, Eric is arrested, and Bill goes to the monks headquartered high above Barcelona to beg forgiveness. This was sledgehammer piety that didn't sit well with viewers. Corman's *The Trip* is now considered a milestone because it allowed the audience to make up their own morals.

Hallucination Generation was nowheresville, man.

THE HAPPY HOOKER GOES HOLLYWOOD (1979)
Produced by Menahem Golan and Yoram Globus
Directed by Alan Roberts
Written by Devin Goldenberg
Starring Martine Beswicke, Adam West, Phil Silvers, and Edie Adams

And why not? Especially since *The Happy Hooker* (1975) was all but sterilized in its translation from dirty book to pristine screen. Lynn Redgrave, of all people, starred as infamous prostitute Xaviera Hollander in the white-washed version of her sizzling career. This first film was definitely "PG" and, as such, made some good money. Golan and Globus saw a chance to make even more cash with an R-rated sequel.

So deciding, long-time English exploitation film actress Martine Beswicke (who can claim such Hammer Studio's horror films as 1968's *Slave Girls* and 1971's

Dr. Jekyll and Sister Hyde to her credit) starred as Hollander in this completely fictional soft-core romp. The plot proceeds from the premise that the notorious brothel madam has the film rights to her life story bought by Hollywood's biggest mogul William B. Warkoff (Phil Silvers).

Xaviera is flown to California and is met by hot-blooded Warkoff Studio director Lionel Lamely (Adam West of TV *Batman* fame). He shows her a good time in various Los Angeles restaurants, and she shows him a great time in bed. That doesn't make Lamely's previous girlfriend (Lindsay Bloom) too happy, so she secretly videotapes the bedroom action to embarrass her beau.

The trick works and Hollander leaves the employ of Warkoff, but not before signing a contract with small print that says if she decides to make her own movie and doesn't finish before February 25th, the studio boss receives all film rights free. In waltzes youthful wunderkind Robby Rottman (Chris Lemmon, Jack's son), Warkoff's grandson, with his own script adaptation of Hollander's story that the hooker would be happy to make.

In order to raise the needed capital, Xaviera brings in all her East Coast sex talent and sets up a wildly profitable West Coast operation. She fills the cinematic coffers while Warkoff and company plot to sabotage the production. They hire goons to steal the film while Hollander sensuously lures both Lamely and Warkoff's son-in-law (Richard Deacon) to the same hotel room at the same time.

Warkoff's plan fails, but hers works perfectly, up to and including taking the men's clothes and leaving them in dresses. Although no one thinks to call up a friend to deliver the proper attire, they try to leave the establishment in drag and are arrested as transvestites. Finally, Warkoff hijacks the finished film on the way from the lab to the premiere theater. Robby saves the day and the film rolls just in time.

Beswicke was the third to play the part, after Lynn Redgrave in the original film and Joey Heatherton in *The Happy Hooker Goes to Washington* (1977). For what it's worth, Martine wears the part best, and the nicest thing that can be said about this and Golan-Globus' other genre picture, *The Apple*, is that they certainly had their hearts in the right place.

Their company, Cannon Films, conceives very commercial ideas, but then they go ahead and nurture some truly moronic product. As slick as most of Golan-Globus' Cannon movies were, their manner of presenting tried-and-true formulas was extremely tired.

A HISTORY OF THE BLUE MOVIE (1970)
Produced and Directed by Alex de Renzy
Starring Incognito

Enjoy this. It will be your only chance to get X-rated thrills (of a sensual kind) throughout the remainder of these pages. There is no doubt that hard-core sex movies make up a great portion of the exploitation film market, but they are a subject unto themselves. It is far too broad and deep a subject to be incorporated into the odd pictures this book champions.

It would be unfair to ignore them completely, however. Therefore, this all-encompassing title, made by a well-known nudie director. Actually, this is a rather labored little ditty—a documentary that shows clips from stag films dating from 1915 to 1970. Its educational value is on a par with its entertainment value, which may or may not be minimal, depending upon what turns one on.

For the record: first up is *A Free Ride*, circa 1915, which turns out to be anything but, as a prostitute services a john. Next comes 1923's *On the Beach*, which is a pleasing combination of lust and levity. Following in rapid succession are the voyeuristic 1930's *Keyhole Silhouettes*, 1940's *Hula Tease*, 1945's *Smart Alec*, 1950's *The Nun's Story*, and the more recent *Masseuse* (1990).

A wonderful thing about X-rated titles is their "high concept" standings. Given that almost all stag films involve sex, each of these titles is fairly self-explanatory. Such is the case with most feature length sex films as well. It is only recently that they have acquired the heading of "Adult Films" and attempted to do anything beyond the customary bump and grind that could be seen as far back as 1915.

In the early 1980s, more than seventy-five producers and distributors of this fare were pouring their product into the marketplace for a solid and appreciative audience. It was a world unto itself, with its own stars (Harry Reems, John Leslie, Desiree Cousteau, Seka, and many, many others) and "superstar" directors (Gerard Damiano, Jim and Art Mitchell, and others). Some of the talent toiling in those waters managed to break into the mainstream ... with mixed results.

It was Gerard Damiano who directed the high-water sexual mark, *Deep Throat* (1972). Not only was the film full of sexual activity of all different kinds, but it was fairly funny too. Linda Lovelace claimed she was beaten and hypnotized into doing the movie, but there is no on-screen evidence of that. It just looks like everyone was having a lot of cheap fun once a doctor discovers that Lovelace's unsatisfied character's most intimate piece of anatomy had somehow wound up just above her lungs.

Deep Throat was greatly responsible for making porno an acceptable theatrical experience. Once it became a conversation piece, more people had an excuse to go. *The Devil in Miss Jones* (1973) and *Beyond the Green Door* (1972) also had much to do with sex movies' growing respectability, as did the beautifully filmed *Emmanuelle* (1974). But even then, it seemed that the public was more willing to enjoy acts of screen violence than acts of screen love.

The exclusion of almost all X-rated films from this book may not be fair, but even less fair would be the exclusion of the strange dichotomy inherent in exploitation films. These sex movies, for the most part, involve lovemaking, pleasure, and happiness. These were the banned movies. The wildly popular and generally accepted exploitation movies are ones that incorporate cheap titillation, ugly violence, sadistic evil, and general brutality.

Go figure.

THE HITCHHIKERS (1972)
Produced, Directed, and Written by Fred and Beverly Sebastian
Starring Misty Rowe, Norman Klar, Linda Avery, Tammy Gibbs, and Mary Thatcher

Here's proof that the couple who play together make films together. Together with writer Ann Cawthorne, they made this and followed it up with 1975's *Gator Bait* and *The Single Girls* … none of which were cheery looks into the world of women's lib. The latter pictures starred the late Claudia Jennings, who was well in the running for the crown of "Queen of the B Movies" before she was tragically killed in a car accident.

This here flick starred *Hee Haw*'s resident dumb blond Misty Rowe as a sweet young runaway who runs afoul of evil in many denominations. First, she's raped by security guards after doing a little innocent shoplifting and then is taken in by a charismatic hippie cult leader named Benson (Norman Klar). The girl is initially worried that the man's entire cult is made up of slavishly worshipping women, but she learns to emulate them in order to gain the acceptance and affection she can't get anywhere else.

If any, or all, of this reminds anyone of another California cult whose demented boss inspired his helpers to commit mass murder, the similarity is anything but coincidental. It was obvious that the public was drawn with horrified fascination to the Charles Manson killings, so independent filmmakers exploited that interest with untold numbers of swarthy adaptations. That is why these things are called exploitation films.

Instead of leading his girls to death, Benson acts as a modern day Fagin, teaching them to hitchhike and lead their drivers to a predetermined spot for a royal fleecing. Other Manson variations weren't as pleasant. 1977's *Manson Massacre* was a horrid, stupid, cheaper-than-cheap effort directed by "Kentucky Jones." This poor excuse for a film was re-released in 1980 as *House of Bondage*. Anywhere it played should have been called "Theater of Screaming Viewers." It was the lowest of the low.

The Hitchhikers, on the other hand, also serves as a representation of the "pretty-young-hitchhiker-cruisin'-for-a-bruisin'" sub-genre. Every once in a while television (1981's *Portrait of a Teenage Hitchhiker*) and independent distributors (1980's *Pickup*) like to show willing audiences the dangers involved in sticking out one's thumb. Sometimes it is the hitchhiker who gets the hitchhikee in Dutch, such as in *Death Game* (1977), but most often the audience gets to see about forty-five minutes of shoddy abuse once a poor deluded girl gets into the wrong car.

HOUSE OF MISSING GIRLS (1972)
Directed and Written by Jean Francois Davy
Starring Anna Gael, Hans Meyer, Claude Charney, and Michele Levine

What is a nice movie like that doing in a book like this? Especially since it is evident by the writer-director's name that this is not an American film. Well, any distribution company willing to be as mercenary as this deserves a berth in the exploitation annals.

In this case, the now defunct VIP Distributing Company took a Gallic crime thriller, re-edited and redubbed it into submission, plastered this title across the advertising, then laughed all the way to the bank. There is no house of missing girls. There aren't even any missing girls. There is one girl, played by Anna Gael, who becomes an unwilling moll of a possessive, creepy mobster (Claude Charney).

Her rescuer (Hans Meyer) is another kettle of bouillabaisse. He takes her away from all of the evil to his hovel, which is built at the bottom of a hill. When the girl climbs to see what is on the summit, she finds a piano. I'm not kidding. There's a baby grand, and a fool, on the hill.

Laughable, maybe, but this kind of audience subjugation is constantly occurring. In 1982, an Italian crime drama was renamed *Assault with a Deadly Weapon* and shipped out with an ad campaign that prominently featured a policeman with a death's-head skull pointing a gun at the viewer while his uniformed companions beat up a black man and dragged a voluptuous white woman away in handcuffs. Hopefully you weren't as stupid as certain people I could name who spent good money to find out that there wasn't anything remotely similar in the actual, boring, film.

HOUSE OF PSYCHOTIC WOMEN (1973)
Produced by Joseph Giner

SEX, DRUGS, AND ROCK 'N' ROLL

Directed by Carlos Aured
Written by Jack Molina
Starring Paul Naschy, Diana Lorys, Eva Leon, and Maria Perschey

Now is the time to honor one great exploitation actor and one great exploitation importer. The actor is one Paul Naschy, a staple in cheap foreign fright films. The importer is Sam Sherman, head of Independent International, who was one of the industry's leaders in buying lousy, gory Italian, German, and Mexican movies, then turning them into marketable American fare.

House of Psychotic Women was originally a Spanish, vaguely Hitchcockian, murder mystery. By the time Independent International got through with it, it was a vaguely understandable murder movie featuring a brunette with a synthetic hand, a redhead with abnormal sex drives, a paralyzed, wheelchair-ridden girl, a blond nurse with ESP, and a pile of beheaded female corpses with their eyes gouged out.

Even so, it was not an enjoyable viewing experience by any stretch of the imagination. Not only wasn't it very logical or even coherent, but the cheapness of its production was mildly unsettling. Everything was so sordid, the screen practically sweated. The movie was successful in that it left a residue after viewing.

ILSA, SHE WOLF OF THE SS (1974)
Produced by Herman Traeger
Directed by Don Edmonds
Starring Dyanne Thorne, Sandi Richman, Jo Jo Deville, Uschi Digard, and Wolfgang Roehm

Now we're talking. Other movies with outlandish titles may have been teasing or outright lying, but Ilsa was the real deal. The ad campaign spelled it out in no uncertain terms: "Warning. Some Members of the Public May Find Certain Scenes in this Film Offensive and Shocking."

But they weren't going to leave it at that. "(What) you are about to see is based on documented fact. The atrocities shown were conducted as 'medical experiments' in special concentration camps throughout Hitler's Third Reich. Although these crimes against humanity are historically accurate, the characters are composites of notorious Nazi personalities, and the events portrayed have been condensed into one locality for dramatic purposes."

Yeah, baby. So sit back, relax, eat your popcorn, and imagine all the perverted, corrupt evil of Nazi Germany crammed into ninety-five minutes and you've got *Ilsa, She Wolf of the SS*. The time: 1945. The place: Medical Camp Number Nine.

The purpose: training young captives for the field brothels of the German Army. The result: those not pretty or strong enough are handed over to the scientists for experimentation. The warden: SS Officer Ilsa (Dyanne Thorne).

One would think that would be enough to hang the sadistic plot of a movie on, wouldn't one? But no. Ilsa is a monumental sexual monster who conducts experiments of her own on women all day and men all night. In her torture chamber, she tries to prove that females can stand as much pain as males by putting imprisoned girls through abject terror. In her bedroom, she samples a different male prisoner every evening, then has him castrated if unsatisfied.

Her downfall is instigated by a handsome new American prisoner, who is able to satisfy her lusts. In the meantime, one of her female victims plots revenge even though she is slowly dying from an injected syphilis virus. The plot culminates on the day Ilsa is entertaining a visiting member of the Nazi High Command. At dinner, Ilsa has a naked, bound and gagged girl standing on a block of ice with a noose around her neck. As the meal progresses, the ice melts and the victim slowly chokes to death.

After such entertainment at the dining table, the visitor wants equal entertainment in Ilsa's bed. The German officer is pretty kinky himself and gives Ilsa a small amount of her own medicine. After he leaves, she calls the American prisoner to her while the other inmates start their escape. The wily American convinces Ilsa that bondage would be just the thing, then leaves to join the revolt after the commandant is securely tied down.

Once the takeover is complete, the American leaves with his true love—a female prisoner named Rosette—while the syphilis-wracked girl starts executing her tormentors. Before she can get to Ilsa, however, the camp is invaded by tanks. At first, thinking it must be the Allies, all the victims rush to greet them ... only to be mowed down in their tracks.

It is actually the Axis soldiers, making sure that the victorious Allies get no evidence of the atrocities committed there. The last to die is Ilsa herself. Thinking that they have come to rescue her, she smiles, but the other Germans fear more than admire her and are happy to end her life. The movie concludes with the German tanks driving off into the sunset.

"We dedicate this film," producer Herman Traeger had concluded at the outset, "with the hope that these heinous crimes will never occur again."

Well, they reoccurred all right. Just one year later, director Edmonds was back with Dyanne Thorne to resurrect Ilsa. True to his introduction, however, Traeger had been replaced with William Brody. This time it is the present (circa 1976) and it's *Ilsa: Harem Keeper of the Oil Sheiks*. Ilsa is supplying the venomous El Sharif Hakim (Victor Alexander) with kidnapped international beauties. Before they can be handed over, they must be trained, naturally, giving Ilsa ample time to devise all manner of degrading torture.

This perverted paradise is invaded by American diplomat Dr. Kaiser (a Kissinger clone played by Wolfgang Roehm, who was also the twisted General in the previous picture), as well as secret agent Adam Scott (Mike Thayer), who is disguised as Kaiser's top aide. Fearing that one of his captives will blow the whistle, Sharif orders his harem sold, instigating massive plastic surgeries to cover up the various abuses.

Kaiser wants Sharif to give the United States more oil. Ilsa wants the handsome Scott to give her whatever she wants. The Sheik can handle the diplomat, but the secret agent turns out to be too much for the dominatrix. Since he can satisfy her, Ilsa's lust turns to devotion. Kaiser leaves, his mission a failure, but not before ordering the secret agent to get the fuel lines open by any means necessary. Fearing both Adam's prowess and Ilsa's infatuation for him, Sharif orders her to kill him. Instead, she shows Scott where the rightful Arab ruler is held captive. This young boy, the child of the Sheik's brother whom Sharif killed to gain power, is locked in a pit of excrement.

Before he can be rescued, Sharif's guards capture Scott and Ilsa. The harem keeper is given to a leper as a sexual plaything, while the agent is bound with his head in a cage of tarantulas. The girl escapes in time to mount a revolt and save her love. Arming the eunuchs, she has them led by her pair of twin black lesbian assistants, Satin (Tanya Boyd) and Velvet (Marilyn Joy). They make quick work of the opposition since they enjoy ripping off men's private parts with their bare hands.

After ample bloodshed, the Sheik is captured, bound and gagged. At this point, Ilsa's evil nature gets the better of her. Seeing the opportunity to wrest all the kingdom's power for herself, she plans to reinstate the nephew as a puppet ruler. But first she must eliminate her threat of exposure by Sharif.

There is only one white slavery victim left: a poor girl who has been given a booby-trapped anti-pregnancy device set to explode at the height of passion. Ilsa promises the girl freedom if she will make love to the tied-up Sheik. Unable to escape or warn the girl through the gag, Sharif is destroyed along with his reluctant lover as the bomb goes off.

This sort of thing isn't easy to cover up. Scott makes a deal with the new ruler before he leaves. First, America is welcome to all the oil it wants at popular prices. Second, Ilsa takes the boy's place in the prison pit of excrement.

The Ilsa movies were pits of depravity, eagerly and professionally served up to an audience consisting of "gore junkies, sadism fans, and sexual deviates" (according to the *Gore Gazette*). Of course, one doesn't have to be one of those three to enjoy the two "official" Ilsa movies, but it certainly helps. At least they delivered what they promised with a certain "joie de morte."

They were not the last we saw of Ilsa, however. *Ilsa the Tigress of Siberia* staggered out in 1977, disappointing many who saw this tepid tale of our favorite she-devil lording over a gulag and a prostitution ring. Faring relatively better was the infamous Jesus Franco's "homage," first known as *Greta the Torturer* and *Wanda the Wicked Warden* before it finally reappeared in 1979 as *Ilsa the Wicked Warden*. By any name, it starred Dyanne Thorne, whose Greta/Wanda/Ilsa was now making life miserable for W.I.P. victims in South America.

If possible, this one was even sicker than the prior few, what with chests being used as pin-cushions, eyes being gouged out then eaten, and prisoners being forced to use each other's tongues for toilet paper. This is one film that could be rated "Y" for "Yuch."

Interestingly enough, except for the presence of Thorne, Greta/Wanda/Ilsa had the exact same cast and scenery as Franco's other cult favorite, *Barbed Wire Dolls* (1979). They were probably made at the same time, since it is obvious that Franco loves his job. It's probably advisable not to see any of these films on a full stomach. Or, for that matter, an empty one.

LIVING NIGHTMARE (1977)
Produced by Group 1
Directed by William Hawkins
Music by Francesco De Masi
Starring Sirpa Lane, Carl Sisti, Robert Post, Christy Borg, and Mike Morris

While on the subject of the Third Reich, there's this sterling specimen of producer versatility. When this movie first appeared, it was called *Nazi Love Camp #27* and, as such, was tremendously successful in the South. For some reason, no one seemed as eager to see it in more northerly climes. But Group 1 was a company that never said "die." At least not to its audience.

After some study, it was discovered that Yankees didn't look so kindly upon Nazi exploitation movies, even though almost any thick paperback with a swastika on the cover is best seller material. Not questioning their findings, the company simply eliminated all mention of Germany, Hitler, World War II, or concentration camps from their ad campaign. It was the exact same movie, only now titled *Living Nightmare*, and sporting a nifty new poster featuring three pretty, nearly naked girls in a non-descript room.

"What is the worst act a woman can be forced to commit ... ?" the poster asked, "Again and again and again ...?"

The best touch, however, was an unsigned review quote. "Overwhelming suspense ... mind-boggling terror ... totally erotic...." It makes little difference that no critic is taking credit for the quote. Group 1 got its point across, and successfully established a trend for mercenary movie-marketing-rave-review-creation that is popular to this very day as scores of tenuously legitimate "prozacritic-quote-whores" eagerly supply studios with whatever they want to hear.

Living Nightmare was as popular up north as *Nazi Love Camp #27* was down south. The company's cunning extends to the film's official synopsis as well. Although the entire movie is based on Nazi atrocities, the copywriter skirts the issue by terming World War II "a terrible series of events." The concentration camp now becomes a "women's prison," and "beautiful young girls are put through merciless and degrading acts" rather than being assaulted by the Third Reich.

Anne (Sirpa Lane), our heroine, manages to survive the "crescendo of action, death and destruction" and sees her wardens get their comeuppance. But as Group 1 points out, and I quote, "for her, life is ended. But what matter, after all she has been through, is life really worth living?"

Funny ... I was going to ask them the same thing.

MALIBU BEACH (1978)
Produced by Marilyn J. Tenser
Directed by Robert J. Rosenthal
Written by Celia Susan Cotelo and Robert J. Rosenthal
Starring Kim Lankford, James Daughton, Susan Player Jarreau, and Michael Luther

Thank heaven! After all the ignominy of the last few films, here is some good clean (or only slightly smudged) fun. Producer Tenser had a habit of backing up solid teen entertainment, and her teaming with Cotelo and Rosenthal was a fortuitous one, since the writing/directing pair were also responsible for the cheery *Pom Pom Girls* (1976) and *The Van* (1977).

All three efforts are empty-headed visions of the good life in teenage-infested Southern California, complete with an unthreatening conflict, some practical jokes, and loads of sleek young girls in bikinis. For the record, *Malibu Beach* stars Kim Lankford as a bodyguard who handles kiddies by day, but hangs out in music clubs, makes out around beach campfires, and skinny-dips with her boyfriend (James Daughton) by night.

The only sour note in their rosy world is a bodybuilding beach bully (Stephen Oliver) who keeps putting Daughton down. It takes him about seventy minutes to realize the bully is just an immature braggart, but in the meantime there's drag racing action and chauvinist fun with a dog who snatches bikini tops.

All in all, these are the most harmless, most enjoyable of all the sex-oriented exploitation fare—direct descendents of the Frankie Avalon/Annette Funicello *Beach Blanket Bingo* series … only with more skin.

MONDO TEENO (1966)
Produced, Directed, and Written by Norman Herman
Narrated by Burt Topper

At the time, it wasn't funny. Today, most of these sort of heartfelt documentaries about the anti-establishment youth movement of the 1960s look incredibly strange. But during that turbulent decade, young people were discovering the magic of filmmaking and were dumping their hearts, brains, and spleens onto celluloid. The result was a few exceptional rock docs (like 1969's *Woodstock*), and many of the dumbest, most pretentious excuses for meaningful messages ever witnessed.

There was almost no limit to the sincere absurdity, like *Hippie Revolt* (1968), a film by Edgar Beatty that proudly announced: "all the narrative commentary was improvised at the moment of recording." Then there was Jack O'Connell's *Revolution* (1967), starring the lovely Today Malone and her male co-star "Little Jesus."

But *Mondo Teeno* says it all, or at least tried to. "Mondo" means "world" in Italian. It was a word audiences became familiar with after the surprise success of *Mondo Cane* (World of Strangeness) in 1963. Suddenly all sorts of odd efforts sprouted "Mondo" titles, including *Mondo Topless* (1966) and *Mondo Cannibale* (1979).

Mondo Teeno was a compilation of rites of passage, concentrating on the drug scene in the U.S. and the U.K., pre-marital sex in France and Sweden, and teen prostitution in Italy and Japan. Harking back to the good ol' days of the 1940s, the film climaxed with the birth of an unwed mother's baby.

The 1960s were a turbulent but important decade. It's too bad that films like this make it look ridiculous.

MOVIE STAR, AMERICAN STYLE (1968)
Produced by Robert Carcamico
Directed by Albert Zugsmith
Written by Graham Lee Mahin and Albert Zugsmith
Starring Paula Lane, Del Moore, and T.C. Jones

When Italian director Vittorio de Sica's lovely comedy *Marriage Italian Style* (1963) took America by storm, there was no stopping a torrent of inferior, but like-titled films getting booked into theaters. This was the weirdest of them all.

Originally called *LSD, I Hate You!*, it starred Paula Lane as wildly neurotic film star Honey Bunny, who is packed off to a sanitarium after the latest of many feeble suicide attempts. There, the extremely strange Dr. Horatio (Del Moore) uses her and his other patients as guinea pigs for his new hallucinogenic treatment.

Although the movie is rife with what the producers called "LSD sections" filled with strange camera angles and extreme color tones, the film is stolen by T.C. Jones playing wildly camp dress designer Skippy Roper, who races in and out of scenes as if he were in a road company of TV's *Project Runway*.

MS. 45 (1981)
Produced by Navaron Films
Directed by Abel Ferrera
Written by Nicholas St. John
Starring Zoe Tamerlis, Albert Sinkys, Darlene Stuto, and Jimmy Laine (Abel Ferrera)

This was a rarity: a heartfelt but 100 percent exploitation film. It is especially unusual considering the same team's first film. Ferrera and St. John were New York University graduates who slapped together a tacky little hunk of trash called *Driller Killer* in the late 1970s. Ferrera used the pseudonym Jimmy Laine to star himself as psychotic artist Reno Miller, who wanders around lower Manhattan, eliminating anyone who gets in his way with a handy Black and Decker electric drill.

In lieu of believable plot or dialogue, Ferrera dumped screen blood and guts all over the place, making *Driller Killer* a particularly relentless exercise in the "gross-out" school of filmmaking. Surprisingly, everyone behind the camera seemed to learn from the experience, because *Ms. 45* ranks as one of the closest near-misses to exploitation classic status of any film since the mid–1970s.

Zoe Tamerlis stars as Thana, a mute, hauntingly beautiful girl who works in New York's garment district. On the way home from work one night she is brutally raped by a masked man (Jimmy Laine — who is actually the pseudonymed director). As if that wasn't enough, she gets home only to interrupt a burglar … who rapes her a second time.

Unable to stand it, she manages to smash in the robber's skull with an iron. But then she is unable to tell anyone about her attack, and unsure as to how to deal with the corpse in her apartment. Her decision to hack him up, put him in plastic bags, and keep him in the refrigerator, until she can drop off the Glad bags one by one, drives her insane.

She takes the man's .45 caliber automatic and starts killing whichever man propositions her. After awhile, she can no longer wait for someone to come to her. She dresses up as a prostitute and goes after them. It is an ultimate form of entrapment with an automatic death sentence. She murders more than five men—some more deserving of their fates than others—until it comes time for the office Halloween party.

In another example of the irony Ferrera and St. John fill the film with, she goes as a nun. Once there, the inevitable happens and she starts blasting away at every male in the place. Her best friend Laurie (Darlene Stuto) comes up behind her with a huge cake-knife held at crotch level and then drives it pointedly up into Thana's back. Mortally wounded, the girl spins around, but is unable to kill a fellow female.

Ms. 45 is not subtle, but it is effective. Ferrera and company really seemed to care how the picture looked and what it was about. Although slightly hurt by some overblown performances, the major roles—especially that of Tamerlis—are right on the money.

Navaron's second film is important because it shows that exciting exploitation can come from the heart as well as the gut, brain, and wallet. An exploitation movie does not have to be brainlessly brutal—it can have a moral backbone that makes all the violence that much stronger. An exploitation film does not have to suffer from creative thought. Relevance and meaning can only make it all the more effective.

Abel Ferrera went on to an eclectic, fascinating career as a writer, producer, director, and composer, while his star changed her name to Zoe Lund, and worked as a model and actress until her untimely death from drug-related heart failure in 1999.

NOCTURNA: GRANDDAUGHTER OF DRACULA (1979)
Produced by Vernon Becker
Directed and Written by Harry Tampa
Starring Nai Bonet, John Carradine, Yvonne DeCarlo, and Tony Hamilton

The success of Frank Langella as Dracula in the long-running Broadway show (that concentrated on satiric campiness rather than shivering creepiness) from 1977-1980 led to several vampire burlesques. *Love at First Bite* (1979) starring George Hamilton was far more successful than this—the saga of Dracula's disco-loving granddaughter.

Famed belly dancer Nai Bonet both executive produced and starred in the lightweight lampoon that took a few affectionate jibes at bloodsucking legends. As in Hamilton's movie, hard times have befallen Castle Dracula. In order to pay property taxes, the mansion has been converted into the Hotel Transylvania—run by the Count's granddaughter, Nocturna (Nai Bonet). The Count himself (the ever lovable John Carradine, who gives great spice to the role) is still in the basement in his crypt, with his teeth and fangs in a glass by his casket's side.

In order to make more money, Nocturna books a band into the establishment to entertain the guests, only to fall in love with one of the musicians (Tony Hamilton). The music hath charms to soothe the savage beast and, much to her surprise, Nocturna finds that she does not want to empty the man of plasma … and she can see her reflection when she dances.

Enamored of the thought of lovemaking with her human, she follows the rock group to New York, with an enraged and betrayed Dracula right behind her.

Nocturna's first stop is the crypt of Jugulia (Yvonne DeCarlo, then best known for her stint on TV's *The Munsters*), an ex-love and victim of the Count. Since she lives under the Brooklyn Bridge, it is just an easy hop, skip, and flap to the disco where the group is playing. Jugulia is supportive of the relationship, but Dracula arrives to place a curse on all concerned. To save her love, Nocturna agrees to return to her homeland. But before that can happen, Jugulia releases the victims from their spells, and Nocturna's love rips a neon "t" from the disco sign to use as a cross against the aged vampire.

Defeated, Dracula turns into a bat and flies off. The love Nocturna feels for her beau convinces her that she has become human. The film ends with the lovers together, waiting for the sunrise. The audience is left wondering whether its rays will give her a tan or destroy her in the time-honored method of vampire killing.

This movie had neither the humorous style of *Love at First Bite* nor the fabulous frisson of probably the best vampire movie of them all, *Horror of Dracula* (1958, directed by Terence Fisher and starring Peter Cushing and Christopher Lee). Although the disco atmosphere had some cinematic suggestions to connect it to a vampire tale (only opening at night, frenetic splashes of shadow and light, beautiful women under the thrall of a fascinating human monster, etc.), Nocturna ignored the major possibilities to settle for a facile fable.

PARADISE (1982)
Produced by Robert Lantos and Stephen J. Roth
Directed and Written by Stuart Gillard
Starring Willie Aames and Phoebe Cates

Another rule of exploitation filmmaking is that every major film success begets imitators. A constant danger is copying a major studio's original too closely or too soon. A movie called *Great White* (1982) learned that the hard way when Universal, the company that made *Jaws* (1975), managed to keep this very similar shark saga from being seen.

Reports are that Columbia Pictures, the owners of the remade *Blue Lagoon* (1980), tried to repress *Paradise*, an Avco Embassy release, but was not as successful. They shouldn't have tried. If anything, *Paradise* only made *Blue Lagoon* look good. In some cases, the same reviewers who groaned in critical pain over the major movie trumpeted its relative glories as compared to this unofficial clone.

All this is not to say that *Paradise* was bad. It was pleasing to the eye and did not threaten the brain a whit. It also had something that *Blue Lagoon* did not: Phoebe Cates, just before she would usher millions of young men into puberty via her legendary appearance in 1982's *Fast Times at Ridgemont High*.

While *Blue Lagoon* had Christopher Atkins and Brooke Shields being marooned on a tropical island as children, *Paradise* had teen actor Willie Aames (late of television's *Eight Is Enough*) and teen model Phoebe Cates running into the desert to get away from a sheik who desires to place the girl into his harem at any cost.

Four-fifths of the movie's remainder concerns Aames' and Cates' fun-in-the-sun, while one-fifth concerns the sheik's obsessive search for the girl. Whenever he is about to find the kids' oasis, they simply move on to the next until Aames realizes it is time to stand and fight.

By then the attractive and well-developed children have discovered the joys of adulthood, thanks to the coaching of two chimps named Doc and Eve. When the apes hold hands, so do the teens. When the apes kiss, so do the teens. When the apes suddenly sprout a baby, the teens have their work cut out for them. It is a classic case of "human see, human do." This doesn't say much for the much-vaunted human intelligence.

Paradise is a dream for anyone who likes to see good-looking teenagers giggling, making out, running around, and showering with little or no clothing on. Unlike Brooke Shields, Cates isn't above taking her clothes off for the camera. Much was made of the fact that Shields used a stand-in for her movie nude scenes even though she had posed naked for a still photographer years before.

Pubescent skin aside, *Paradise* has the distinction of being an exploitation of an exploitation. *Blue Lagoon* seems to have been made specifically for the teen crowd, which reports say make up the majority of modern filmgoers, and dirty old men, who make up the majority of exploitation film lovers. *Paradise* seems to have been made for the exact same crowd, utilizing nearly the exact same ingredients: two pretty leads and lush photography. It is enjoyable to watch both for that, and the fact that it is such an obvious copy.

REVENGE OF THE CHEERLEADERS (1976)
Produced by Richard Lerner and Nathaniel Dorsky
Directed by Richard Lerner
Written by Ted Greenwald, Nathaniel Dorsky, and Ace Baandage (sic)
Starring Jerii (sic) Woods, Rainbeaux Smith, Helen Lang, Patrice Rohmer, and Susie Elene

That last name under the screenplay credit should give one a good idea of the humor level in this amiable, generally watchable representative of the "cheerleader" movie. These high school and college girls, whose only responsibility seems to be whipping sports fans into a frenzy of home team patriotism and lust, have always been a fascination to exploitation filmmakers and an attraction to audiences. After all, where else besides dance clubs can you go for some innocent glimpses of skin, bumping, and grinding?

The major distinction between cheerleader movies and the likes of *Malibu Beach* is that while the latter film is somewhat coy about premarital sex, these cheerleaders are out and out sensual sirens. At Aloha High School, the site of the squad's revenge, no one, on the one hand, raises an eyebrow over the fact that the girls regularly shower with the basketball team and engage in the ultimate amorous activity in the hallways.

The cheerleaders (Jerii Woods, Rainbeaux Smith, Helen Lang, Patrice Rohmer, and Susie Elene), on the other hand, raise their eyebrows and other things over the fact that their liberal establishment may be merged with the strict Lincoln Vocational School. Realizing this calls for drastic action, they spike the lunch spaghetti with drugs on the day several school board members are touring.

The place goes wild. Adults and students alike partake of an *Animal House*-esque food fight in the cafeteria (two years before *Animal House* premiered) and a bubble-bath orgy in the locker room. Unfortunately, the girls are too busy enjoying themselves to take incriminating pictures, so, once the narcotics wear off, the horrified adults are even more intent on merging the wacky school with the straight one.

This delights one Walter Hartlander (William Bramley)—the de rigueur real estate developer who wants to use Aloha High as the site for his new shopping center—but horrifies new principal Hal Walker (Norman Thomas Marshall), who replaces the girls with less amorous cheerleaders. This leads to disaster during the all important basketball game between the dreaded Lincoln Vo and Aloha. The home team crowd and players just can't get up for the game with the new unit, which inspires the fired girls to mug their replacements during halftime and take their place.

Thanks to their reappearance, Aloha goes on to win, and the school board agrees with Walker that the moral fiber of the school has improved. Thus the merger is called off. That makes Hartlander so unhappy that he bribes school nurse Beam (Eddra Gale) into dynamiting the school's main building and kidnapping Walker so it would look like he did it.

The cheerleaders know better and trail the nurse to Hartlander's hideout to rescue their principal. All's well that ends well at Aloha High, as the girls continue to rule their school with immorality. All's well that ends well at the box office as well, since *Revenge* was as effective as its 1973 predecessor, *The Cheerleaders*, made by the same team and distributed by Monarch Releasing.

Albeit slapdash, these films weren't mindless, and even showed some moments of true wit. Perhaps not a huge amount of thought went into them, but a bit obviously did, making them more agreeable than the mercenary norm. Thanks, Ace Baandage!

SATAN'S CHEERLEADERS (1977)
Produced by Alvin L. Fast
Directed by Greydon Clark
Written by Greydon Clark and Alvin L. Fast
Starring John Ireland, Yvonne DeCarlo, Jack Kruschen, John Carradine, and Kerry Sherman

Clark and Fast come from the "William Sachs School of Filmmaking." Like the director-writer of *Galaxina*, they have a history of getting legitimately workable ideas—in this case, an inspired one—and then putting those ideas on screen in the most tepid manner imaginable.

How could anything with this title and concept be anything but a comedy? Easy, when Clark and Fast are in control. It is one part teenage "T and A" picture to three parts supernatural film. It promises to be all kinds of fun, what with pretty pom-pom girls' heads spinning and spewing green pea soup, but instead it is a woefully tame telling of what happens when the devil gets hot for a high school girl without benefit of expensive special effects.

The trouble starts when Billy (Jack Kruschen), an abnormally uptight school janitor, gets teased by Benedict High cheerleaders Patti (Kerry Sherman), Chris (Hillary Horan), Debbie (Alisa Powell), and Sharon (Sherry Marks). It seems as if

Billy just happens to be a new member of the local small-town satanic cult and completely overreacts to the innocent banter.

His vengeance takes place after the cheerleaders' bus breaks down on the way to the first game of the season (it never fails to amaze how Satanists manage to make mechanical motors do their evil bidding).

Billy is waiting with his car and promises to give the group a ride to the end zone—only to take them to the twilight zone instead, represented by a painfully plain satanic altar in the middle of the woods. The producer's idea of special effects is to have everyone freeze in place while eerie sound effects are played. Only Patti gets to move, with blank expression, to the stone slab so that she can, as the producer puts it, "mate with Satan."

None the worse for wear, everyone breaks out of their trance to find Billy dead of an apparent heart attack and Patti about as lifeless as the movie itself. She uses the excuse that the janitor died while trying to rape her. Buying that explanation, the girls wander around in search of help, only to find John Carradine playing a bum who knows directions to the sheriff's house.

Carradine is such a wonderful actor that his constant appearances in these dreadful opuses aren't as pitiful as they might initially seem. Even in the most ridiculous of circumstances, his strength of character and acting ability shine through. Such is not the case with poor John Ireland and Yvonne DeCarlo—who play the sheriff and his wife, who turn out, in the most expected of plot twists, to be the cult's high priest and priestess. The film kills time with some uninspired "Satanists-get-girls, Satanists-lose-girls, Satanists-recapture-girls" meanderings until it's finally time for the black mass.

To the surprise of probably no one, Patti turns the tables on them, since she's now the dark one's fave. She sends two dogs for the throats of Ireland and DeCarlo, who are probably pretty happy to get out of the picture around now. While the other girls celebrate their "escape," Patti smiles the wicked smile of a secret cult leader.

Sadly, what could have been a fine send-up of both horror and teen films was a mediocre bore. The tragedy of *Satan's Cheerleaders* is that it didn't have to hold together, it didn't have to be original, it didn't really even have to make sense. All it had to be was fun, but it was not.

TANYA'S ISLAND (1980)
Produced and Written by Pierre Brousseau
Directed by Alfred Sole
Starring D.D. Winters, Richard Sargent, and Don McCleod

This project had everything going for it; a producer willing to experiment slightly, a talented director with a proven track record, and two of the most personable new stars seen in many a moon. The first star was D.D. Winters, a Canada-based model whom Brousseau had spotted in a magazine. The other was "Blue," a monster suit designed by Rick Baker (*American Werewolf in London*), built by Rob Bottin (*The Thing*), and worn by mime–actor Don McCleod.

All they needed (and all they didn't have) was a decent script. What resulted was a boring, indifferent muddle with great possibilities. Winters plays Tanya, a model who is kicked out of the apartment she shares with her moody, ridiculous boyfriend Lobo (Richard Sargent). She then fantasizes that she's on an island with this huge hairy beast which she names Blue, after the color of his eyes.

This results in an extremely successful pairing, in that Winters is a very attractive and personable presence, while the beast suit that Baker, Bottin, and McCleod collaborated on is tremendously successful in displaying a wide range of realistic emotions. After an initial Blue rape and subsequent mutual lovemaking, their idyllic paradise is invaded by Lobo, who proves to be far more savage than the animal Blue. That's the moral, get it?

Though many understood, very few cared. The movie ends with Tanya coming out of her fantasy, only to meet a man with the same kind of eyes Blue had. By this time, it seems that only a few weren't overcome by apathy since the audiences had to entertain themselves with Winters' shape and McLeod's strength. The poor guy suffocated in the unventilated suit, was hit with rocks, and actually shot with a real arrow (when the special effects people couldn't convince the crew that the effect could be realistically faked).

It seems as if Brousseau had a concept in mind that no amount of reasonable argument could shake. Director Sole and collaborators Mick Garris and Rosemary Ritvo tried to make the effort more entertaining, but reportedly the producer was determined to make a dry, serious retelling of *Beauty and the Beast* (1946) meets *Lord of the Flies* (1963). He got what he wanted, but not enough paying customers seemed to share his enthusiasm.

TEENAGE MOTHER (1968)
Produced by Jerry Gross and Nicholas Demetroules
Directed and Written by Jerry Gross
Starring Arlene Sue Farber, Frederick Riccio, Julie Ange, and The Young Set

The mighty Mister Gross returns with this wonderful opus of twisted affection and "now-you-see-it, now-you-don't" morals. Back in the 1960s, many exploiters still felt the necessity of sugar coating their movies with "socially redeeming values." This film was little more than a "birth movie" under the guise of a love story.

It was very little more, considering it only lasted seventy-eight minutes. But those seventy-eight minutes were full of sure-fire ingredients. Arlene Sue Farber stars as Arlene Taylor, a nice enough girl who is sent into paroxysms of jealously when a forward-thinking Swedish sex education teacher (Gross vet Julie Ange, who suffered through *Girl on a Chain Gang*) keeps her boyfriend Tony (Howard Le May) after school.

So worried over what the teacher might do, Arlene elicits the interest of Duke Markell (Frederick Riccio), the local hood, bully, pusher, and pornographic picture salesman. She follows that up by pretending to be pregnant in order to get Tony to marry her. He's willing, but must deal with a plan by Duke and pornographic picture supplier Henry Kaplan (David Vancelette) to discredit the sex ed teacher.

Duke tries to rape the teacher, then tries to rape Arlene after the shamed girl fights with her shocked parents and runs away from home. Tony arrives in time to soundly thrash the creep, while the teacher shows an actual childbirth film to the school board to convince them that sex education belongs in the classroom.

Well, that does it. The school agrees that the teacher should remain, Arlene admits she was only fooling about her pregnancy, and the police pounce on Duke and the pornographer. The critics pounced on Jerry Gross for this blatant attempt to return the joys of birth movies to the viewing public. But for anyone who liked this sort of thing, the producer didn't disappoint.

One who learned his lesson well was David E. Durston, who went to work for Gross in 1971. The very next year, Durston wrote and directed *Stigma* (1972), the first, greatest, and only movie trumpeting the joys of syphilis. Philip Thomas, Harlan Poe, Josie Johnson, Connie Van Ess, and famed New York disc jockey "Cousin" Bruce Morrow were just a few of the actors who had to deliver the bare educational facts on V.D., while some exposed their bare bodies in order to get it.

When a movie is as plainly exploitative as this, it can be fun to watch the remarkably obvious filmmaking wheels squeal across the screen. The subject may be no laughing matter, but the mercenary intent of the producers may be so patent that the audience is left with little choice but to laugh.

TENDER LOVING CARE (1975)
Produced by Chako Van Leeuween and Don Edmonds
Directed and Written by Don Edmonds
Starring Donna Desmond, Michael Asher, Leah Simon, Tony Victor, and Anita King

To reiterate and remind: thus far there have been women in prison pictures, prostitute pictures, hippie pictures, X-rated sex pictures, bikini-girl pictures, and cheerleader pictures. This is a nurse picture, a nurse picture made for Roger Corman by Ilsa creator Don Edmonds, and a pretty good nurse picture in the wake of such other New World Productions as *Student Nurses* (1970), *Private Duty Nurses* (1972), *Night Call Nurses* (1972), *Young Nurses* (1973), and *Candy Stripe Nurses* (1974).

This was the first film the producers/distributors did after they had run out of words to put in front of Nurses. All these films were cut from the same cloth. There was a little female frontal nudity from the waist up and the back down, there was a lot of rampant affection and some lovemaking, and there was some corruption and criminal activity. Donna Desmond is the center of attention here as a new nurse on her first day of hospital service.

Complications include an addicted doctor (Tony Victor), who uses one of Donna's roommates (Leah Simon) as his connection. She's caught red-handed, and blackmailed by a male nurse, which leads to the addicted doctor killing him. A parallel plot has Desmond investigating the suspicious death of a boxer (John Daniels).

By the fade-out, the addicted doctor and his lady love are killed, but the boxer's murderer is served up to justice. Nurse Desmond is thereby inspired to continue to devote her life to the helping of others. This, along with almost every other Corman-released picture, adheres to the formula of delivering a tiny message among the huge melodrama.

Now is as good a time as any to mention that Corman practiced his particular brand of minutely moral filmmaking in such other sexploitation sub-genres as the "rape film" (hugely successful in Japan) *Jackson County Jail* (1977); the "teacher movie" (1973's *Student Teachers*, 1976's *Summer School Teachers*); the "girl-grifter film" (1977's *Great Texas Dynamite Chase*, 1978's *Moonshine County Express*); and the "stewardess picture" (1973's *Fly Me*).

If a female could fill the job, Corman's New World Pictures could film it.

TOWER OF SCREAMING VIRGINS (1968 and 1972)
Produced by Wolf C. Hartwig
Directed by Francois Legrand (pseudonym of Franz Antel)
Written by Kurt Nachmann (based on the novel *The Tower of Nesle* by Alexandre Dumas)
Starring Terry Torday, Jean Piat, Uschi Glas, and Frank Olivier

The author of *The Three Musketeers* and many other great works must not only be turning over, but spinning, in his grave. Not only is this not an American film, it is a West German, French, and Italian co-production. Why is it here? Because of the title, of course.

By now certain people might be bellowing in abject rage about the rampant male chauvinism (and self-imposed Preface rule breaking) so far displayed. These people will be happy to know that, not only are there no screaming virgins in the tower, there are actually screaming men. Hey, men can be virgins too, you know (so I've heard).

It seems that the Queen of France (Terry Torday) had a bad habit in medieval days of disguising herself and two handmaidens so that they could lure unsuspecting males into a tower for some illicit lovemaking … and murder. Much to their chagrin, they made the mistake of trapping intrepid Captain Bouridan (Jean Piat), who fights his way out—killing many of the Queen's hired assassins—only to return and confront the corrupt monarch.

He reveals that he is really Lyonnet de Bouronville, who fathered two other illegitimate children years before, and that one of those kids was unknowingly murdered by her just hours before! The Queen is understandably upset by this news, but not so much that she doesn't order the rest of her thugs to make mincemeat out of her ex-lover. He holds them off magnificently until the cuckolded King shows up with his men. Knowing how rotten things could be for a treacherous, adulterous Queen in the royal dungeon, she hurls herself off a handy parapet.

Beside the pandering title, this was a pretty entertaining and energetic hour and a half with Piat handling his fighting chores nicely. But Maron Films—the American distributor of the movie (which was originally called *The Tower of Forbidden Love*) didn't think people would pay to see something called *Tower of Shouting Swashbucklers*. So Virgins were uncaged to save yet another film.

UNHOLY ROLLERS (1972)
Produced by John Prizer and Jack Bohrer
Directed by Vernon Zimmerman
Written by Howard R. Cohen and Vernon Zimmerman
Edited by Martin Scorsese
Starring Claudia Jennings, Louis Quinn, Betty Anne Rees, Roberta Collins, and Alan Vint

Just when you thought all the female occupations were covered, along comes this "women's roller derby movie." This effort has the distinction of starring the late Claudia Jennings, another *Playboy* Playmate of the Year. Her director, unfortunately, can stand alongside William Sachs and Greydon Clark in the "Good Idea-Lousy Realization" category.

Actually, that isn't quite fair. This and subsequent Zimmerman films (1981's *Fade to Black* for instance) show a better grasp of technique than many others, but he seems to be just as lacking in the plot motivation department as all the others. His characters have a little depth, but seem to do things just because they need to move things along.

The 1981 film was especially disappointing in that it was about a troubled young boy who disguises himself as movie heroes in order to exact vengeance on those who've wronged him. What could have been an incisive, or even wildly entertaining, satire was just a pedestrian murder movie with no real bite, flair, style, or flash.

Unholy Rollers holds no such promise, and therefore is the more successful of the two. The movie charts Jennings' rise from factory worker to roller derby queen and back again. Her downfall is assured by her growing interest in off-track squalor and violence. But women bashing each other on or off skates didn't seem to hold the same attraction as women in varying states of dress tending patients, serving airline snacks, cheering on school teams, getting into jail, or escaping out again … despite *Unholy Rollers'* extraordinary editing. Wonder whatever happened to that film splicer?

VAMPIRE HOOKERS (1979)
Produced by Robert C. Waters
Directed by Cirio H. Santiago
Written by Howard Cohen
Starring John Carradine, Karen Stride, Lenka Novak, and Katie Dolan

Another great idea gone astray … but a perfect place to point out that it's actually hard for ideas like this not to go wrong. That's the catch-22 inherent in all high-concept concepts. Once a title like this has been conceived, how can the film possibly live up to it (just ask the doomed crew who subsequently mounted *Bordello of Blood* in 1996)?

Contrary to the impression that has perhaps already been given, it is not that easy to flesh out a one-note conceit like this one. Once the existence of vampires who disguise themselves as prostitutes is established, the plot must take off from there in an interesting or involving manner, while still maintaining the flavor of the title so as to not disappoint the audience.

Vampire Hookers does not even nearly succeed. John Carradine has the unenviable job of playing yet another Count Dracula type, who sends his voluptuous victims up to lure unsuspecting men to his crypt for draining. The whole approach is so middling that it is actually difficult to decide whether the story is meant to be taken seriously or as a joke.

About the only interesting sidelight is that when Capricorn Three Films sold this to MPM Films, the name and approach were changed. The new version, now called *Cemetery Girls*, was saddled with the tagline: "They Rise At Night For More Than A Bite," followed by the somber warning: "Due to the unusual subject matter and explicit presentation of this motion picture, only mature adults should attend."

If they had reached out to "immature adults," the flick might have been more successful.

THE VIRGIN WITCH (1972)
Produced by Ralph Solomans
Directed by Ray Austin
Written by Klaus Vogel
Starring Ann Michelle, Vickie Michelle, Patricia Haines, Neil Hallett, and Keith Buckley

Pretty classy, pretty entertaining, and just plain pretty, this film is one of the more enjoyable of the sensual supernatural fare, because it knows what it's about and it just goes ahead and does it with very little self-indulgence or self-consciousness.

Ann Michelle plays a very attractive English girl who is initiated into witchcraft in modern-day England. The coven's craft is fairly clever. The high priestess is a lesbian who heads up a model agency. Procuring the best lookers available, she hands them over to the high priest, who is also an M.D. Under the guise of examination, he deflowers the girls and proclaims them "white witches"—those who should continue on the path of righteousness.

Ann, however, likes the idea of harnessing the powers of darkness, and works diligently toward a mastery of the black arts. One of her methods of doing this is by sleeping her way to the bottom—hopping into bed with anyone who gets in her way so she can enchant them into submission.

The film is filled with watchable weird touches, the neatest one occurring when Ann casts a spell on the lesbian by staring at her photo. The picture of the smiling model agency boss burns up and then immediately reappears — only this time the picture shows the woman with a terrified expression.

FOR ONE WEEK ONLY

★★★ HELD OVER BY POPULAR DEMAND ★★★
John Waters

Today he is an award-winning Broadway musical inspiration, sought-after talk show guest, and out-spoken advocate of gay rights. But once upon a time this fantasy-oriented, blood-thirsty spawn of exploitation was a walking bad taste machine. He made his living trying to demolish audiences with demented glee, spotlighting weirdos, rejects, and exotic oddballs to his heart's content.

He started making sixteen millimeter movies in his native Baltimore, including *Hag in a Black Leather Jacket* (1964), but his first film that got any interest outside his circle of friends was *Mondo Trasho* (1969). Made for two thousand dollars with no dialog, it starred the charismatic Divine—a heavyweight transvestite—as a Jayne Mansfield-esque star who runs over a young girl. Her adventures in a laundromat, insane asylum, and a park lead to her slow motion demise in a pigpen.

The title, content, and Waters' hustle garnered the film perhaps more attention than it deserved, but the nascent director fully intended that would never be the case again. His follow-up, *Multiple Maniacs* (1970), was his first foray into synchronous sound. Divine led the way again, this time playing the co-owner of the "Cavalcade of Perversion Traveling Freakshow." Instead of bearded ladies or two-headed cows, they displayed homosexuals and drug addicts … before robbing, and sometimes murdering, their audience.

The movie industry metaphor was hard to miss, but then Waters buckled down on the plot, which saw Divine murdering her husband and eating his guts before being attacked by a giant lobster. Appetite now slaked and hopelessly insane, she is ultimately gunned down by the National Guard. Don't you just love happy endings?

As crazed as these early efforts were, they were only the hoary hors d'oeuvres to what many consider Waters' masterpiece, *Pink Flamingos* (1972). According to reports, it was Divine who finally convinced the young filmmaker to go for broke. "The time has come to stop fooling around," s/he said, so Waters started compiling a compendium of the most unforgettable things he could afford to do in one picture. Most of them appear to be in this ground-and-toilet-breaking 1972 opus.

As a public service, here's the plot. Two families are vying for the title of "The Filthiest People Alive." One is led by Divine, her insane son Crackers (Danny Mills), a bleached-blond friend (Mary Vivian Pearce, the star of *Hag in a Black Leather Jacket*), and Mama Edie, a nearly toothless, egg-worshipping crone who sits in a playpen wearing only her bra and panties. The other family is the Marbles: Connie and Raymond (Mink Stole and David Lochary), who like picking up hitchhiking girls, having their butler (Channing Wilroy) rape them, then selling their babies to lesbian couples.

As hard as the white slavers tried, there was really no comparison between Divine's natural, organic sleaziness and the Marbles' desperate attempts at hideousness. So Connie and Ray resort to dirty tricks to psych-out Divine and company. But anyone that disgusting is not easily swayed, even by the likes of mail-sent excrement, chicken bestiality, and arson.

After their mobile home is destroyed by fire, Divine finally pays back the Marbles in kind. They are captured, tried, and killed at a press conference for all the low-grade tabloids, and then Divine does what has made the movie the legend it is. Waters structured the entire movie around this scene. He conceived the act before any other part of the story, and he was intent on filming in one continuous, uncut sequence.

A small dog defecates. Divine immediately picks up the canine waste and eats it.

There are other directors who might conceive of such an idea (see *Salo* in Chapter Three), but there is probably no director and transvestite muse who could conceive and film such a moment with as much ... well, love.

Pink Flamingos shot Waters from the lower depths of underground filmmaking into the stratosphere of arthouse eccentricity. Although called "the prince of puke," he is actually "king of sleaze." What makes him and his work so interesting is the obvious enthusiasm and even joy he takes in it. Although he created vistas of violent, extravagant absurdities on film, he doesn't swear by them. Well, he might utter a few obscenities, but what does that matter in the audacious light of *Pink Flamingos*?

Waters didn't create the nation's bad taste, he just lets his characters revel in it. He films it all in the manner it deserves—crudely. This is not to accuse Waters of high art; far from it. It is just an acknowledgment that Waters knows what he likes, and knows how to translate it to film in an entertaining way. He has a twisted good time, and passes it on to his audience.

After *Pink Flamingos*, there wasn't much to say on the same subject, but Waters went ahead with more fantasy-oriented visions for Divine to star in. *Female Trouble* (1974) was next, and it didn't disappoint his new legion of fans. Divine plays Dawn Davenport, who runs away from home because she didn't get a new pair of high heels. She's raped by a construction worker, who is also portrayed by Divine (without her female get-up).

That forced mating produces a daughter whom Divine supports by mugging, stealing, and tricking. She works her way down to modeling for two beauty parlor owners (David Lochary and Mary Vivian Pearce) who see crime as beauty. After her face is splashed with acid and she chops off the hand of the attacker (her leather-clad aunt portrayed by egg lady Edith Massey), the parlor people see her as even more beautiful.

The path to perfection is traversed when Dawn strangles her daughter (Mink Stole) on the stage of a Baltimore night club, and then riddles the audience with machine gun bullets. The apex of beauty is achieved when she is subsequently electrocuted for her crimes. That's another thing about Waters—he's a sucker for happy endings.

More and more critics were beginning to understand that as well. He was making films for connoisseurs of bad taste while discovering that there were plenty of them out there. His next movie, *Desperate Living* (1977), suffered from the death of actor David Lochary due to a drug overdose, and the absence of Divine (who was touring with a play entitled *Women Behind Bars*).

Instead, Susan Lowe starred as Mole McHenry, a lady wrestler living with a murderess who drowned a babysitter in dog food. Together they overthrow the mythical town of Mortville where criminals can live as long as they suffer the abuses of Queen Carlotta (Edith Massey).

As he made each movie, Waters became more proficient with the techniques that needed to evolve. Still, he kept all his budgets ridiculously low, which resulted in his films garnering profits with far more ease than their major studio brethren.

Still, he realized that he could not maintain his lifestyle for long without breaking out of the arthouse ghetto. Without tapping a wider audience he couldn't hope to survive in style while only making a film every two years. His ticket to ride was *Polyester* (1981), arguably his most accessible comedy—if that isn't a contradiction in terms. He describes it as "*Father Knows Best* gone mad"—and it is the first movie in "Odorama."

Divine is back, this time as Francine Fishpaw, a sweet-tempered housewife who has to deal with a brutal, cheating husband who runs an X-rated theater (David Sampson), a foot fetishist son (Ken King), and a nymphomaniac daughter (Mary Garlington). Lighting up her life is playboy Tod Tomorrow (Tab Hunter, who with Waters helped put the memory of *The Arousers* to rest).

Francine tries to keep her good Catholic life in line while constantly sniffing out problems. The sniffing came in whenever a number appeared on the screen. Each member of the audience got an Odorama card with ten "scratch and sniff" scents on it. When the celluloid number flashed, the viewer scratched and sniffed the corresponding spot on the card. These smells included everything from pizza to old sneakers to roses to the more pungent aromas of things one might expect in a John Waters film.

Besides that winning gimmick, *Polyester* was more controlled, polished, and generally slicker than anything he had done before, but with little sacrifice of lunacy. Only this time the craziness is identifiable, recognizable, and heavens-to-murgatroid, even empathetic. It was also his ticket out of exploitation land. Following thereafter came *Hairspray* (1988), 1990's *Cry-Baby* (with Johnny Depp), *Serial Mom* (1994), and others, each less outrageous, and more mainstream, than the last.

It is Waters' blessing, and curse, that he lives in a society that caught up with the sickest things he could imagine. He no longer requires people eating bodily waste when there are things like TV "Nooz," "Reality TV" and R-rated gross-out movie comedies around. With the nasty now the norm, John Waters can sit back, relax, eat popcorn, and laugh at what he helped create.

CHAPTER TWO
VIOLENCE

They really don't have a name. Mick Garris, Hollywood-based expert on such things, called them "knife-kill movies." Harlan Ellison, famed author of science (and other types of) fiction, adopted that phrase himself. Author John McCarty termed them "Splatter Movies" in his book of the same name. Fans have come to know them as "slasher films," while, more recently, critics have termed them "torture porn."

By any name, these exploitation films—filled with the blood of human savagery—first created a controversy worthy of their graphic gore. Roger Ebert, screenwriter of *Beyond the Valley of the Dolls*, and his original (and finest) on-screen partner Gene Siskel, condemned most of them on their television shows. Writer Ellison has spent many columns attacking them in various magazines. Parents and teachers all over the nation once abhorred their existence—blaming them for the dehumanization of their children and the increase of real-life violence everywhere.

But, in reality, they are really "murder movies," and nothing new. These are the films that exist for no other purpose than to graphically kill as many victims as possible without the benefit of a valid plot or motivation ... and to relieve audiences of their aggressive tension. These films glorify gore-encrusted psychotic murderers ... and serve as an excuse to get couples to clutch at each other. These films release tension without the actual horror of, say, a multi-car pile-up or the Roman Coliseum.

Many viewers and reviewers lump them into the "horror film" genre, but that's not true. Horror is fear of the unknown. Terror is fear of the known. The moniker "murder movies" is not only more alliterative than "terror flicks," but it also differentiates them from extremely graphic horror movies, where the slaughter is caused by supernatural or alien means. It also distinguishes them from the violent, but otherwise laudable, *Jaws* (1975) or *Dirty Harry* (1971).

Ellison saw these films as a backlash against women's liberation. While it is true that most of the corpses littering these movies are female, it is to his horror that both men and women viewers cheer the deaths of both innocent men and women on screen. So what went on here? Why are more people than ever paying good money to see bad movies where nice human beings—who, in some rare cases, have never done a single negative thing in their on-screen lives (and in others have made the terrible mistake of having premarital sex)—are slashed, chopped, hacked, stabbed, garroted, beheaded, impaled, shot, strangled, and other gruesome things?

There are some explanations that come quickly to mind. First, teenage males are relatively certain that their dates will be crawling all over them by the end of these gross-out exercises. Second, pre-teens and teenagers enjoy things they know their parents find bewildering at best, disgusting at worst. What was not immediately understandable was why the 1980s and '90s generations appreciated these vicious entertainments the way prior generations loved the Beatles and the generation before went gaga over Elvis.

Third, there seems to be something in all our hearts that is gratified by watching someone better looking and better off get theirs in no uncertain terms. This again brings into focus the difference between the film that abuses its characters and those that debase and degrade them.

Once more, the film that falls into the abuse category is one that pushes and torments its characters until they have little choice but to fight back or die. Those films that debase and degrade the characters defeat those protagonists even before they have begun. They render the characters' entire existence meaningless so that they exist simply to be butchered.

Sad to say, there's always a small percentage of society who will respond negatively to any stimuli—whether they refuse to believe we landed on the moon or, in their infinite wisdom, recreate the "Russian roulette" sequence from *The Deer Hunter* (1978). Thus was the phrase "don't do this at home kids" born. But, in the huge majority of cases, these movies did, do, and will serve the same positive function all exploitation films do: relieving tension or pent-up hostility.

Unfortunately, a side effect is fostering and maintaining such anti-productive attitudes as: women are fodder, there's no use in trying, and people are less than garbage. These side effects will become clearer as we discuss movies that fall into this category.

Warning: If you cannot look directly into a veal parmigiana dinner without getting queasy, this chapter may not be your pound of flesh. The plot descriptions will be as subtle as possible without losing the flavor of the film concerned, but in terms of some of the movies, that's not saying much.

To paraphrase the words of Margo Channing (Bette Davis) in *All About Eve* (1950): Hold onto your stomach. This is going to be a bumpy ride.

★★★ HELD OVER BY POPULAR DEMAND ★★★
Herschell Gordon Lewis

As reported earlier, different exploiters went different ways. While Russ Meyer combined his love of breasts and buffoonery, Herschell Gordon Lewis—a "nudist camp" contemporary—went goofy on gore.

His road toward the most single-mindedly violent films of the time was not a direct one. He made a variety of sexploitation films in the late 1950s and early 1960s, the most famous of which was *Lucky Pierre* (1961)—which had the distinction of being one of the first nudie movie films in thirty-five millimeter.

But his first step toward the films that would make him semi-famous was *Scum of the Earth* (1963)—"The Motion Picture Your Cashier Will Never Forget!" That was just part of an advertising campaign that was said to have had a comic book version available to theaters as giveaways.

"From the shadows of their sordid haunts ... they slither like predatory beasts ... to stalk their prey! Hell is their only address and they offer you a cheap substitute for fulfillment ... in exchange for your soul!"

Clocked at a breathless, nearly incomprehensible seventy-one minutes, this "Davis Freeman" opus, directed by Lewis, was derivative of some other schlock efforts of the time. What the poster called "Depraved, Demented, Loathsome, Nameless, and Shameless" was actually the rather tame story of some pornographers using teenagers as models and pushers. There was some threatening with knife and gun to keep the girls in line, but there was nothing to light the fires of those Lewis was to call "the gorehounds."

But Lewis was inspired. He decided that nudity was not the way. He no longer wanted to turn anyone on—he wanted to gross them out. He intrinsically understood the Puritan foundation upon which the United States was built. He realized that Russ Meyer would always have trouble with those Puritans. Sex excited them in ways they couldn't completely control or understand. Violence excited them in ways they could.

In less than a week, he filmed the movie that started it all. It was the milestoned *Blood Feast* (1963), and it more than made up for lost time.

"It started as a low, agonized gasp and built in force until it bounced off the walls in an ear-splitting crescendo. Then it was choked off in one shuddering sound. The smooth gore-splattered body writhed in a straining, undulating dance, forming a tableau of madness incarnate. Now a chain rattled, rusty steel rasped on rusty steel. A nubile woman's voice pleaded. The plea was answered by ghastly, raucous laughter. The mutilation began."

Now here was something "new." European Grand Guignol theaters had been filled with it for decades, but never had the likes of this crept onto American film screens. *Blood Feast* was introduced to exhibitors with the above quote, written in a drawing of a blood-splattered book. It was new in that no one had ever gone as far as Lewis did with the extremely graphic violence in this film. It was amazing because it did not lie to the prospective patrons. Everything advertised was not only accurate, but in some cases, the film went beyond expectations.

"An Admonition," the ads warned. "This is no publicity stunt warning. If you are the parent or guardian of an impressionable adolescent, do *not* bring him, or permit him, to see this motion picture." No lie there. The producer, identified on the credits this time as David F. Friedman, had found Connie Mason, an extremely attractive girl who worked for *Playboy* and couldn't act to save her life. Thankfully, she didn't have to. As the representative heroine, she was the one character who was never slaughtered in Lewis' films. But it was open season on almost everyone else.

Stalwart Thomas Wood played Pete Thornton, a man on the trail of a certifiable mental case, a caterer (played by Mal Arnold) who thought he was the reincarnation of an ancient Egyptian named Ramses. And Ramses had a bad habit of ripping vital organs out of the bodies of once vital women. But really, the plot hardly mattered. What did matter was Lewis' approach. The two highlights of the movie's seventy-five minutes are the ripping out of a girl's tongue and a girl's brain.

There was no "cutting away" (all puns intended) with the camera here. Using a system of hoses filled with home-made blood (from a base of Kaopectate), Lewis had the gore splashing around for all to see. A sheep's tongue was stuffed into *Playboy* Bunny Astrid Olsen's mouth, along with some cranberry sauce, and then the actor hauled the whole thing out in glorious full color.

Those who didn't throw up, laughed. Yes, laughed. For sheer outrageousness in style and content, no one could beat Herschell Gordon Lewis. His films were so completely obvious, so totally mercenary, and so unconcerned with anything besides ultra-violence, that they are really quite funny for anyone who can handle the noxious annihilation depicted.

It seemed as if many could. *Blood Feast* was booked into the regular circuit of grindhouses, and word got around that this, finally, was the real deal. Satiated exploitation audiences filled the theaters. It was a huge success. On a cost-to-profit basis, this picture did better than the likes of *Star Trek*. Costing less than fifty thousand dollars, it grossed upwards of seven million over the years.

It put a cool million into Lewis' pocket alone—a sum he subsequently lost on business deals outside the motion picture industry. But in the meantime, it was decided that he should follow *Blood Feast* up with a movie even more extreme. With a budget four times the size of *Blood Feast*, work started in St. Cloud, Florida on Lewis' magnum opus: *2000 Maniacs* (1964).

Here was a picture ready-made for the South. In comparison to his other movies, *Maniacs* was even literate. Six northern couples are driving to Florida when a weirdo with binoculars spots them from up in a tree.

"They are a-here," he calls in a ludicrously thick accent. "Theys a-comin'!"

With that cue, another madly grinning redneck places a detour sign on the interstate, leading the couples to a small town filled with, seemingly, the sweetest of southern hosts. The inhabitants stay inordinately cheery even when they start slaughtering their guests in the most prolonged and outlandish of ways. It seems that this is a ghost town of Civil War residents who were raped, murdered, and pillaged by Union troops in 1865. So, once every hundred years, the whole place reappears to pay the north back in kind.

This "Bloody Brigadoon" was Lewis' excuse to film his most wholesale display of cheery sadism thus far. While people were being chopped up in the foreground, he'd have children stringing up cats in the background. Nothing that could be done quick and cheap was beyond his imagination here. With an eighty-thousand-dollar budget, this was probably his most accomplished film, but to no avail.

For while audiences were ready to lap up his buckets of blood, the motion picture regulatory system was not giving in without a fight. *Blood Feast* had taken them by surprise. It was so popular that even non-grindhouse theaters were beginning to book it. The censors put a stop to that by making sure *2000 Maniacs* stayed in the nudie houses where it had no chance of breaking into the mainstream.

Lewis learned his lesson well. He slammed out more than thirty movies in the next nine years, each one made for the sheer blood-spilling joy of it. Lewis encapsulated the meaning of exploitation. Whatever seemed to work he would do, taking nothing seriously. All he wanted to do was have fun … and make money.

His next idea of fun money was *Color Me Blood Red* (1965), in which an insane painter needs the blood of his models to create just the right shade of crimson. But then Lewis' powers of inspired ugliness seemed to elude him for the next few years, even though he made the likes of *A Taste of Blood* (1967) and *Something Weird* (1968) —both written and produced by James F. Hurley. These just didn't have the same touch of excremental excitement his earlier films had.

It wasn't until *The Gruesome Twosome* (1968) that Lewis regained his murderous mojo. This tender tale of a wigmaker and her homicidal hair-supplier-son was filled with his patented brand of imaginative mayhem. By this time, what Lewis had started snowballed to the point that no one could stop it. And, naturally, the man who kick-started it took advantage of his newfound notoriety. His subsequent movies were even more vivid than his initial work.

The Wizard of Gore (1970) portrayed a magician who did incredible things to his female assistants on stage … only he wasn't using illusions, as the audience thought. That title soon became the director's own moniker for all concerned. But with power comes responsibility, and Lewis had gone about as far as he could go, but him being him, he decided to go out with a bang (and boom, and hack, and slash).

Lewis' initial swan song to images sadistic was *The Gore Gore Girls* (1972), which celebrated the Age of Aquarius in white, blue, but mostly red. Henny Youngman, of all people, starred as strip joint owner Marzdone Mobilie, whose go-go girls were terminated by a lot more than a pink slip. One girl was hammered to death with a meat tenderizer, another hacked with a meat cleaver, a third's wrinkles were permanently flattened with an iron, and the *pièce de résistance?* A girl's face was French-fried in a pot of boiling oil.

Fop-around-town Abraham Gentry (Frank Kress) solves the case amid such suspects as a man who constantly smashes squash with his fist, and a lesbian women's lib gang. The killer turns out to be (spoiler alert) envious waitress Marlene (Hedda Lubin), who was scarred early in life and attempts to make all pretty girls look like her. The tome's tone has already been established, so the film is capped by Marlene's suicidal plunge from a balcony … then a car runs over her head.

"Poor Marlene," Gentry eulogizes in the film's last line. "That's her all over."

That's Lewis all over as well. He was a surprising combination of cutthroat businessman, self-deprecating gentleman, and fun-loving filmmaker. At heart, it seems as if he was simply a straightforward, uncomplicated, mercenary moviemaker with hardly a thought toward what effects his films had. The gore pictures garnered an audience and attention, so that is all that seemed to concern him.

To his credit (for the Puritans at least), he has tried to make other kinds of films with actual messages, like *Year of the Yahoo* (1972), which had a surprisingly accurate and ever-timely political statement. Written by Allen Kahn, it traced the senatorial campaign of country-western singer Hank Jackson (Claude King), as a bunch of marketing types controlled his image.

A more familiar Lewis message might be found in *This Stuff'll Kill Ya*, released the same year. Written, directed, and produced by Lewis, it was a moonshiner-versus-revenuer picture with the added spice of a religious fanatic murderer mixed in. While young Carter (Terence McCarthy) tries to decide whether to leave the backwoods for civilization, people are literally getting stoned to death and crucified by a guy named Grady (Ray Sager), until his own face is blown off by a shotgun at close range.

To Lewis' debit (as far as the Puritans are concerned), he started a cinematic tradition that was soon to overtake him. Just as *Blood Feast* proved so successful it outgrew its grindhouse origins, gore-fests soon left Lewis behind. Once it seemed permissible for the mainstream to get in on their profitable production, their gruesome effects were a thousand times better, their scripts tighter, and the acting far superior.

Lewis, meanwhile, moved on to where the money was greener. Since he couldn't beat marketers, he joined them, writing several books on the industry. In 2002, at the age of seventy-three, he returned to filmmaking with a sequel to *Blood Feast*, among other things. But by now, like so many pioneers of perversion before him, his efforts pale in comparison to what passes before our eyes today.

To be honest, Lewis is not really to blame for these types of pictures. It is the audience who goes to see them that makes the movies a success. It is much easier to blame the filmmaker and the distributors for "allowing" these movies to be seen, but, without a profit, the films would not be made. The answer, as always, is not in our movie stars, but in ourselves.

ALICE SWEET ALICE (1976)
Produced by Harristown Funding Ltd. and Richard K. Rosenberg
Directed by Alfred Sole
Written by Rosemary Ritvo and Alfred Sole
Starring Linda Miller, Niles McMaster, Paula Sheppard, Tom Signorelli, and Brooke Shields

This is the film where director Sole showed great promise before helming *Tanya's Island*. The great promise was shown in subject matter and approach. The former concerns the murderous tensions in a middle-class, devoutly religious New Jersey family, which results in the murder of their youngest daughter on her Communion day, circa 1961.

In fact, this movie was originally called *Communion* when it, and its paperback novelization, were first released. Since then, it has taken on two more titles and added relevance. *Alice Sweet Alice* is its most recognized name, which relates to the character of Alice (Paula Sheppard), the murdered girl's older sister, who is the most likely suspect.

The relevance came with the success of Brooke Shields, who played the murder victim at the tender age of nine—just about at the same time she posed nude. The film's unflinching approach was responsible for creating its cult status, and, perhaps, alienating a major audience. Of course, all the title changes didn't help.

The first came in 1977 when Allied Artists tried their hand at distributing the odd effort. The second came in 1981 when Dyna-Mite Entertainment (the same company who bought a lot of Hammer Films' backlist, including 1974's *The Satanic Rites of Dracula*) re-re-released it as *Holy Terror*. In each case, Sole's film remained the same thought-provoking, ahead-of-its-time thriller.

Sole worked hard to create an atmosphere of fear and pain, the two emotions he thinks strict religion creates. When people are hurt in this movie, they are hurt bad—in places that he felt would elicit both a conscious and subconscious reaction. One woman is stabbed in the foot. A man is repeatedly struck in the mouth with a brick. In one of several unforgettable scenes, Alice herself strangles a cat.

Sole photographed all this with the help of John Friberg and Chuck Hall in a stark, jarring, way. Taken as a whole, the movie is worthy of its attention because Sole made a murder-filled movie for reasons other than just exploiting an audience. He was extremely graphic for a purpose. Too bad that purpose ran directly counter to the Puritan nee Catholic agenda.

Sole was trying to say something about the lie many live, and the pious hypocrisy many subscribe to. He deserved much better for his efforts. After the fustercluck of *Tanya's Island*, he made *Pandemonium* in 1982 (a.k.a. *Thursday the 12th*), a woefully unfocussed satire of slasher movies, after which he forged a far more rewarding career as a writer and production designer.

BLACK ANGELS (1972)
Produced by Leo Rivers
Directed, Written, and Photographed by Laurence Merrick
Starring Des Roberts, John King III, Linda Jackson, Clancy Syrko, and Beverly Gardner

Lucky us. This chapter has barely started and already here's an introduction to two violent exploitation staples: the motorcycle gang picture and the blaxploitation pic. Roger Corman's *The Wild Angels* (1965) may have been the "official" start of the former formula, while famed photographer Gordon Parks' *Shaft* (1971) and Melvin Van Peeples' *Sweet Sweetback's Badass Song* (1971) basically gave blessings to the latter.

While there have been other biker gang efforts, most notably *The Wild One* (1954), starring Marlon Brando and Lee Marvin, Corman's movie was the first of the really unruly dramas documenting the brutal abuses of various motorcycle gangs. Van Peeples, in the meantime, spent much of his own money to make his angry statement about the state of being black in America.

While Van Peeples' movie made a great deal of money on a cost-to-profit basis, as well as making many towns sweat over its volatile subject matter (a black man violently victimized by white police, then exacting his revenge before escaping), Parks' reworking of hard-boiled detective sagas to fit a modern, black, superhero played by Richard Roundtree was something everyone of any color could, and did, enjoy.

Suddenly it was profitable for veteran exploiters to film racial and motorcycle matters. The inventive and tenacious names listed above hit upon the idea of combining the forms. The only thing the white motorcycle gang called the Serpents hated worse than the black motorcycle gang called the Choppers was the police lieutenant named Harper (Clancy Syrko). The one thing Harper wanted more than a raise was to see the gangs wiped off the face of the earth. Johnny Reb (John King III) was going to see to it that Harper got his wish.

After Chainer (Des Roberts), leader of the whites, kills a black, he feels so good that they accept renegade biker Reb into their ranks. The Choppers almost succeed in killing Chainer in an ambush, but Reb saves his life. That calls for a party, where the ever-resourceful Johnny produces a bag of uppers. These uppers turn out to be bummers because they are really downers.

Frenchy (John Donovan) then finds out that Reb is as fake as the pills. He's a black passing for white. But, as the rest of the gang passes out, Reb silences Frenchy with a well-placed switchblade and calls on the Chopper cavalry. The Serpents may be drowsy, but the attack sobers them up enough to fight back. They slaughter each other long enough for Lieutenant Harper to get a good vantage point at the top of a hill. The end.

By 1974, producers were depending on gimmicks to get people in for the same old rigmarole. Notorious director Matt Cimber (best known for his multiple Razzie Award winner *Butterfly* in 1982) cast five real-life black football players and one black baseball player to portray the members of a peaceful, law-abiding unit of Vietnam vets called *The Black Six*, who had to contend with a racist bunch of Caucasian Hell's Angels.

However, the real winner in the blaxploisbiker sweepstakes was *Black Gestapo* (1975), an unusually bold story of black victimizing black. Rod Perry stars as the original leader of The People's Army of Watts (PAOW), a group dedicated to keeping white mobsters from poisoning their community with drugs. But when white racketeers (led by director Lee Frost in an on-screen role) begin really putting on the pressure, a violent black militant played by Charles P. Robinson takes over the PAOW.

Of course you know this means war, which escalates after Perry's girlfriend is raped and the PAOW cuts off the rapist's offending parts with a razor. The good guys finally emerge triumphant, but not before Robinson is totally corrupted by power. He and his men turn out to be the worst oppressors of all.

It remains for Perry to come roaring back into the action just before Robinson manages a wholesale takeover of Los Angeles by his new army of storm troopers. With clips of Hitler's original Gestapo edited in, Perry manages to blow up the PAOW's training camp and serve Robinson his just desserts … making the ghetto safe for big-time white pushers everywhere.

VIOLENCE

BLOODY BIRTHDAY (1980)
Produced by Jerry Olsen
Directed by Ed Hunt
Written by Barry Pearson and Ed Hunt
Starring Lori Lethin, Melinda Cordell, Julie Brown, Susan Strasberg, and José Ferrer

Here's a story of three suburban kids who mastermind and execute a murder spree simply for the hell of it. The unlikely excuse for the children's weirdness is that all of their mothers gave birth simultaneously during a total solar eclipse. I don't know about you, but that would certainly do it for me.

While some psycho might get away with shooting people in real life because they "don't like Mondays," gorehounds usually require either cool gore effects or a cutting edge attitude. Ed Hunt's movie had neither. Debbie (Elizabeth Ho), Curtis (Billy Jacoby), and Steven (Andy Freeman) start by slaughtering a teenage couple in a cemetery, then kill the sheriff when he comes too near the truth.

Next goes their schoolteacher when she refuses to exempt them from homework. Meanwhile, their friends Timmy (K.C. Martel) and Joyce (Lori Lethin) begin to suspect something is going on. What tips the high school girl off is a horoscope she prepared on the trio, which shows they have no feelings.

Debbie's older sister Beverly (Julie Brown) makes the mistake of finding her sister's diary and gets croaked by the trio. The final straw is when Joyce stumbles upon the boys strangling a classmate. They maintain that no one will believe her even if she talks. Incredibly, she then collects her brother Timmy and goes over to Debbie's house when called as a babysitter. Once there, the kids discover that the place has been turned into one big booby trap. They manage to escape the home and capture the two boys, but the movie ends with Debbie still free and unsuspected.

More disturbing than the film's content was the fact that many talented actors were involved. Poor Susan Strasberg, and even Oscar-winning José Ferrer, took money to appear in this travesty. But while *Bloody Birthday* was not widely seen, Columbia Pictures' *Happy Birthday to Me* (1981) was. As one of the major studios' first incursions into splatter films, Melissa Sue Anderson of TV's benign *Little House on the Prairie* (1974-1983) used this study in sadism as her "image-changing" role, while the great Glenn Ford (*The Big Heat, Blackboard Jungle, Superman*) sullied his reputation with it.

Although Columbia was not above distributing this, they still sought to maintain a veneer of respectability, so they quoted their fallen director J. Lee Thompson (*The*

Guns of Navarone, for pity's sake) as saying, "What attracted me was that the young people stood out as vivid, individual characters. The difference between a good chiller and exploitative junk, at least in my opinion, is whether or not you care about the victims." What was he going to say? That the difference between a good chiller and exploitative junk is the size of the check?

This, mind you, from a man having a skewer shoved down one of those victim's throats, while shoving the face of another in spinning motorcycle spokes—all in service of a plot that has a pretty young murder dupe suffering perfectly-timed short-term amnesia after being repeatedly chloroformed throughout her life.

Sadly for all, the real star of the film was Tom Burman, the special effects make-up man, who called what he did for this production "graphic repulsion." Well put.

THE CORPSE GRINDERS (1971)
Produced, Directed, Edited, and Music by Ted V. Mikels
Written by Arch Hall and Joseph L. Cranston
Starring Sean Kenney, Monika Kelly, Sanford Mitchell, and Ann Noble

This is T.V. Mikels in the good old days. The movie is so weird, it's wonderful, especially in comparison with the derivative dross of the two aforementioned *Birthday* movies above. Many consider it T.V.'s masterpiece. Many others consider it vile. There's no reason it can't be both.

Here's the deal: Landau (Sanford Mitchell) and Maltby (L. Byron Foster) become so angry at their backer (after he turns off the cash right after they build their cat food factory) that they shove him into the meat grinder and mix in the results with their pussycat product. This particular shipment proves so popular with felines that the duo keep a grave robber on staff to supply them with fresh bodies. The only problem is that cats raised on a diet of "Lotus Cat Food—For Cats Who Like People," come to like people too much.

After an old lady is killed by her pet, Dr. Howard Glass (Sean Kenney) and his nurse Angie Robinson (Monika Kelly) enter the scene to do a full-scale investigation. All roads lead to Lotus Cat Food, and, while Landau manages to pull the wool over Glass' eye, Nurse Robinson returns after hours to size the place up. She finds the lecherous Maltby alone, since Landau is out eliminating the grave robber. His services are no longer required because, one, he knows too much, and two, the company has just hired a full-time executioner.

Maltby doesn't care, for all along he was planning to abscond with the money. Only now he wants all the money and the luscious Robinson as well. That doesn't sit well with Landau, who returns just in time to mix his ex-partner in with tomorrow's batch of Lotus. At that opportune moment, Dr. Glass reappears, stage right, just in time for Landau to wound him. But before Landau can stuff them into the grinder, a private detective hired by the backer's widow saves the day.

Most critics didn't get the joke. "(This) ranks with the most repugnant things I have seen on screen," critic Donald L. Mayerson even went so far as to say. And taken as a straightforward murder movie, he might have had a point. But the cat food factory locale and the very concept of killer cats driven mad by a potent meal mix is not something the majority could take very seriously.

Besides, Mayerson's condemnation was music to gorehounds' ears. *The Corpse Grinders* was a perfect way for gorehounds to revel in nastiness without suffering pangs of moral guilt (which most never heard of anyway). It sure beat Little Friskies.

CYCLE SAVAGES (1970)
Produced by Maurice Smith
Directed and Written by Bill Brame
Starring Bruce Dern, Chris Robinson, Melody Patterson, Lee Chandler, and Virginia Hawkins

There were some actors who were regular contributors to the exploitation cause. People to whom regular gorehounds respond as only they can to one of their own. Actors whose very presence leads veteran filmgoers to believe what they are about to see is the best in demented drama.

Bruce Dern was one of those actors. After seeing him getting bludgeoned to death in *Marnie* (1964), create problems in the gothic *Hush Hush Sweet Charlotte* (1964), take a ride with *The Wild Angels* (1966), get shot up in *The St. Valentine's Day Massacre* (1967), take LSD in *The Trip* (1967), beat up Charlton Heston in *Will Penny* (1968), get killed by Clint Eastwood in *Hang 'Em High* (1968), get tied to the business end of a cannon in *Support Your Local Sheriff* (1969), and do all sorts of damage in *Bloody Mama* (1970), it was great to welcome him back in this motorcycle movie that did much to waste his talents, but heighten his reputation.

This time he is in the company of Chris Robinson, who proved too good-looking to remain making bad movies forever. While his penchant for changing his hair style and hair color kept him in exploitation circles for quite some time (most notably in *Stanley*, a sublimely dumb 1972 film about a psycho Vietnam vet with a poisonous pet snake), he wound up as Rick Webber, one of the leads on television's *General Hospital*.

Back in 1970, however, Robinson played a sensitive artist who makes the mistake of sketching biker Bruce Dern and his buddies. On the debit side, Dern fully intends to break the artist's hands, but on the plus side, his nymphomaniac girlfriend has a sister who is as sweet as the day is long (Melody Patterson, of *F Troop* fame).

Dern never does get to crush Robinson's hands in a vice, as he originally planned, but the artist does get Melody's hands in what one assumes is future marriage, and it sure is fun to watch Dern eat the scenery. *Cycle Savages* is a good title that takes on a certain sassy, fabulous ring to it once the middling, toothless movie bearing its name is over.

DEAR DEAD DELILAH (1972)
Produced by Jack Clement
Directed and Written by John Farris
Starring Agnes Moorehead, Will Geer, Michael Ansara, Dennis Patrick, and Anne Meacham

Here's how it worked. The great female stars of the 1940s were out of work in the 1960s. Then studios discovered if they starred the once grande dames in over-baked potboilers with a sadistic streak, heads would turn (and roll, at least on screen). First there was *Whatever Happened to Baby Jane* (1962), then *Hush Hush Sweet Charlotte* (1964). Then, of course, studios went too many times to the well, resulting in increasingly unimpressive fare such as *Whatever Happened to Aunt Alice* (1969), *What's the Matter with Helen* (1971), and *Who Slew Auntie Roo* (1971)—none of which lived up to the power of the two gothic originals.

So once the whole fad blew over, Southern Star Pictures released this similar tale penned and helmed by fine novelist Farris, who later wrote *When Michael Calls* and *The Fury* (both of which were made into movies). The movie did not match the power of his books, basically because it doesn't require a film crew to write a novel. What Farris could do comparatively effortlessly with words would take an extreme, expensive effort to reproduce on screen. So this story of a reformed ax murderer didn't quite have what it took.

Patricia Carmichael played the unusual heroine: a plump, graying, repressed murderess who has just been released after twenty years in a mental hospital. Coincidentally, a student (played by Robert Gentry) accidentally knocks her down while she's watching him play college football, so he invites her home for first aid.

The house is made of classic stuff: an aging southern mansion lorded over by an aging southern matriarch played by Agnes Moorehead (who made a latter-day career out of appearing in these things). The basic bone of contention is more than a half-million dollars buried by the dead patriarch. Someone wants it bad enough to part people's heads with an ax.

Spoiler alertingly, Carmichael is the red herring, while Gentry is the slaughtering son who wants it all for himself. Strangely, it is not these two who face each other at the climax. Rather it is the higher-billed Moorehead who gets to plug her progeny with a nearby gun before expiring herself from an earlier-inflicted wound.

Realizing that the tepid effort needed a little more poison in the pudding, the distributor hauled out the then-hoariest advertising cliché available. "Local exhibitors should arrange for a one-million-dollar insurance policy," they suggested, "to cover viewers should the picture prove too suspenseful. A midnight show for women only is recommended." But their marketing master stroke came on the poster and in newspaper ads. "You Pay For The Whole Seat," they declared, "You Only Use The Edge!"

The ad campaign matched the movie for familiarity. Unhappily, they were destined for mediocrity.

DOCTOR BUTCHER, MEDICAL DEVIATE (1982)
Produced by Terry Levene
Directed and Written by Frank Martin
Starring Ian McCulloch, Alexandra Cole, Sherry Buchanan, Peter O'Neal, and Donald O'Brian

What a great press package this oft-titled effort had! "Terror grips New York City in the aftermath of a series of macabre crimes. Four cemeteries and eleven hospital morgues have been vandalized in the last month, leaving over one hundred bodies disturbed. The police suspect that some bizarre death cult may be involved and ask Dr. Stevens of the Columbia Medical School to help. ...With the help of Laurie Miller, a beautiful anthropologist from New York University, he traces the crimes to a mysterious and elusive physician...."

"His name is Dr. Butcher, M.D., and he has perverted ... medicine for his own maniacal means. He performs diabolical surgical experiments ... in the belief that he can bring dead bodies back to life. When Laurie discovers the truth, Dr. Butcher imprisons her, intending that she be his next victim. In a spectacular climax, Dr. Stevens rescues Laurie from Dr. Butcher's murderous scalpel. They escape, blowing up ... his laboratory in the process."

Sounds good, doesn't it? That's the official plot synopsis of the "Aquarius Releasing Corporation Presentation of an Aquarius Productions Film." On the same press release is a picture of the poster. "He is a depraved, sadistic rapist; a bloodthirsty, homicidal killer ... and He Makes House Calls!" Beneath that is a painting of a corpse, the New York skyline, Dr. Butcher, a Bellevue Hospital sign, and a frightened but beautiful girl in a low–cut mini–nightgown.

It looks cool. It sounds great. It seems like a gorehound's dream. It has little or nothing to do with the actual film.

To put it bluntly, Terry Levene is one of the great schlock showmen. He knows what people want, but from time to time has trouble giving it to them, so his ads tell little white lies.

Doctor Butcher was actually a 1979 Italian film called *Queen of the Cannibals*, which was about flesh eaters on an island off the coast of Africa. Feeling that it didn't have what it took, Levene got in touch with Roy Frumkes, who had made an abortive project in the mid–1970s called *Tales that Will Rip Your Heart Out*.

Levene took a quarter of the latter and seventy-five percent of the former and came up with this winner. It made a great deal of money, but confused those who weren't dissatisfied. It is unfortunate that those disgruntled viewers weren't told the far more entertaining story of the film's creation. That, after all, is classic exploitation at it's best (or worst, depending upon your point of view).

DON'T ANSWER THE PHONE (1981)
Produced by Robert Hammer and Michael Castle
Directed by Robert Hammer
Written by Robert Hammer and Michael Castle
Starring James Westmoreland, Flo Gerrish, Ben Frank, Nicholas Worth, and Pamela Bryant

DON'T GO IN THE HOUSE (1981)
Produced by Ellen Hammill
Directed by Joseph Ellison
Written by Joseph R. Masefield, Ellen Hammill, and Joseph Ellison
Starring Dan Grimaldi, Robert Osth, Ruth Dardick, and Charles Bonet

DON'T LOOK IN THE BASEMENT (1974)
Directed by S. F. Brownrigg
Written by Tim Pope
Starring Rosie Holotik, William Bill McGhee, Jesse Lee Fulton, and Robert Dracup

DON'T OPEN THE WINDOW (1976)
Directed by Jorge Grau
Written by Sandro Continenza, Marcella Coscia, and Jorge Grau

VIOLENCE

Starring Christian Garbo, Raymond Lovelock, Fernando Hilbeck, and Arthur Kennedy

I was always hoping that the likes of these would be followed up with such films as *Don't Chew with Your Mouth Full* or *Don't Track Mud on My Nice Clean Floor* or, best of all, *Don't, Just Don't*.

But the actual plethora of "Don'ts" was instigated by Hallmark Films, an independent production and distribution house that became known for murder movies that fluctuated greatly in content and style. While one would be gritty, nasty, realistic, and gross, the next might be slick, uninvolving, unbelievable, and dull. One thing that remained consistent, however, was the publicity campaign. Once Hallmark settled on a winner, they didn't let go easily.

One of their campaigns that seemed to hit a responsive chord was for *Don't Look in the Basement*, a fairly good effort concerned with murders at a psychiatric hospital. The characters were eccentric, the heroine personable, and the plot engaging and unusual. Brownrigg was to be commended for a valiant try with what was obviously a very small budget.

The other films, on the other hand, should have their wrists slapped with a meat cleaver. Hallmark didn't like wasting any successful ploy, no matter if it had to stick in pablum instead of pulp. *Don't Open the Window* was a nonsensical retitling of *The Living Dead at Manchester Morgue* (1974), which was also known as *Breakfast at Manchester Morgue* when released abruptly in the States. It tells, in very uncertain terms, of a machine that both kills insects and revives human dead, and what chaos these dead bugs and reliving people cause.

The only familiar face in the cast is that of Arthur Kennedy, who did a variety of foreign films to keep solvent. Hallmark managed to make money with this subterfuge as well, but it was just one of the many instances that wound up ruining their credibility with the audience that kept them working.

... the House was released by Film Ventures International, who obviously thought that their success was assured by borrowing a page from Hallmark's book. The film certainly received some prestigious bookings—like the Cinerama Theater in Manhattan, but it would have helped having a halfway decent film to back up the promotion.

Dan Grimaldi played Donny, yet another psychotic momma's boy who had been a victim of child abuse. The most telling moment in his young life came when mommy dearest stuck his hand onto a burning stove. Naturally, this led to the boy mummifying his mummy and building a metal cremation room so he could fry anyone who reminded him of his parent. Unfortunately for the populace at large, anything with two legs, long hair, and breasts reminded him of his mother.

... the Phone was Crown International's responsibility and they, too, did quite well by it—even though it was a mass of leftover clichés from prior murder movies. James Westmoreland starred as Chris, a disturbed Vietnam vet who called his intended victims to make sure they were home before coming to strangle them with some Vietnamese coins in a stocking.

The only other notable sidelight to the film is that its ad campaign included the phrase "Don't Answer the Phone ... He'll Know You're Alone," the latter part of which became the title for Metro-Goldwyn-Mayer's entry in the exploitation swillstakes: *He Knows You're Alone*. Originally called *Blood Wedding*, this disagreeable ditty of destructiveness (written by Scott Parker) concerned a demented murderer who sought out brides-to-be because his own fiancée left him at the altar. She became his first victim.

Tom Rolling played the man known only as "The Killer"—a blank-eyed psycho who stalked the betrothed. Caitlin O'Heaney played Amy, who was all set to marry Phil (James Carroll) when the killer starts his hunt. She is saved by ex-beau Marvin (Don Scardino—enacting the part as a twisted scamp). Even though the murderer is never run completely to ground (saving him for an abortive sequel, no doubt), Amy prepares to marry Marvin when Phil shows up, knife in hand, and murder in mind. Here we go again, *Twilight Zone* style.

On the basis of all these films, there's a new movie just crying to be made. *Don't Go in the Theater*. Thankfully, there's a happy ending. Don Scardino became a very successful TV director (*The West Wing, Law & Order, Rescue Me*) and producer (*30 Rock*), while movie director Edgar Wright (*Shaun of the Dead, Hot Fuzz, Scott Pilgrim Vs. the World*) was so inspired by this sub-genre that he created a satiric trailer for *Grindhouse* (2007) called, simply, *Don't*. It was one of the best things about the film(s).

DRIVE-IN MASSACRE (1976)
Produced by Gail Films
Directed and Written by Stewart Segal
Starring Jake Barnes, Catherine Barkley, Adam Lawrence, and Patricia James

Just when you thought it was safe to go to the movies, along comes this dumb little ditty that is either a chaotic classic of the genre or just another good idea gone bad. Considering its tacky tone and texture, there's no reason it can't be both.

Someone is making a habit of decapitating, slashing, strangling, and stabbing teen lovers night after night in a California drive-in theater. The local police have many suspects to choose from: the mentally-handicapped groundskeeper, the theater owner with a machete fetish, and the sadistic night watchman driven bonkers by the cruddy films he sees.

But the murder mystery plot is just a red herring for director Segal to produce as many unconvincing slaughter scenes as he can cram into seventy-two minutes. Every opportunity to effectively satirize or develop the clever concept is wasted in order to mount yet another tired "stalk and slice" sequence. That, after all, is what people are paying to see, right?

To top it off, everything that served as story is simply thrown away at the end of the film so he can pull the old switcheroo that master schlock-artist William Castle used in his classic *The Tingler* (1959). For you see, the Drive-In murderer was never found, and it has just been learned that he is in the theater where the movie is playing at this very moment ... !

Actually, this is not a bad movie, it's just a painfully plain one. The idea was rife with possibilities, but the producers ignored them in order to stick with what they felt was marketable. This situation displays another truism of the murder movie trade. Most people jumped on the brutal bandwagon because it's easy. It takes no great thought or talent to make these films. All one needs is a good distribution deal and the execution of some poor darling about every fifteen minutes.

FEMALE BUTCHER (1972, 1973, and 1975)
Produced by X Films and Luis Films
Directed by Jorge Grau
Written by Juan Tebar, Sandro Continenza, and Jorge Grau
Starring Lucia Bose and Ewa Aulin

What's good for the cooked goose is good for the gory gander. It is not recently that murder movies' thoughts have turned to predominately female victims. Women have been cinematic sacrificial lambs since the silent days. It has always been sublimely suspenseful to place a girl in peril. The main difference between then and now is that the relief used to come when the damsel in distress was rescued. More recently it seems that the release comes when her young life is savagely terminated.

Any movie that portrays a female victimizing her sisters is somewhat unusual, and any movie with a title like *Female Butcher* gets an A for effort. Only this one, from the same guy who brought us *Manchester Morgue* a.k.a. *Don't Open the Window*, has also been called *Legend of Blood Castle*, *Countess Dracula*, and *Lady Dracula*.

All of them were the Spanish-Italian co-production detailing the life and crimes of Hungarian Countess Bathory, whose day wasn't complete without bathing in the blood of virgins. Lucia Bose does the honors here, with her victims including actress Ewa Aulin, a nicely delineated blond who played the title role in the star-studded (Richard Burton, Marlon Brando), but weak, sex farce *Candy* (1968).

It would be unfair not to mention that Grau is more than just a competent filmmaker. Both his included films show some fine attention to visual detail, but he too suffers from disinterest in anything non-exploitative. It just seems too hard for producers to realize that the context in which their violence occurs can serve to make the image stronger.

FOXY BROWN (1974)
Produced by Buzz Feitshans
Directed and Written by Jack Hill
Starring Pam Grier, Antonio Fargas, Sid Haig, and Juanita Brown

FRIDAY FOSTER (1975)
Produced and Directed by Arthur Marks
Written by Orville Hampton
Starring Pam Grier, Yaphet Kotto, Godfrey Cambridge, Thalmus Rasulala, Eartha Kitt, Jim Backus, Scatman Crothers, Ted Lange, Carl Weathers, Julius Harris, and Rosalind Miles

LADY COCOA (1976)
Produced and Directed by Matt Cimber
Written by George Theokos
Starring Lola Falana, Gene Washington, Alex Drier, Joe Greene, and Millie Perkins

Women's lib and racial equality unite in this comfortable, but ultimately misleading, trio of movies chosen to represent a once-thriving blaxploitation sub-category. The story is that one day various American International producers walked out of their offices and there, sitting at their own reception desk, was Pam Grier.

No doubt lines like "Baby, we're going to make you a star," and "Today the secretarial pool, tomorrow the world," were bandied about as the statuesque female was promoted into the ranks of lights, cameras, action.

Russ Meyer could be credited as one of the first to discover Grier's on-screen charms since she was seen in *Beyond the Valley of the Dolls*, but she soon found a place in the heart of down-n-dirty film lovers everywhere as the star of *The Big Doll House* (1971), *Women in Cages* (1971), *The Big Bird Cage* (1972), *Hit Man* (1972),

Black Mama White Mama (a women's lib version of 1958's *The Defiant Ones*), *The Twilight People* (1972), and *Scream, Blacula, Scream* (1973).

Also in 1973, she starred in *Coffy*, directed by that old workhorse Jack Hill. Hill had been in the business for some time, having films like 1963's *The Terror* (starring Boris Karloff and Jack Nicholson) to his credit, so he generally knew what he was doing. And what he was doing with *Foxy Brown* was another black-woman-versus-murderous-drug-pushers movie to milk the success of *Coffy*.

Foxy Brown did better than the trick, thanks to the more memorable title. And foxy Grier was a revelation, taking on white enemies who had the bad manners to kill her boyfriend. Hill mixed the sexual, violent, and racist elements like a well-tossed salad, teaming Grier with the likes of Antonio Fargas ("Huggy Bear" of *Starsky and Hutch*), Terry Carter ("Sgt. Broadhurst" on *McCloud*), Peter Brown ("Chad Cooper" from *Laredo*) as an innocent-looking but vicious hood, and the ever-wonderful Sid Haig (more than a hundred TV and film appearances) as yet one more white villain.

Haig is another exploitation perennial who didn't seem to be champing at the "big time" bit like some of his contemporaries. A hulking man with stringy hair, bulging eyes, rough skin, and a huge smile, he seemed content to play all his various eccentric parts with enthusiasm and skill. It is always a pleasure to see him in one light-headed film after another.

The movie itself is striking in its use of sexual, rather than firearm, weapons. Grier plays a game of "who's best in bed" throughout the film, culminating in the castration (figuratively and, in one case, literally) of her Anglo-Saxon foes. By the end, all the pushers, black and white, know better than to fool with Foxy.

Grier returned the following year in more violent blaxploitation tales, including *Sheba Baby, Bucktown,* and *Friday Foster*. The third is the most unusual of the trio, in that it was based on a nationally syndicated comic strip about a black news photographer who fought evil above and beyond the call of her city editor.

Once more she is in strong company, including Eartha Kitt as a couture clothier, Godfrey Cambridge as a fey felon, Ted Lange (of *The Love Boat*) as a preening pimp, and Yaphet Kotto as Foster's able assistant.

Her latest assignment leads to her being an eyewitness to a terrorist attack on Thalmus Rasulala, playing a reclusive billionaire. She discovers a Washington scandal and cover-up ... while she uncovers up for a variety of lovers and suspects. Whenever she gets out of bed and into trouble, Kotto is there to do the rough stuff. Everything is done in R-rated superhero style, concentrating on the lighter aspect of all the dark doings.

It was about this time that Grier started making noise about wanting a better lot in Hollywood—better parts, better movies, and, in the words of Aretha Franklin, more thespian R-E-S-P-E-C-T. Some people scoffed, but she struggled valiantly on, scoring high marks for her work as the homicidal hooker with a razor in her teeth in *Fort Apache, the Bronx* (1981), starring Paul Newman. But her moment of true acceptance came with her role in Walt Disney Productions' *Something Wicked This Way Comes* (1982), based on the book by Ray Bradbury.

No more blaxploitation for her, except in such exceptional cases as Quentin Tarantino creating the title role of *Jackie Brown* (1997) just for her. She remained a valued and respected presence in films and TV throughout her long career. Lola Falana, meanwhile, seemed happy with her self-proclaimed position as "Princess of Las Vegas." Ever a welcome guest on a variety of talk shows and the talk of variety shows, Falana rarely appeared in films. A notable exception, unfortunately, was *Lady Cocoa*, put together by the now familiar Matt Cimber. Falana was basically window dressing to the action antics of Gene Washington, playing one of her two bodyguards.

Cocoa, see, is the state's star witness against her ex-boyfriend—a mobster played by James R. Watson. Part of her deal to squeal includes a day out of jail. A day where Watson does everything he can to stick her six feet under. Doing his best to stop him is Washington as patrolman Doug, who works in the company of veteran cop Ramsey (Alex Drier). The highlight of the complications is a chase between Doug on foot and two fake honeymooners in a car. The most unusual facet of that fight is that both are trying to cut each other off inside a hotel. Doug blasts away at the killers as they drive through the lobby and hallways before crashing into the swimming pool.

The battle doesn't stop there. Although the fake husband is drowned, the fake wife is also a fake woman. Ripping off his wig, he hauls out a gun and the two continue to go at it until Doug blasts the transvestite down. But even then his troubles aren't over, for it turns out that, surprise surprise, even his partner is in the corrupt employ of Watson. But Doug finally eliminates everyone between Falana and the witness box.

These types of pictures were enormously popular with action audiences even though they were essentially false at the core. The various black actors were happy for work, of course, but only on rare occasions (such as *Shaft* and *Cotton Comes to Harlem*) was the creative talent the same color. For the most part, the writers, directors, and producers were Caucasian exploiters anxious to make a buck.

Eager patrons, no matter what their color, didn't seem to care—in some cases delighting in the stereotypes, no matter what their color. For anyone lucky enough to have been part of the experience at its height, any blaxploitation theater viewing was an amazing experience to say the least.

VIOLENCE

★★★ HELD OVER BY POPULAR DEMAND ★★★
Wes Craven & Sean S. Cunningham

Now these are not bad guys. In fact, both of them are very nice men who have done their best over the years to make meaningful movies filled with the milk of human kindness. However, the crass and commercial interests of audiences have conspired into making them two of the most important contributors to the "cinema of sickness." Alone and together, they have produced films that are milestones in murder movie country.

Cunningham was a theater producer in New York while Craven was an ex-high school teacher toiling in the bowels of the motion picture industry, looking for a way out of the editing room. By happenstance, they were put together to work on one of Cunningham's first films: coincidentally and ironically named *Together* (1970).

Produced (with Roger Murphy), directed, and written by Cunningham, this movie established what was soon to become one of the man's best-known trademarks. "A pseudo-documentary on feelings and sex," the *Film Journal* evaluated, "that keeps talking about the importance of feelings over sex, yet keeps showing sex without any feeling. A hot-selling item … but still an unfulfilling movie for those who want either good information or good sex."

Cunningham could have been commended for at least attempting not to cater to the prurient interests of a sex-thirsty audience, but Hallmark Releasing put together a simple but effective ad campaign that utilized a rear view of a hippie couple with their hands in each other's pants. Cunningham Films was thereby launched.

Their launching was given a blast from the release of *Last House on the Left* in 1972. Hallmark was so enamored of the returns from *Together* that they dropped some money in the men's laps with instructions to make a no-holds-barred horror movie. To them, horror meant the sort of evil men do to their victims, rather than the horror that monsters do to women. But horror meant more to Craven, who wrote the screenplay in a few days.

It was so simple, so savage, and so scintillating that Hallmark doubled their advance money, and Cunningham got cracking. The story seems like simplicity itself. Two girls walking in the woods are set upon by a gang of thugs who delight in sexually and physically torturing them to death. To the killers' everlasting mortification, their unknowing next stop is the home of the murdered girls' family.

No shrinking violets these. The family of the dead girls prove to be more than a match for the punks, whom they dispatch in fitting fashion. This is one coarse, graphic, ugly, powerful movie, yet it is essentially impossible not to be taken in by the parents' gory quest for vengeance. It is of some significance that Craven wasn't satisfied to merely slaughter the innocents as so many other filmmakers had done.

Beyond the fact that the movie included sensationalistic things that had never been shown before, the secret of its success, of course, lay in the killers getting their comeuppance in kind. After seeing him ripping out his victims' entrails and participating in necrophilia, to see the villain's offending organ bitten off comes as truly perverted punctuation.

As sickly satisfying as the picture was, Hallmark did it one better with one of the most effective ad campaigns ever created. It was they who came up with the title, reportedly borrowing from Stanley Kubrick's movie version of Anthony Burgess' *A Clockwork Orange* (1971). In it, the protagonist's bully boys attack the "last house on the left" of a dead end street.

It was also Hallmark who might have borrowed the key phrase of the campaign from the advertising on Herschell Gordon Lewis' *Color Me Blood Red*. On that poster are the words "You Must Keep Reminding Yourself It's Just a Motion Picture!" On the *Last House* ads is the admonition; "To avoid fainting keep repeating, it's only a movie ... only a movie ... only a movie ...."

Brilliant, bloody brilliant, and enormously workable too. Even those who wouldn't go to see the movie on a bet knew of the ad campaign, but Hallmark didn't stop there. Each poster carried the legend "Mari, seventeen, is dying. Even for her the worst is yet to come," and the warning: "Not recommended for persons over thirty!"

The reaction was swift, certain, and controversial. The infamous Roger Ebert proclaimed it "a sleeper about three times as good as you would expect." The criticism against it was just as voracious. Elsewhere it was called morbid, shameful, and repugnant. But that only fueled the fire at the box office, as gorehounds started crawling out of the woodwork to hoot when the girls are killed and howl when the killers get theirs.

The ever-resourceful Hallmark covered itself against the wealth of bad publicity that flooded its way as well. In a widely seen disclaimer added to the poster that was titled "Can a Movie Go Too Far?", they defended themselves in a way that would have made Perry Mason proud. "Yes," they answered their own question, then asked themselves "why?" The answer came after the distributor compared *Last House* to Ingmar Bergman's *The Virgin Spring* (1960).

"Yes, you will hate the people who perpetrate these outrages—you should! But if a movie—and it is only a movie—can arouse you to such extreme emotion then the director has succeeded. Violence ... is not condoned ... far from it! The movie makes a plea for an end to all ... the inhuman cruelty that (is) ... a part of the time in which we live. We don't think any movie can go too far in making this message heard and felt!"

Hallmark probably got the "Rationalization of the Year" award for their heartfelt performance. And they made a bundle on the picture ... while those who enjoyed this type of thing had a good old time, and the aghast tastemakers screamed in rage.

Then, as was common with Hallmark, they squandered their advantage by overworking the campaign on every subsequent horror movie they released. *Don't Look in the Basement*, while a decent film, didn't deserve the "it's only a movie" moniker, nor did *The House that Vanished* (1974), which was a fairly high-class English ghost story that contained no ingredients worthy of warning.

Hallmark wasn't the only company that abused the concept, however. Cinemation Industries released *The Horrible House on the Hill* (1974) with the suggestion "If you get too scared, try telling yourself ... it can't happen to me ... it can't happen to me ... it can't happen to me...."

Other companies weren't content to just steal the ad campaign. Some took the title as well. Central Park Distributing released *The New House on the Left* (1975), which was a German film with the same plot as the original *Last House*, except that the revenge takes place on a train.

Replacing the "it's only a movie" here was a hilarious "Seal of Consumer Awareness" that read: "The price of admission to this motion picture is only the down payment. The balance will be extracted from your nerves minute by minute."

It wasn't long before *Last House on the Left II* came out, only Cunningham, Craven and Hallmark had nothing to do with it. Actually it was a retitled re-release of Mario Bava's masterwork *Twitch of the Death Nerve* (1972). Ironically, although originally stylish enough to be bought, edited, and distributed by a major studio, it wasn't until this was re-released as a *Last House* rip-off that gorehounds were able to see Bava's original with all its violence intact.

Meanwhile, Cunningham and Craven had gone on to other things. Although they tried to sell a variety of meaningful movies close to their hearts, no one was buying. They finally had to split up to pursue other goals. One result was the 1975 release of *The Case of the Smiling Stiffs*, produced and directed by Cunningham. Although this X-rated movie was made in 1971 from a script by Bud Talbot entitled *The Case of the Full Moon Murders*, it wasn't until mid-decade that it was shown in its full X-rated glory. For the record, it was a funny satire of *Dragnet*—only with sex supplied by Harry Reems and other porno stars.

Craven's progress was highlighted by *The Hills Have Eyes* (1977), which proved to be a slightly calmer extension of the concepts he introduced in *Last House*. Peter Locke produced this story of a civilized family deciding to fight for their lives against a barbaric family in the American desert. After what Craven calls his "white bread" family's station wagon and trailer break down in a desolate area, they are set upon by cannibalistic mountain weirdos.

Instead of spending his time choreographing one murder after another, Craven chronicles the pitched battle between natural savages and those forced to become savage when their thin veneer of civilization is stripped away. With the help of their family dogs, and a rational female member of the savages, the "nice" family wins, but only after becoming as vicious as their attackers. Once again, Craven's spin on the traditional, easy, exploitation route marked him as a man to watch. And, naturally, the film's relatively huge success didn't hurt either.

So, the status quo was maintained until 1980. That was when Cunningham was becoming dissatisfied. He had managed to make a few movies that were positive and upbeat, but was frustrated at the nation's apathetic response. *Here Come the Tigers* (1978) was little more than an inexpensive version of *The Bad News Bears* (1976). *Kick*, or, as it was later known, *Manny's Orphans* (1979), had essentially the same theme, only soccer had replaced baseball.

But, finally, Cunningham was fed up. He wanted to make a movie that would propel him into the first-class cabin of motion pictures. He wanted to make a rip-snorting, knock down, drag out success that would give him some leverage in the industry. What resulted was a script by Victor Miller called *Friday the 13th* (1980).

What Cunningham wanted, and got, was a roller coaster movie—one with predictable and expected shocks—only with violent murders replacing explosions and gunfights. The more obvious and foreshadowed the shocks were, the better. That's the way he planned the film and that's the way he filmed it—using friends, associates, and local help in his home state of Connecticut.

The movie begins in 1958 when two camp counselors, who are making out away from a bonfire, are gruesomely murdered. Twenty-two years later, Camp Crystal Lake is all set to reopen, with a whole new batch of young, nubile camp counselors, when somebody starts picking them off again, one by one.

But it is not just that they get picked off, it's how they get picked off that is the main concern here. The first gets her throat slit. Another gets her throat punctured from beneath the bed she's lying on. The then-unknown Kevin Bacon gets a pick-ax in an important part of his anatomy, I believe. The supposed hero (played by Harry Crosby, Bing Crosby's son) gets an arrow in the eye, among other places. The main course comes when the prettiest girl gets an ax full in the face.

This is not the makings of a day at Disneyland, but Cunningham does bring everything back full circle as, spoil alertingly, the last survivor, Alice (Adrienne King), finds out that nice Mrs. Voorhees from next door (Betsy Palmer in yet another image-changing role) is actually a vengeance-bent hag who's determined to get all the counselors for letting her mongoloid son drown while they were making out.

Things look bad for Alice until she grabs hold of a nearby bladed implement and separates Mrs. Voorhees' head from her shoulders. In shock, she falls into a rowboat, which then floats out into the middle of Crystal Lake, where she is found the following day (Saturday the 14th) by rescuers. Ah, but Cunningham saves the big jolt until last. Rising up from out of the water behind her is the mongoloid himself, Jason Vorhees, corroded and flaking from more than two decades underwater.

Once her rescuers reach her, however, all hint of his attack is gone. Alice is taken away while the camera remains on the placid surface of Crystal Lake. At last, air bubbles break the surface. The End ... or is it?

Of course it isn't, but first things first. Cunningham was sure he had one exploitable piece of prime meat here, and he hired a New York publicity firm to make sure the right people saw it. The right people included various gorehounds, fantasy film reviewers, impressionable friends, and major studio executives. Then, the enterprising public relations team did their darndest to make sure that, whenever a powerful distributor saw the film, the screening room was packed with "screamers."

It worked, in spades. To even the producers' surprise, the venerable Paramount Pictures, home of *The Godfather* and *Star Trek*, bought the film for distribution and then, to everyone's surprise, took to the film's promotion like maggots to a corpse. They replaced the previous publicity concept—block letters spelling the title crashing through glass—with a bloodthirstily pragmatic campaign.

The new poster had the outline of a figure holding a bloody hunting knife. Inside the outline was a painting of the woods at night with some counselors standing around. The legend spelled it out plainly. "They are doomed."

The television commercials and coming attraction trailers were even more direct, accurate, and sadistic. Structured as a well-edited body count, it essentially told the viewer outright: "Come watch them die."

Some within, and without, the studio may have thought that the marketers and makers should have been ashamed, but no one was prepared for the extraordinary amount of money the film made. Even Sean Cunningham was not prepared for the phenomenal returns his mercenary movie raked in. Satisfied that he had achieved what he set out to, Cunningham concentrated on more respectable projects (most notably *A Stranger Is Watching*, his tepid 1982 movie adaptation of Mary Higgins Clark's career-making bestseller), while Paramount all but screamed for a sequel.

They didn't have to wait long. Steve Miner, a long-time Cunningham associate (who edited *Case of the Smiling Stiffs* and associate produced the first *Friday the 13th*), was given Paramount's blessings to produce and direct *Friday the 13th Part II* (1981) under the subtle advertising banner: "The Body Count Continues."

Writer Ron Kurz immediately established yet another cold-blooded tradition. Although Cunningham's original was buoyed by his "roller coaster" approach and the fact that sweet, innocent Alice survived the onslaught, the first thing that happens in number two—the very first thing—is that Alice gets an ice-pick in the eye.

All bets were off. All classic story structure was deep-sixed. All morality was on hold. Talk about debasing and degrading characters, *Friday the 13th Part II* wrote the book. These characters aren't representations of human beings, they're plastic shooting-gallery targets that pump out blood and gore when touched.

This was probably the ultimate "people as biodegradable garbage" movie and, as a touchstone to show how far out of touch the crew was, they were reportedly disappointed when the ratings board demanded an entire forty-two seconds edited from the eighty-two-minute slaughter fest—eliminating what they considered their proudest moment: the impalement of two copulating teens by one spear that goes through both their bodies.

Here's the rest of the bad news: Jason Voorhees (Warrington Gillette) is not dead after all. He's alive and out to get those who did him and his mother wrong. First stop is Alice's house (still played by Adrienne King, but not for long), then it's back to Camp Crystal Lake for more fun. Hammers are slammed into skulls, barbed wire is sawed through throats, and machetes are slammed into faces, with an inner-forest shrine to Jason's dead mother as the focal point.

Not content with cloning the first part, minus any identifiable conflict, Miner and Kurz also borrow some things from *Psycho* and *The Texas Chainsaw Massacre* (whose section is coming up). There's a kid in a wheelchair who represents the latter while the strange disembodied voice of Mrs. Voorhees is present to remind one of the former.

And once again, there remains but one survivor—a good girl named Ginny (Amy Steel), whose boyfriend disappears with what looked like a mortally-wounded Jason. Anyone want to bet how long she survives? In the decades that followed, there were a dozen movies, a TV series, books, comics, and even toys celebrating, generally, Jason's murders, but specifically, the monetary profit to be accumulated from films that only require an unusual executioner and a growing group of young victims to be eradicated.

Meanwhile, Wes Craven had gone on to two of the genre's greatest contributions, starting with *Nightmare on Elm Street* (1984), which, like it or not, firmly established the "slasher sicko as witty hero" concept. Freddy Krueger was not just an undead monster who attacked innocents in their dreams, but a possible child molester/killer who attacked innocents in nightmares he instigated. But in movie executives' infinite wisdom, wouldn't it be great if he was the most powerful, imaginative, clever, amusing character in the entire series? In other words, wouldn't it be great if he was, essentially, the films' hero? Huh? Wouldn't it?

That approach ultimately being too redundant for him, Craven labored until he helped come up with yet another genre-bending concept. *Scream* (1996), written by Kevin Williamson, managed to pull off one of the most impressive hat tricks in the industry. One, it worked as a legitimate slasher film. Two, it also worked as a legitimate satire of slasher films. And three, it actually worked as a play-fair whodunit, with a female detective who doesn't get slaughtered in the first scene of the sequel. And to think, rumor has it, that Craven was this close to not directing it.

But we digress. The question remains: why did *Friday the 13th* eschew the profitable lesson of *Last House on the Left*, as well as many other far more profitable films that incorporated irony, intelligence, exhilaration, and heroism? Why did the skeletal formula of nice young people getting slaughtered by an inhuman monster who seems unkillable become all the rage?

Two reasons. One is that this kind of film is easy. When there's a murderer who can't be killed, there is the easy option of sequels with almost no rethinking necessary. Does anyone honestly believe that the writing of *Friday the 13th Part II* (or three, or four, or five…) took any original thought? The other reason is next. Read on.

★★★ HELD OVER BY POPULAR DEMAND ★★★
John Carpenter

Halloween (1978) is the reason. This independently produced and distributed movie, which cost three hundred thousand dollars, and took twenty days to film, went on to gross more than fifty million—making it, at the time, the single most successful independent feature ever made. It is, in addition, one of the most influential of all exploitation films. Unfortunately, it is influential for the wrong reasons.

The man who is responsible for most of *Halloween*'s success is John Carpenter. Along with Dan O'Bannon (as co-writer, star, production designer, and special effects man), Carpenter made *Dark Star* (1974)—a marvelously inventive movie that could stand on its own as comedy, science fiction, or satire. Made for sixty thousand dollars with several University of Southern California students (Brian Narville, Cal Kuniholm, Doug Knapp, Joe Sanders) and the contributions of artist Ron Cobb (production designer for 1982's *Conan the Barbarian*), model animator Jim Danforth, (1985's *Day of the Dead*) and model maker Greg Jein (1977's *Close Encounters of the Third Kind*), the movie that was originally called *The Electric Dutchman* caught the eye of distributor Jack H. Harris.

Harris is another master of the exploitative art, but he also loved science fiction, so he was willing to take a chance on Carpenter's esoteric, funny film. The highly influential *Dark Star* looks like the sort of sci-fi feature the TV crew of the original *Rocky and Bullwinkle* would have made if they were let loose. In other words, Carpenter used the picture's very cheapness as one of its main attributes.

Dark Star is the name of the arrowhead-shaped spaceship on a twenty-year mission to destroy suns that are about to go supernova. To do this, they have a bunch of computerized "thermostellar" bombs in their hold that can think for themselves. Up in the control room are four very eccentric spacemen driven nearly bonkers by the long mission.

Since their Captain died early in the trip, Doolittle (Brian Narville) has assumed command, even though he visits the cryogenically frozen, telepathic Captain for advice. Boiler (Carl Kuniholm) is a bearded, macho jock type. Pinback (Dan O'Bannon) is a mistake … literally, since he's a man who came on board accidentally twenty years before and has since taken over the real Pinback's place. Powell (Joe Sanders) is a dreamer—a man who almost never leaves the observation bubble, never stops staring into the beautiful reaches of star-studded space, and longs to surf again in California waters.

The major complication arises when one of the bombs gets stuck with the countdown already begun. Doolittle must talk it out of detonating, and almost succeeds using psychology and religion. The latter ploy proves his undoing when the computer concludes that it is God and remembers that the Lord said "Let there be light."

With Boiler and Pinback killed by the explosion, the space-suited Doolittle and Powell grab two slabs of floating debris and surf into the nearest planet's atmosphere. Although they are burned up, it makes for an exhilarating finale.

"I thought that once it was out, the film industry would come rushing to my door and carry me off on their shoulders to another film," Carpenter told me. "So I was somewhat shocked and depressed that no one paid any attention. No one really cared. No one really considered it a legitimate film. It may seem like a successful cult movie now, but for me it was a four-year struggle."

More years of struggle were ahead, the high point being the sale of a script called *Eyes*. "The original story had a woman 'linking' into the Skid Row Slasher," Carpenter explained. "It's somebody you never see—kind of a faceless force—

and you slowly realize he's getting closer and closer to her. But that was too grim for them."

"Them" was Columbia Pictures, who refashioned Carpenter's original into *The Eyes of Laura Mars* (1978), starring Faye Dunaway. In their version, Mars still sees what the killer sees, only this murderer is wiping out all Laura's friends, and, spoil alertingly, turns out to be both the cop investigating the crimes and the man Mars is in love with (Tommy Lee Jones).

It was a bad movie, to say the least, but Carpenter didn't suffer by it. His name was on a major motion picture, and he had directed *Assault on Precinct 13* (1976) in the meantime. The promise he had shown in *Dark Star* paid off in this snappy, crackling and pop thriller of a nearly deserted police station under siege by a kinky street gang. *Assault* was all but swallowed up in the sea of American cinema without causing a ripple, but people went crazy over it in Europe and at film festivals.

"It was the first film where I had to meet a schedule and shoot in thirty-five millimeter and Panavision and Metrocolor and stuff like that," Carpenter recalled. "I think we had twenty-five days. After we wrapped (principal photography), I cut the film myself in three months, did the sound effects, and the music, then released it. It was sold as a black violence film, so no one really paid any attention to it."

But it was good enough to get Warner Brothers interested in another Carpenter script called *High Rise*. In 1978, producer Richard Kobritz bought it for TV and let the screenwriter direct it under the title *Someone's Watching Me*. Like *Eyes*, it concerned the stalking of a woman by a faceless dread.

"It's a recurring theme of mine. I think it's a very frightening idea. It's the essence of paranoia: he, it, they are going to get me. And whatever it is, it's completely evil," Carpenter said. "Two weeks after I finished the TV movie, I started preproduction on *Halloween*."

Ah, the now infamous *Halloween*. It was a little movie, hatched as the brainchild of producer Irwin Yablans. "Irwin had an idea to do 'the babysitter murders,'" Carpenter remembered, "and I went along because I wanted to make movies. At one point Irwin called up and said 'How about calling it *Halloween* and having it take place on Halloween night?' At that point, this thing really took shape. What a great premise! Not make a movie about a babysitter killer, but make a movie about Halloween night. I sat down with Debra Hill (whom he met when she served as script supervisor on *...Precinct 13*), who was my writing partner and producer, and we produced a script in about eight days. It followed the 'maniac on the loose' premise, but we tried to make it a little bit more. Three weeks later we were shooting. We shot for twenty days, and it fell right into place. It was the simplest movie I ever made."

Simple, maybe, but it became much more than the little movie originally envisioned. It starts with youngster Michael Myers (no relation to the author) putting on his Halloween mask and eavesdropping on his pretty older sister making out with her boyfriend. As soon as the boyfriend leaves, Mikey goes right into the kitchen, picks up Mommy's best carving knife, and turns his shapely sister into a sack of stabbed flesh.

Fifteen years later, the town of Haddonville has gotten over the shock of the senseless murder, but the Myers house is still considered haunted. On the Halloween anniversary of Judy Myer's death, Laurie Strode (Jamie Lee Curtis) and her friends (Nancy Loomis and P.J. Soles) prepare to baby-sit. Unbeknownst to them, Michael (Nick Castle) has taken advantage of a rainstorm to ambush the car driven by his sworn enemy Dr. Sam Loomis (Donald Pleasance) and come back to town armed with an over-the-head mask (which was later revealed in real life to be a store-bought *Star Trek* "Captain Kirk" mask) and another butcher knife. For some reason, he fixates on Laurie and spends the rest of the movie killing her friends.

After strangling the two other girls and knifing their boyfriends, Myers—also known as "The Shape"—starts terrorizing Laurie and her two young charges, who have spent the time watching science fiction and horror movies on TV. Her maternal and survival instincts coming to the fore, Laurie lets Mike have it in the neck and then, later, the eye with a darning needle.

In both cases, the Shape goes down, but not for the count. There's just no killing the once-little, now-big devil.

He finally seems fated to wrap his hands around Laurie's neck when Dr. Loomis appears in the nick of time and pumps six .357 Magnum shells into his chest at point-blank range. The Shape flies out of French doors, over a balcony railing, and slams onto the ground. But when Loomis goes back to check after comforting the hysterical girl, Myers is nowhere to be seen. The movie ends on a macabre note of "is he or isn't he the Boogieman?"

"All it was," Carpenter said of his groundbreaking film, "was a stylistic exercise strung together with a threadbare plot. That's why it was so much fun." Many people agreed with him, because when *Halloween* premiered on Halloween of 1978, it garnered exceptional reviews and warranted long lines at the box office. Most everyone seemed to enjoy its ability to be spooky without being gory. It was a perfect chiller to warm up dates on a cold October night. People laughed, gasped, and screamed right on cue. Carpenter had them in the palm of his cinematic hand.

At that time no one could foresee what real horrors this innocuous number was to wreak. No one seemed to realize that, taken at its most basic level—beyond the fact that Carpenter had a firm grasp on cinematic style, beyond the fact that Laurie

Strode was pictured as a capable, strong heroine—*Halloween* is nothing more than a man who can't be killed killing innocent victims all around him for, apparently, no reason at all.

While influential, Pulitzer Prize-winning critic Roger Ebert reportedly sent Paramount a letter admonishing them for the distribution of *Friday the 13th*, he was vocal in his admiration for *Halloween*, even though that movie introduced all the stylistic formulas that he found so abhorrent in the former film.

Without *Halloween*, there probably wouldn't have been so much dependence on the use of the killer's "point of view" camera angle (the camera serving as the character's eyes, seeing what he sees, and just generally making the audience into the murderer). Without *Halloween*, there wouldn't be so many film murderers who seem impossible to destroy. Without *Halloween*, there wouldn't be so many major studio movies that are centered around the stalking, torture, and death of innocent young women—again, for, seemingly, no reason at all.

Well, that's no reason to condemn *Halloween*, is it? After all, is it the film's fault that so many derivative clones have utilized all its bad aspects without incorporating the good? No, of course not. Not at first. Unfortunately, the evidence of *Halloween II* (1981) only serves to blow the whistle on its predecessor and taint its true colors.

It's not as if Carpenter broke off all creative connection to the sequel as Sean Cunningham did with *Friday the 13th Part II*. He and Debra Hill wrote and produced the follow-up. And when first-time director Rick Rosenthal reportedly failed to deliver the proper shocks, Carpenter returned to film gruesome inserts.

At first, the project sounded enormously promising. Hill went on record saying that "chopping off people's limbs isn't scary, it's disgusting." Carpenter was quoted as saying that elaborate ways of killing people didn't matter—it was the filmic style that counted. Universal took over the distribution chores, and a lion's share of the backing, so it looked like the level of quality the first film established would be maintained.

Something definitely happened between the platitudes and the actual production, because every positive aspect of *Halloween* is missing from its sequel, and all of the negative aspects are multiplied. Laurie Strode, again played by Jamie Lee Curtis, is turned from a strong survivor into just another screaming, running, crawling, whimpering victim. The style was patented *Friday the 13th* and *The Gore Gore Girls*; hammers to the head, faces into boiling water, knives to the throat, and hypodermic needles to the eye. And the Shape (this time filled out by Dick Warlock) just keeps coming, despite being repeatedly shot, sliced by glass, and finally, immolated in the fiery finale.

The plot, which serves as a framework to all these knee-jerk jolts, takes up where the first movie left off. It is still Halloween night, and the Shape has just fallen from the balcony with six slugs in his chest. Strode is in no condition to do anything but be taken to the hospital. Taking but a moment to steal another kitchen knife, Michael isn't far behind.

From there, it's just one contrived set-up after another as the super strong, super fast killer wanders about the unbelievably dark, empty corridors of the medical facility killing guard after doctor after nurse in his obsessive hunt for Laurie. One could only hope that Carpenter and Hill would somehow give dimension and meaning to the first movie, but all they did was reveal that Laurie was actually Myers' other sister who was adopted after Michael's killing of Judy.

That only sorta kinda explains why he's obsessed with her. It doesn't explain the most important thing: how has her kid brother suddenly turned into a homicidal superman? Why can he take knives, bullets, fire and loads of other obstructions in the subsequent sequels and just keep going? "He's the Boogieman" just doesn't cut it (all puns intended) anymore.

The truly ironic thing is that the answer is right there in the first *Halloween* movie. Seemingly unbeknownst to either Carpenter or Hill is that they originally made a totally play-fair murder mystery movie with all the clues to the solution in plain sight. I had hoped that Hill and Carpenter had picked up on it when the director was quoted as saying he wanted to "clear some things up" in the sequel, but was grossly disappointed to see the essentially mindless gore-fest instead.

I repeat, however, that there is an answer. Although the many sequels have muddied the waters, the original's solution gives the whole concept depth, reality, and excitement beyond the predictable "stalk and slaughter" sequences. It could have opened the way for one of the most exciting climaxes in murder movie history, but it was not to be.

If you watch the first movie closely, you'll see that when Dr. Loomis and the nurse drive onto the stormy sanitarium grounds, seemingly all the patients are wandering around the lawn, as if released from the facility. Then note that every time Laurie kills the Shape in the original film, she leaves the body … apparently so he can leap up and surprise her, and the audience, again. You'll also see that the only time he breaks off his attack is when she nearly pulls the mask from his face.

Is that because he's afraid she'll recognize him as her brother? I say, given the evidence, it's actually because he's afraid she *won't* recognize him. Because, as anyone from Sherlock Holmes to Hercule Poirot to Columbo would tell you, the killer is *not* Michael Myers. Or should I say, the killers, plural? The *mastermind* is Michael Myers. The murderers are the other homicidal maniacs he recruited in the asylum, who, after each successive one is killed, is dragged away, and the Cap'n Kirk mask is put on the next.

The insane have taken over the asylum, indeed, and how cool would it have been had Laurie and Loomis tracked Michael to his lair?

But John Carpenter moved on. *Halloween III* (1982) dumped Michael Myers and was originally written by Nigel Kneale, a great British science-fiction writer who created the excellent *Quatermass* films (1956's *The Creeping Unknown*, 1957's *Enemy from Space*, 1968's *Five Million Years to Earth*, and 1981's *The Quatermass Solution*). Subtitled *The Season of the Witch*, it was rewritten and directed by Tommy Lee Wallace, scripter for *Amityville: The Possession* (1982) and production designer for *Halloween*. With a poster that reads "Witchcraft enters the computer age," it promised to launch the series into a different direction.

Of course that was not to be either. The attraction of having a masked, unkillable murderer who merely has to show up and slaughter an estrogen-heavy cast of unknowns was too great for easy-money studios to ignore. The ominous threat of Michael Myers to good writing started something that is not nice, and has created a never-ending night *he* came home.

His creator, meanwhile, carried on, with style, making some good movies (1981's *Escape from New York*, 1984's *Starman*, 1988's *They Live*), several arguable efforts (1982's *The Thing*, 1983's *Christine*, 1986's *Big Trouble in Little China*), and a bunch of, let's say, other ones.

HAPPY MOTHER'S DAY, LOVE GEORGE (1973)

Produced and Directed by Darren McGavin

Written by Robert Clouse

Starring Patricia Neal, Cloris Leachman, Bobby Darin, Tessa Dahl, Ron Howard, Simon Oakland, Thayer David, Joe Mascolo, and Kathie Browne

I so did not want to include this movie. It's written by the man who directed *Enter the Dragon* (1973). It's produced and directed by the man who starred as *Kolchak the Night Stalker*, and played the father in the beloved *A Christmas Story* (1983). It stars a bunch of A listers. By any criteria, it has no right to be in this book.

But the movie ... the movie! It's just too deliciously demented and misguided *not* to be in this book. Award-winning Ron Howard of *American Graffiti* (1973) and *Happy Days* stars as Johnny, a teenager who returns to his home town in Nova Scotia, Canada, to discover his true parentage. He's actually the illegitimate son of café owner Ronda (award-winning Cloris Leachman), who gave him up for adoption to a fanatically religious couple immediately after birth.

No one in his fishing village is happy to see him. Most are reeling from the recent murders of four residents. Eddie, Ronda's current beau (award-winning Bobby Darin in his last movie role), shows his displeasure by beating the boy to a pulp. No matter the situation, Ronda won't reveal Johnny's father, and Eddie continues to strenuously suggest that the teen get out of town.

Stubborn as the day is long, Johnny goes for help to Ronda's estranged sister, Cara (award-winning Patricia Neal), a poverty-stricken, bitter hag who wants little to do with Johnny or his quest. Her daughter Celia (Tessa Dahl, real-life daughter of Neal and award-winning writer Roald Dahl) is another matter. A tall drink of water with knockout eyes, she wants a lot to do with Johnny and confides in him.

Confidence number one includes showing him her attic hiding place where she spies on her playboy neighbor Mr. Piccolo (award-winning soap opera actor Joe Mascolo) and his current babe, Crystal (Kathie Browne). A good thing too, because shortly thereafter Mr. Piccolo, his mistress, and Eddie the boyfriend turn up seriously hacked to death in a deserted summer home.

The sequence of their discovery bears repeating because some sweet woman is checking out the house for possible rental, only to open the door to find the first bloody body. Screaming, she backs up into another room, which secrets the second stiff. Now thoroughly panic-stricken, she stumbles into the remaining second-floor room to find corpse number three. Finally, she gets it through her shell-shocked skull to get the hell out of there.

That's enough to get Johnny really going, so he confronts Cara, demanding to know both his father's and the murderer's name. Cara, who has finally seen the error of her taciturn ways, reveals that his father was actually her husband, George, but, upon discovering that George was having an affair with Ronda, the then-pregnant Cara killed him and dumped the body where it would never be found.

And if that weren't enough, Cara then tried a home self-abortion. Celia was born anyway, none the worse for wear except for what Cara calls a "small mental disorder" that only recently causes the sweet-faced girl to reduce the neighbors into chopped chuck. Not at all happy about her mother's confession, Celia shows up, butcher knife in hand, and gives it to her mother's neck, business side first.

Having nothing better to do, she then attacks Johnny, who manages to quiet her down and hand her over to the authorities (award-winners Simon Oakland and Thayer David). His quest complete, Johnny leaves town for an award-winning career as a beloved movie director, with only five people dead in his wake.

As might be gathered by this flippant description, this film was both a half-baked and over-baked stinker, made all the more laughable by its creators' pedigrees. All involved did their best to pretend it never happened, but today it remains a uniquely warped viewing experience.

VIOLENCE

HELL NIGHT (1981)
Produced by Irwin Yablans and Bruce Cohn Curtis
Directed by Tom De Simone
Written by Randolph Feldman
Starring Linda Blair, Vincent Van Patten, Peter Barton, Jenny Neumann, and Suki Goodwin

This is just one of *Halloween*'s spawn—a minnow in an ocean of killer whales. It represents producer Irwin Yablans' on-going attempts to recreate the success of his original blockbuster idea. He tried to capture a little of the same gold with the faddish, already dated *Skatetown U.S.A.* (1980) and the totally misguided *Fade to Black* (1980), only to find that it was too little too late. The same disease afflicted this limp effort.

Following the example of other school-based murder movies like *Prom Night* (1979), *Terror Train* (1980 ... and both starring the indefatigable Jamie Lee Curtis), *Graduation Day* (1981), *Final Exam* (1981), *Student Bodies* (1981 ... ostensibly a comedy helmed by Mickie Rose), and even *Night School* (1982), *Hell Night* traces the deaths of fraternity and sorority pledges Seth Davis (Vincent Van Patten), Jeff Reid (Peter Barton), and Denise Dunsmore (Suki Goodwin), and the terror inflicted upon the lone survivor Marti Gaines (Linda Blair).

It was a long way from *The Exorcist* (1973) for Linda Blair. After starring in the movie that started it all (in part), she saw the monetary necessity to appear in pale plagiarisms like this, not to mention *Roller Boogie* (1979). In any case, in order to join Alpha Sigma Rho, the pledge quartet must stay overnight in the Garth Mansion, where the infamous Garth children were born. One was deformed, another was mongoloid, the third deaf and dumb, and the last a full-fledged monster. Virgil Garth, the head of the clan, was so distraught over the situation that he killed everyone involved, including himself. Only the body of the little monster was never found....

Anyone reading this far can fill in the rest. The only other thing one might need to know is that the fraternity and sorority presidents (Kevin Brophy and Jenny Neumann) take one of their members along (Jimmy Sturdevant) to sneak into the mansion where some previously rigged scare tactics are waiting. Naturally, the joke is on them when the Garth monster starts breaking heads because the script told him to.

The monster gets his after falling on the high spear-like fence that had previously kept the frightened pledges captive. As doltish and derivative as this is, it is almost worth the price of admission to see the actors making believe they can't climb the fence so the film has some reason to continue. The stridently forced nature of that scene almost makes the tedium worthwhile. Almost, but not quite.

HOMEBODIES (1974)
Produced by Marshal Backlar
Directed by Larry Yust
Written by Howard Kaminsky, Bennett Sims, and Larry Yust
Starring Peter Brocco, Frances Fuller, Kenneth Tobey, Wesley Lau, and Irene Webster

Every once in a while, a decent little film rises from the dross—a clever, effective, meaningful movie that is also eccentric, unique, and completely incapable of finding a mass audience. This is one of those lovely little movies.

A select group of some of the best elderly actors available starred in this bloody black comedy about the disenfranchisement of the aged. A cheerily callous social worker (Linda Marsh) is the intermediary between a half-dozen old people in a condemned tenement and the construction company set to knock it down to make way for a skyscraper. As the pitiful old folk count the days to the demolition of the place they always knew as home, a construction worker accidentally falls to his death. When the work stops for a day, the half-dozen residents get an idea on how to postpone the destruction indefinitely. With firm resolve, they set about a series of sabotage that results in three more deaths.

Finally, one goes to what she thinks is the source of the problem and stabs her. When the others discover that the social worker is dead, they rally together again to eliminate anyone who would threaten their residence. The owner gets dropped into the hardening concrete cornerstone of the new building before some of the frail killers begin to have self-doubts.

That signals a complete deterioration of the plan, as the initial murderer (Paula Trueman) feels compelled to silence any opposition. The others rally around her victim's husband (Ian Wolfe), who feels that their own lives and their friendship is more sacred than even their homes. They leave Trueman in the building as they go in search for a new life.

Director-co-writer Yust handles all of the dark deeds with just the right touch of affection and righteousness. Even though the elderly assassins do dastardly things, there is still the impression that they are far more sinned against. The construction workers, social worker, and businessmen convincingly represent a world more interested in progress than people. The odd "heroes" of *Homebodies* seem to represent all that is delicate and special and that which deserves to be cherished rather than stamped out.

Nonetheless, it too was swallowed up by the disintegration of the independent exploitation film genre. Perhaps its only monument was that maybe someone from Pixar saw it and got the idea for *Up* (2009)?

I DISMEMBER MAMA (1975)
Produced by Leon Roth
Directed by Paul Leder
Written by Herschel Burke Gilbert
Starring Zooey Hall, Geri Reischl, Joanne Moore Jordan, and Marlene Tracy

Now we're talking. This was a great example of the pact between exploitation filmmakers and their audience. Once something is named this, how could any self-respecting gorehounds not go—even if they are 99.9 percent sure the actual movie will stink? How is any movie, no matter what it is about, going to live up to a title like that?

So amazed that anything could possibly be called that, *Screen World 1975* listed the film as *I Disremember Mama*. It seems as though, rather than risk comparison with its fabulous title, the eighty-one minutes of movie that come after its moniker lights up the screen, are almost completely indifferent.

Once Albert's (Zooey Hall) mother complex is established, he illustrates its ill effects by carving up women he considers to be impure. Given that his definition of impurity is anyone who shows even the remotest affection toward anything, the female population has cause for concern.

In his ever-continuing fight to eliminate rancid reputations from the world, he dispatches three girls and one male troublemaker to a higher plane before coming upon his idea of perfection: a nine-year-old girl. Falling deliriously in love, he does everything to protect her virtue from the smutty presences of her older sisters, but by the time the climax comes, he figures it has all been for naught. The police are closing in on him, represented by a no-nonsense detective played by Greg Mullavey (a great underrated actor with more than a hundred and fifty roles on his resume), and the adolescent is showing signs of puberty.

Thankfully, death claims him before he's able to dispatch his underage paramour. He leaps out of a building clutching a naked mannequin. But what does it matter? He died to give the world that terrific title.

By the way, he didn't dismember mama. Just another example of false, but inventive, exploitation advertising.

I SPIT ON YOUR GRAVE (1979)
Produced by Joseph Zbeda
Directed and Written by Meir Zarchi
Starring Camille Keaton, Eron Tabor, Richard Pace, and Anthony Nichols

It's a shame to keep bringing up critic Roger Ebert, but given his Pulitzer Prize and TV shows, he has become the last vestige of real film critics in this age of quote whores (the interchangeable "prozacritics" who never saw a movie they didn't love). In addition, Ebert was, until recently, about the only mainstream reviewer who ever had a history of enjoying, positively reviewing, and even remotely understanding exploitation films (except kung-fu movies, of course, which he blindly condemned throughout).

Be that as it may. One of the most talked-about episodes of his original *Sneak Previews* series with the late Gene Siskel was their murder movie special that condemned the likes of *Friday the 13th* while singing the praises of *Halloween*. But the duo saved their biggest rocks for this movie, proclaiming it probably the worst picture of its kind.

Its tale is a classic success story. Israeli entrepreneur Zarchi originally made it for next to nothing in Connecticut under the title *Day of the Woman*. The plot was as rudimentary as it was derivative. An attractive woman played by Camille Keaton (who is directly related to silent film comedian Buster Keaton) comes to the backwoods for rest and relaxation. What she gets instead are the unwarranted attentions of three crude chauvinist pigs and a repressed, almost retarded, bespectacled wimp.

While she is floating in the middle of a huge lake in a rowboat, the boys come by and drag her craft to shore. There follows a painfully long scene of ripping off her bathing suit and raping her. They leave her there, beaten and bare. Naked, she stumbles back to her rented cottage, only to find the same men waiting around for more.

And, indeed, more brutalization follows as the guys talk the nerd into "proving he's a man." These guys are the worst actors imaginable, somehow making their performances all the more real. The illusion of depravity is further heightened by the male characters' attitude. They act as if this was why the girl had come to town—simply to fulfill their sadistic lusts before they throw her away. They even give the impression, simply from the way they march in and do whatever they want, as if they had done this sort of thing before.

In short, the three main instigators act like obnoxious king cocks (i.e. roosters), strutting around as if the universe was made for their defilement. After they leave the girl the second time it's *Last House on the Left* all over again, only Camille doesn't need her family's help. The remainder of the movie has her personally making mulch piles of her despoilers.

As apt a title as *Day of the Woman* was, it did not attract the audience that would make it a success. The fact of the matter is that there were not that many female gorehounds back in the day, which should surprise absolutely no one. Although veteran exploitation audiences seem to get just as big a kick when some poor guy is on the receiving end, producers maintain their concentration on feminine victims.

So it was up to the aptly named Jerry Gross Organization and *Sneak Previews* to save the day. The master movie packager pulled the film out of distribution, took the title of a 1964 French-imported picture called *I Spit on Your Grave*, and worked up a whole new ad campaign. The poster was a masterpiece of cunning ingenuity. Its centerpiece was the richly colored photo of a bruised, scratched woman taken from the back. One could see just how battered she was because all she was wearing was a flimsy, ripped, one-piece undergarment of some nature—exposing most of her back and rear as well as all her arms and legs. Clutched tightly in her bloody right hand was a butcher knife. To further heighten the tension, she is not holding it by the handle, but by the blade.

"This woman has just cut, chopped, broken and burned five men beyond recognition ... ," it said at the top of the poster. "But no jury in America would ever convict her." Gross, always the master of understatement, had struck again. There are only four men killed in the picture. But what matter? Gross stuck the movie back into circulation, and it did good business.

But it took *Sneak Previews* to really push the picture into the stratosphere. Before Ebert and Siskel's vehement condemnation, hundreds of gorehounds and gorehound theater exhibitors had never even heard of the flick. Whenever any person the exploiters see as "mainstream" comes down on a picture that hard, they figure it has to be good.

I Spit on Your Grave delivered. It was everything *Sneak Previews* said it was and more. It was numbingly dumb and brutally boring. In other words, despite the subject matter, it was a guilty pleasure that could be seen and laughed at. Without all the shouting, many prospective patrons wouldn't have gone to the film.

Some need a rationalization to allow themselves to be titillated by anti-social behavior. Ebert and Siskel had given them a reason to see what all the fuss was about. The snowballing effect of the attention served to thrust the film into the public eye. Once there, it's hard to get out ... like a hair.

The best way to hurt these pictures is to ignore them. Let them play out their course to their regular viewers and just die. The worst thing that can be done is to create new viewers by pointing at the offending picture and screaming. That only serves to draw a crowd every time.

THE INCREDIBLE TORTURE SHOW (1977)
Produced by Alan C. Margolin
Directed and Written by Joel M. Reed
Starring Seamus O'Brien, Viju Krem, Lynette Sheldon, Karen Fraser, and Louie Dejesus

"*See:* the flesh eating cannibal women! *See:* the iron tourniquet that screws your brain! *See:* the living dart board! *See:* the orgy of screaming virgins! *See:* the sickness that will make you retch!"

Now here's a rarity: a total gross-out ad campaign that doesn't exaggerate. Anyone expecting to see a pale shadow of what the poster promises was no doubt surprised when this cheap flick did all of it and more.

Seamus O'Brien starred as Sardu the Great, a theatrical impresario who presents a Grand Guignol show to the public in a rundown Greenwich Village theater in the Soho section of Manhattan. The movie opens with his admonition to the audience. "If you are bored by it, pretend it is real. If you are excited by it, pretend it is fake."

Sardu then proceeds to do nasty things to his on-stage assistants, including almost all the delights listed above. Eyeballs are plucked out, then eaten, a lady's backside is used as a pincushion with the bull's-eye being exactly where one might expect, and in the highlight of the show, a girl's head is drilled into, and her brain literally sucked out through a straw. Ta-da!

But Sardu isn't content to rest on his laurels. Having been a white slaver in Europe and having collected cages of unwilling, naked assistants off the streets of New York, he fixates on a prima ballerina (Viju Krem). Her kidnapping brings down the wrath of her football star boyfriend, who hires a detective to find her.

All this culminates on the night Sardu's show is to be reviewed by a *New York Times* critic. By then Sardu has maligned, berated, vilified, and just generally mistreated the dancer into brainwashed submission. While she is out doing a dance that climaxes with her trampling the critic to death, the cop bursts into the cage of naked women … who promptly eat him. Their appetites not slaked, they then escape and repay Sardu and his dwarf assistant for all their tender loving care.

There's no getting around it. This is one sick movie. Even the ratings board couldn't avoid that conclusion and gave it an "X" for violence. That limited its bookings, but not its appeal. It made money for the American Film Distribution

Corporation, but Troma Incorporated saw a way to make even more. They hired a couple of very pretty girls and did a new poster with the title *Bloodsucking Freaks*.

Their cunning extended to screenings at the Cannes Film Festival, which led to Rex Reed reviewing it in his column, and an "R" rating, even though not one second of nudity and gore was excised. This variation of—and, in its way, an homage to—Herschell Gordon Lewis' *The Wizard of Gore* stands as both a highlight and a lowlight in murder movie history. Once seen, it is nearly impossible to forget. No matter how hard one tries.

INVASION OF THE BLOOD FARMERS (1977)
Produced and Directed by Ed Adlum
Written by Ed Kelleher and Ed Adlum
Starring Jack Neubeck

This is acknowledged as one of the great classics of schlock cinema, and Ed Adlum stands as one of the most unconcerned, most shameless makers of this stuff—even though he only has three such films to his credit.

The first was *Blonde on a Bum Trip* (1968), which is exactly what it sounds like, but it was this second feature that really catapulted Adlum into the pits. Once a rock and roll writer for *Creem* magazine, he penned this stirring saga of an upstate New York druid cult who held people captive in order to use their blood in an attempt to revive their queen.

Farmers was lauded by exploitation experts for its amateur acting, Neanderthal direction, and phony gore effects. Everyone agreed that the exaggerated, sickening sound effect that blared on the soundtrack whenever the bodily fluid was pumped out of the victims was worth its weight in fool's gold.

Even after such a beloved endeavor, Adlum went on to one bigger and better things, since he had somehow convinced the members of the coin-operated amusement machine (read: pinball and video games) industry to back his ventures. His next film could have been even better than the *Farmers* if only it looked cheaper and were just a bit more outrageous.

Nevertheless, *Shriek of the Mutilated* (1974) makes a nice bookend to Adlum's film career. Calling upon sexploitation director Mike Findlay to helm this one, it tells the elaborate story of Dr. Ernst Prell, who has convinced four of his college students that they can help him capture a Yeti—the fabled Abominable Snowman. Like dolts, they go along.

Prell is played by Alan Brock, an actor from the 1930s, who became an agent midway through his career. This change probably put him in the proper state of mind to appear in this. Getting back to the action, the five hunters go to Boot Island where they meet up with Dr. Karl Werner (Tawn Ellis, one of the stars of 1954's *Cat Women of the Moon*). Together with his mute Indian manservant Laughing Crow (Morton Jacobs), they are the only residents of the island.

Firmly convinced that the capture of a Yeti is possible because an early spring thaw has prevented the monster from getting back to the mainland, the group begin their adventure. No sooner do they start than one of the students is killed by a big, hairy white beast. The very next morning, the first victim's girlfriend is killed as well.

Only two students are left: Keith Henshaw (Michael Harris) and his girlfriend Karen Hunter (Jennifer Stock). When Karen finds out that the two doctors had been old school friends, she begins to suspect the worst. When Keith traces the sounds of bestial cries to a tape recorder and speaker system, he finally knows something is wrong.

Neither has time to learn from these discoveries as Keith is knocked out and Karen set upon by not one, but two big, furry white Yetis with sharp claws and vampire teeth. She manages to hold them off from the bathroom and is just about to escape when she finds her way blocked by an ax-holding Laughing Crow.

His expression makes it quite clear that the ax is not meant for her pursuers, so Karen promptly keels over—frightened to death. Keith finally wakes up and walks in to find Prell and Werner supping as calm as you please, only their meal consists of choice cuts from the first dead student. It is explained that they lead the "Vauderi" cannibal cult and occasionally pick prime students to go through the Yeti charade in order to supply food.

A quick look into the closet at the Yeti suits verifies their story for Keith. Once again Laughing Crow bops the kid on the back of the head, but once again Keith wakes up and manages to slip away while the entire Vauderi outfit comes over for a feast.

Keith brings a cop back in time to see the dinner table surrounded by weird guys and the nearly naked body of Karen on the cutting board. It is then that the cop reveals that he too is a cult member and the only reason Keith found him was that he was on the way to the banquet. The entire group drag the boy over to his dead girlfriend's side as Laughing Crow pulls a ceremonial cloth from her naked body and turns on the electric knife.

The camera moves in on him as he speaks the movie's final line: "Mr. Henshaw ... white meat or dark?"

What more can be said?

VIOLENCE

KEEP MY GRAVE OPEN (1980)
Produced and Directed by S.F. Brownrigg
Written by F. Amos Powell
Starring Camilla Carr and Gene Ross

Have you heard the one about the guy who keeps getting calls asking for "Joe"? He answers the phone and hears, "Is Joe there?" He replies, "'There's no Joe here,'" and hangs up. The phone rings again and a different voice asks, "Is Joe there?" and the fellow says, "Wrong number," and hangs up again. Immediately there's a third call, and the addled answerer picks it up only to hear, "May I speak to Joe?" He yells, "No!" and slams the phone down. Of course, it rings again. The fellow rips the receiver off the hook, ready to scream some obscenity when he hears, "This is Joe. Any calls for me?"

This is the murder movie version of that joke. After the atmospheric *Don't Look in the Basement*, Brownrigg didn't make lightning strike twice in this nonsensical excuse for uninteresting bloodletting. Each successive incident makes less sense than the last, instead of the other way around.

It starts with a hitchhiker who spots a dark gothic mansion with one light on upstairs. He knocks on the unlocked door, but no one answers, so he enters and ransacks the kitchen. Finding what he wants, he leaves, makes a campfire outside and starts to eat. He hears a noise, turns toward it and gets a sword shoved through his torso.

The next day a woman known only as "The Lady of the Mansion" (Camilla Carr) calls out to an unseen occupant named Kevin with the catch words "I'm back," then leaves tea outside his door, confessing that she always loved him, loves him now, and will always love him, as well as protect him any way she can.

She does this by bringing people into the house so they can be killed by an unseen force. The Lady seduces a young man who's murdered, then a hooker is hired to take care of Kevin. She goes into his room only to find the Lady disguised as a man waiting for her with murder in mind. Things get so out of hand that the delirious Lady finally commits suicide. At her lonely grave is a tall, handsome man who goes back to the mansion, enters and calls upstairs, "I'm back."

Yeah, but is Joe there?

THE LOSERS (1970)
Produced by Joe Soloman
Directed by Jack Starrett
Written by Alan Caillou

Starring William Smith, Bernie Hamilton, Adam Roarke, Monica Phillips, and Allan Caillou

Not to be confused with the 2010 movie of the same name, this was the natural culmination of all the biker movies that had been made before it appeared. After *Hell's Angels on Wheels* (1968) starring Jack Nicholson and many real life Hell's Angels, as well as *Born Losers* (1968), the biker epic that introduced Tom Laughlin as "Billy Jack" to the world, this movie took some of the best rough-and-tumble actors for an adventure reminiscent of *The Dirty Dozen* (1967) and *The Wild Bunch* (1969).

It seems as if Presidential advisor Chet Davis (played by this film's director Jack Starrett, who went on to co-star as the mean sheriff in the original *Rambo* movie, *First Blood*) has been taken hostage in Cambodia by the Red Chinese. The CIA has been empowered to recruit five Hell's Angels who are suicidal enough to get him back. Among the men put under the care of the Army officer in charge are Adam Roarke (who starred as a Hell's Angels leader in the aforementioned Jack Nicholson pic) and William Smith.

Smith is one of the greatest loved film villains of all time, with almost three hundred roles to his credit. The devotion of his small legion of fans is legend, and some of his greatest roles are milestones in the exploitation canon. He went on to wider acclaim as the venomous Falconetti in *Rich Man, Poor Man* (1976), the barbarian's father in *Conan* (1982), and Clint Eastwood's friendly boxing nemesis in *Any Which Way You Can* (1980), but his followers will never forget his magnificent fight scene in *Darker than Amber* (1970) starring Rod Taylor.

In this adaptation of John D. MacDonald's "Travis McGee" novel, Taylor as McGee squared off against Smith as a tanned psychotic hoodlum who wore a blond wig. It stands as one of the most brutal fight scenes in history as the two smash each other all over a luxury liner and then swing two-by-four boards at each other on the dock.

But getting back to *The Losers*, these five bikers live up to the movie's name as they brawl with men, and bed down with women, all during their training period. Bernie Hamilton, later to star as *Starsky and Hutch*'s police superior, played their army commander, but even he couldn't control them. The amassed Red Chinese found it relatively simple, however. Although astride souped-up bikes (courtesy of the Army Corps of Engineers), all were cut down in slow motion by the enemy during the finale.

It was a rough, but entertaining time, with barely restrained condemnation of America's involvement in the Vietnam conflict bubbling just below the movie's surface. If analysts wanted to go out on a limb, the bikers could be said to represent all of the crude, corrupt influence of the United States on the torn Southeast Asian nation. That is, if anyone wanted to read between the fights. But most were content to just watch the violence.

MANIAC (1981)
Produced by Andrew Garroni and William Lustig
Directed by William Lustig
Written by C.A. Rosenberg and Joe Spinell
Starring Joe Spinell, Caroline Munro, Gail Lawrence, Kelly Piper, Carol Henry, and Tom Savini

Well named. This infamous pile of mean-spirited slaughter has its fans, but there's a gigantic difference between a filmmaker wallowing in blood in order to release the audience's tension and a movie that serves just to get the filmmaker's sadistic rocks off.

Co-scripter and popular actor Spinell (*The Godfather, Taxi Driver, Rocky*) himself stars as Frank Zito, a bloated, coarse-skinned hunk of slime, who sees his dead, hated mother in many women. Since she used to lock him in the closet, he now feels obliged to hunt down pretty women in order to murder, strip, then scalp them. He drapes their clothes and hair on mannequins around his claustrophobic Manhattan apartment.

The wealth of detail the scriptwriters and director inject into each murder is telling, but the real star here is special make-up effects artist Tom Savini. Savini, the nicest, most dedicated and talented guy one is apt to meet, is also responsible for some of the most distasteful effects on record.

Before this, he had realized the graphic content of *Dawn of the Dead* (we're coming to that) and *Friday the 13th*. After this, he labored on the likes of 1981's *The Prowler* (a rip-off's rip-off if ever there was one) before moving up to 1982's *Creepshow*. Many see *Maniac* as Savini's crowning achievement (although he's now better known as an actor) since the film never shied away from overdoing the ugliness in close-up and slow motion.

Zito garrotes a girl's boyfriend on the beach before doing her in, rips open another's boyfriend with a shotgun blast to the head at close range through a windshield, pushes a machete through a girl's chest from the back in a subway washroom, binds and gags a model on her bed in a spread-eagled position before planting a switchblade in her chest, and just generally has a merry old time while sweating and bugging out his eyes.

Between all this oily mayhem, he has time to fixate on a beautiful fashion photographer (Caroline Munro) who, incredibly and unbelievably, responds to his overtures. The ninety-minute movie ends in a flurry of confusing incidents. As far as it can be understood, Zito is hallucinating with increasing frequency. In the graveyard where his mother is buried, he (and the audience) sees her erupting out of the ground to grab him. In reality, his mania forces Munro to wound him in order to escape the cemetery.

Stumbling home, his mannequins seem to come to life. All of his female victims are back from the dead to attack him. The sequence climaxes with the blood-coated girls literally ripping his head off. The film proper ends with two cops bursting in to find Zito face down on his mattress. Thinking him dead, they walk out, only for the camera to move in on the killer's face as his eyes snap open.

Welcome to the bottom of the barrel. *Maniac* is the murder movie stripped down to its lowest possible base. There was no fitting revenge here as in *Last House* or *I Spit on Your Grave*. There was no style as in *Halloween*. There wasn't even any struggle between pro- and antagonist as in *Friday the 13th*. *Maniac* is the murder movie naked and personified. It says and shows nothing except a man killing women for no real reason. That is its only purpose.

Enjoy.

MOTHER'S DAY (1980)
Produced by Michael Kravitz and Charles Kaufman
Directed by Charles Kaufman
Written by Warren D. Leight and Charles Kaufman
Starring Nancy Hendrickson, Deborah Luce, Tiana Pierce, Holden McGuire, and Rose Ross

Although an interesting and curious movie in its own right, this also represents another kind of fallout from the success of *Halloween*: the holiday murder movie. After producers had all but worn out the concept of students being slaughtered by faceless or nameless evil, they figured that if the content of John Carpenter's film could be copied, then so could the title.

We've already looked at some birthday efforts. Christmas also had been attacked several times in the past (1973's *Silent Night Bloody Night* and 1975's *Black Christmas*), so exploiters checked their calendars for other suitable dates. What they came up with was a very mixed bag indeed. The ever-reliable Golan-Globus released *New Year's Evil* (1981), which had very little to recommend it. Paramount Pictures released *My Bloody Valentine* (1981), which was the worst offender.

Written by John Beaird and directed by George Mihalka, it borrowed heavily from both *Halloween* and *Friday the 13th*. Instead of a murderous mother killing camp counselors many years later, or a butchering brother trying to wipe out his sister fifteen years after the fact, here a coal miner comes back two decades after pick-axing his two supervisors. His motive was the fact that he had to eat his dead co-workers when caught in a cave-in.

Because of that he cut out his supervisors' hearts and delivered them to the local government in heart-shaped candy boxes with a warning to never hold the Valentine's Day Dance again. Of course it makes no sense, but filmmakers figure audiences will swallow anything a homicidal psychotic says.

Well, guess what? The dance is about to be held again when one of the main organizers has her rib cage opened and heart ripped out. For extra measure, she's stuck to bake in a whirling clothes dryer. As the movie progresses, such delights as the miner's pick-ax going through a man's chin and out his eye are shown, as is a girl's head being shoved onto the end of a pipe so that she becomes a dying faucet.

As had been the case with Paramount's *Friday the 13th Part II*, the Motion Picture Association of America (MPAA) demanded that several seconds be trimmed from this big studio effort in order to get an "R" rating, and once more the filmmakers voiced their disappointment. But really, it's hard to sympathize with filmmakers whose entire movies rest on less than a minute of gore. If any picture's success rests almost solely on the amount of blood shown, it could not have been much in the first place (nor was its 3-D remake, appearing twenty-eight years later).

Most of these films aren't. That much must be clear on the basis of the tired, thin plotlines that have already been described. But *Mother's Day* is a holiday of a different color, thanks to an eccentric point of view and some very convincing acting. The plot, once more, is no great shakes. Two whacked-out hillbillies attack three girls on a camping trip, and drag them to their remote house.

Waiting is their mother, who looks and acts like a sweet old lady, but is actually the most pleasantly and indifferently sadistic and homicidal of them all. Holden McGuire plays Ike, who loves disco, and Billy Ray McQuade is Addley, who loves punk rock. The two are constantly screaming at each other about which musical form is better. Also screaming is the television, which is almost always on (that is, until it's used as a murder weapon)—blaring its trivial melodramas for Mama.

The matriarch is played in a solid, scary performance by Rose Ross, who does all the maternal things for her boys while they bind, gag, collar, and torture their new playthings as part of her master plan to have them rape city girls. It isn't until one of the girls dies that the other two captives unite for escape and revenge. After one boy's head is chopped off and the other gets it between the legs, the pretty survivors stumble away from the backwoods hell.

The ending mars the curious jumble that precedes it by having the mother's sister come leaping out of the bushes in a freeze frame to continue her family's perverted work. Until then, the gruesome goings-on are made bearable by the director/writer's attitude toward the corrupting influences of the mass media. The impression is given that television and music pushed the already twisted family over the edge.

Ironically Kaufman went on to a career writing for television, most notably the kid-centric animated *Dennis the Menace* (1986-1988) series.

PLEASE DON'T EAT MY MOTHER (1972)
Produced and Directed by Carl Monson
Starring Buck Kartalian, Rene Bond, Alicia Friedland, Lyn Lundgren, and Dash Fremont

Many people know about *Little Shop of Horrors* (1960), the Charles B. Griffith-written, Roger Corman-directed relative masterwork about schlep Seymour Krelboin's discovery of a man-eating plant who says "Feed me!" It was scripted in a week and filmed in two and a half days for almost no money at all (even more know about the musical stage and screen version).

Even on that schedule it far outshone this subtly-titled epic, which managed, at a running time of ninety-eight minutes, to be a half-hour longer than Corman's picture, but about a fifth of the inventive fun. The plot sounds ominously similar. Buck Kartalian played Henry Fudd, a forty-three-year-old virgin who lives with his ma and gets his jollies as a peeping tom.

Incredible as it may seem, a local store has a plant on sale with a female speaking voice. Henry buys the plant and puts a lock on his door so his mother won't know. He feeds it bugs and frogs at first, which makes the thing grow so large that it needs dogs and cats to subsist. To supply his new friend's needs, Fudd gets a job at the pound until his mother manages to get inside his room.

Once the movie's title is negated and Henry finds his mother digested, the plant develops a taste for human flesh. The ever-inventive Henry supplies it with the policeman investigating Mrs. Fudd's disappearance, a hooker Henry hires, and a pair of nude lovers to whom Henry offers his room. All during this feast, Henry has been growing closer and closer to his foliage, until he can deny his love no longer. Their relationship is cut short by her appetite, however, and the illicit love ends in a bad case of Fudd-burn.

How should viewers spell relief? C-O-R-M-A-N. If he didn't sue, he should have. Better yet, he probably left it to the fate it deserved: obscurity.

VIOLENCE

THE PROWLER (1981)
Produced by the Sandhurst Corporation
Directed by Joseph Zito
Starring Vicki Dawson, Farley Granger, Cindy Weintraub, and Christopher Goutman

What do this, a cheap independent film called *Nightmare* and a more expensive semi-major film called *The Burning,* have in common? In addition to a pre-fab, ready-cut, almost negligible plot excuse for more murder movie meanderings, they have make-up artist Tom Savini. Actually, the first and third pictures have him officially, while the other only advertises the fact that he supposedly did the gore effects.

This is how far the industry had come in the 1980s. Instead of advertising stars or story, some were advertising the gore. Not only were they advertising, but they were even lying about it. Savini didn't do the effects for *Nightmare.* He maintains that he merely gave the special effects-slash-makeup (all puns intended) crew some advice over the phone. Whether he did or did not is actually pretty immaterial, except to murder movie enthusiasts.

Rest assured, fans, that Savini personally did the effects for the others back-to-back. *The Prowler* was first in production, first in the theaters, and first in the hearts of gorehounds everywhere. It was another example of the rip-off's rip-off syndrome, in that it was actually *My Bloody Valentine* by way of *Friday the 13th.* And if they hadn't changed the original title from *The Graduation,* it might have been a rip-offs' rip-off's rip-off from the all too familiar *Graduation Day.*

This time the initial murder occurs forty years in the past, when a soldier receives a "Dear John" letter from his love. He comes back to his little hometown, armed with a pitchfork, to find his girl in the back seat with another man on the night of the graduation dance. He makes quick work of the two and disappears. Years and years and years later, the Graduation Dance is finally being resurrected again … and so is the murderer.

This time he's in an army uniform and the pitchfork is his specialty. Interestingly, to me at least, is that once holidays and school locations were used up, the exploiters' attention turned to the implements of death themselves. The prowler shows initiative by, one, cutting the throat of a beautiful girl in a swimming pool so the fake blood can really spread out, two, driving his war knife through the top of a boy's head so it comes out his chin, and three, blowing a head apart with a point blank gunshot. Oh, happy day.

While the discussion is on rip-offs, *The Burning* should be mentioned. Not only does it have Savini, but also a camp location in common with the endlessly aforementioned *Friday the 13th*. The murderer in question on this trip is Cropsy (Lou David), a horribly deformed handyman who had almost been immolated by a practical joke gone wrong five years earlier.

Now he's back with scissors and shears to gain vengeance on the campers who did it to him. There is not one, but two nude love scenes that end in death for both participants, and a wealth of extremely unlikely places and positions for both murderer and murderee to end up. By the fade-out, a literal raft-full of victims are done in.

Once more, the most important ingredient in these pictures is not the acting, the story, nor the direction; it is the special gore effects. Because these films do not try to develop or vary the previously established clichés, nor are they original in any way, shape, form, or intent, they deserve the relative box office oblivion they received.

THE PSYCHO LOVER (1971)
Produced, Directed, and Written by Robert Vincent O'Neil
Starring Lawrence Montaigne, Joanne Meredith, Elizabeth Plumb, and Sharon Cook

There can be no argument that Alfred Hitchcock's *Psycho* is one of the great cinematic achievements of all time. With little violence, and even less blood, the "master of suspense" laid waste to a generation. There are still some for whom taking a shower will never be the same. The exceptional director touched on a subject that had rarely been touched on—and never with such finesse and pure cinematic ability.

But once Hitch let that particular cat out of that particular bag, the subject would be touched again, and again, and again by many grubby hands. Hitchcock had more talent in the fingernail of his pinky than almost all of the subsequent folk had in the bodies of their entire families. But Hitchcock started something that was impossible to stop. *The Psycho Lover* was just one remnant.

A great variety of "*Psycho*-oriented" titles were ground out over the next few decades. There was *Psycho-Circus* (1967), a British/West German collaboration that featured a killer under the big top (much the same as the 1968 Joan Crawford vehicle *Berserk* and 1969's wonderfully named *Night of the Bloody Apes*).

Then there was *Psychomania* (1964), about a college campus killer, and *The Psychopath* (1966), which was written by Robert Bloch—the author of the novel Hitchcock's original movie was based upon. Freddie Francis directed Bloch's script in England, as he had done for Jimmy Sangster's script of *Nightmare* (1964). And like *Nightmare*, an exploitation quickie was to be made years later utilizing the same name.

The *Psychopath* from 1973 is more interesting from a murder movie standpoint. Here was a sixty-two-minute film originally titled *An Eye for an Eye*, about a kiddie show TV host who goes bonkers. Tom Basham plays "Mr. Rabbie," a man who cares about children a little too much. When he finds out that some of his "peanut gallery" are victims of child abuse, he sets out to give the offending parents some of their own medicine … mostly with baseball bats, and, in one memorable instance, a lawnmower (which runs over the head of a mom).

The Psycho Lover pales in comparison. All it has is a rape-murderer played by Frank Cuva, who is under the care of Dr. Kenneth Alden (Lawrence Montaigne). Even after establishing that his patient can't distinguish reality from fantasy, Alden is still unable to firmly establish the man's guilt. More stringent testing is called for.

The opportunity for that very thing arises when the psychiatrist's mistress (Elizabeth Plumb) mentions *The Manchurian Candidate* (1962), in which a person is brainwashed to kill. The doc suddenly sees a way to get rid of his nagging, awful wife (Joanne Meredith). The therapeutic sessions suddenly become exercises in hypnosis during which Alden cements the idea of killing in his patient's brain.

But the doc has left himself wide open. Not only does he telegraph his plan to its intended victim, but he only instructs the hypnotized man to kill the woman he finds in Alden's house. Mrs. Alden pulls the old switcheroo, inviting the doc's mistress for tea. When Alden comes home, he finds his true love and his patient locked in a frozen death struggle. They both had been electrocuted when stepping into the television during their fight.

The film ends on that note, without having to show how the doctor's day, life, and career are completely ruined. Lasting only seventy-five minutes, the movie was barely more than an episode of *Night Gallery, Tales of the Unexpected, Darkroom*, or any of the other inferior fright series that appeared after *The Twilight Zone*.

SALO, THE 120 DAYS OF SODOM (1977)
Produced by Alberto Grimaldi
Directed by Pier Paolo Pasolini
Written by Sergio Citti and Pier Paolo Pasolini
Based on the novel by the Marquis de Sade
Starring Paolo Bonacelli, Giorgio Cataldi, Uberto P. Quintavalle, and Else De Giorgi

The only thing stranger than an unqualified gorehound is an "art movie" lover. As alien as the works of T.V. Mikels, Herschell Gordon Lewis, Russ Meyer, and Andy Milligan are to some, so are the works of Jean-Luc Godard, Alain Resnais, Michelangelo Antonioni, and Pasolini to others. And both factions might look upon each other with equal disdain.

While the exploitation fare could be dismissed as coarse, mindless, and ugly, the art stuff could be seen as pretentious, pseudo-intellectual, and purposely amateurish. However, both factions are extremely vocal and dedicated to their genres. There is nothing quite like seeing one or the other sit through the worst sort of unmitigated clap-trap and then passionately struggle to explain "what the director meant."

Such was the case at the American premiere of *Salo* during the New York Film Festival. Since Pasolini had made such art classics as *Porcile/Pigsty/Pigpen* (1969) and *The Decameron* (1971), some folk figured that his latest work would be right up there with the others. Imagine the surprise when it was discovered that *Salo* was right down there with the likes of the worst gore-fest.

This was a symphony of sadism, a debaucher's dream. It no doubt influenced *Penthouse* magazine publisher Bob Guccione when he mounted his lavish, multi-million dollar monument to bad taste and bad filmmaking, *Caligula* (1979). It was also Pasolini's last film, since he was beaten to death in 1975 by a seventeen-year-old who claimed the director made a heavy homosexual pass at him.

The film took a two-year circumventurous route to America, since it was banned in Italy and closed down in Paris. But it made up for lost time once it finally arrived. Lasting two hours and five minutes, it is a catalog of well-filmed and fairly well-executed (all puns intended) acts of sexual sadism, torture, and murder.

It starred Paolo Bonacelli, Giorgio Cataldi, Uberto Quintavalle, and Aldo Valletti as four Fascist leaders who take the opportunity of a short-lived Salo government takeover to kidnap a bunch of teenage boys and girls. The rules are set with military precision. Every night, brothel madams are brought in to recount their most lurid exploits. All's fair except any hint of normal sexuality. That is punishable by dismemberment.

As the madams speak, the captives are forced to act the tale out. Between the more familiar act of eye-gouging, and the more esoteric displays of organ incineration, the Fascists mouth platitudes about dictators and tyranny. The highlight comes with the film's main banquet in which all the food is bodily waste. Before anyone loses their lunch, Pasolini went quickly on the record saying that it was really all steamed chocolate.

The final part of the movie details the quartet's torture and killing of their victims. That's the plot. Here's the rationalization. The four represent Italy's various corrupt leaders throughout history. All the girls and boys are the Italian people: the easily subdued populace willing to suffer unbelievable and unjust punishments with just a few tears. They are so bland and devoid of personality or emotion that no one cares or pities them even during the worst of it.

Wow. Heavy, huh? Now on to another art film....

SATAN'S SADISTS (1969)
Produced by Dan Kennis
Directed by Al Adamson
Written by Dennis Wayne
Starring Russ Tamblyn, Scott Brady, Kent Taylor, Greydon Clark, and Regina Carrol

A pity this title was already taken when Pasolini got to *Salo*. But now here's a real filmmaker! Al Adamson has lightened audiences lives with *Hell's Bloody Angels* (1970), *Girls for Rent* (1975), and *The Naughty Stewardesses* (1976), among many others. But loads agree that this might very well have been his shining hour and twenty-six minutes.

While other biker flicks pussy-footed around their subject matter, this took the inherent murder and sadism head-on. Russ Tamblyn, the star of *West Side Story* (1961) and *Tom Thumb* (1958), changed his goody two-shoes status by playing Anchor, the baddy two-boots leader of *Satan's Sadists*—the roughest, toughest, blood-thirstiest, shoot 'em firstiest, doggone worstiest hombres west of the Rio Grande ... and I don't mean Mahatma Gandhi (with apologies to Yosemite Sam).

The film opens with the gang coming upon, and killing, a pair of young lovers. That was just the hors d'oeuvre. Their main course is waiting in a desert café. There, a vacationing cop (Scott Brady) and his wife, as well as the diner owner (Kent Taylor) and his wife, await. When the owner insults Anchor's "old lady" Ginny (Regina Carrol), the leader takes all four into the back and kills them.

This causes a dining Vietnam vet (Gary Kent) to seriously consider his position. While Anchor's out back murdering the help, the vet uses his military training to smash a mirror across one biker's face and drown a second in a toilet. Grabbing the beautiful young waitress (Jackie Tailer), the two hightail it to a cave. The motorcycle gang take off in pursuit, only to stumble across a trio of teenage females out on a geology field trip.

Anchor starts the fun by slipping LSD into the girls' coffee and then lets his old lady know that he wants to find a new mama ... by shoving spaghetti and meatballs down her throat. She kills herself by riding her cycle over a handy cliff while the three innocent, freaked-out, students are murdered.

Not content with merely wiping out the three girls, the gang starts turning on each other. Anchor proves himself king of the hill by wrapping a poisonous snake around a friend's neck, burying another under a landslide, and defeating a third in a game of Russian roulette. Finally, the lone Anchor finds the vet and the waitress. He's all set to run them down with his cycle when the ex-soldier hurls a knife into his throat.

Gorehounds found reasons to rejoice over the twelve slayings, four rapes, and two suicides, but critics, not surprisingly, were less than overwhelmed. Especially since Independent International—the distributors—had the bad taste of relating the film to the real-life Sharon Tate murders in their advertising.

A curious sidelight: the addicted member of the gang, called "Acid," was played by Greydon Clark, who was later to give the world *Satan's Cheerleaders*.

SILENT SCREAM (1979)
Produced by Jim and Ken Wheat
Directed by Denny Harris
Written by Wallace C. Bennett, Jim Wheat, and Ken Wheat
Starring Rebecca Balding, Yvonne DeCarlo, Barbara Steele, Cameron Mitchell, and Avery Schreiber

This is a salute to some fine actors, a fine company, and the tenacity and dedication of exploitation filmmakers. The actors are the stars of this film, The company is American Cinema, a feisty independent once stationed in Hollywood. And the tenacity and dedication came from making this movie not once, but twice.

Cameron Mitchell began his film career in 1945, and, for quite some time, he put in exceptional performances in high-class projects. He starred in *Death of a Salesman* (1951), *Les Misérables* (1952), *How to Marry a Millionaire* (1953), *Desirée* (1954), and *Carousel* (1956). But in 1960, he began appearing in foreign films of dubious quality. It wasn't long before he was sticking women's faces against red hot stoves in *Blood and Black Lace*, an Italian/German/French co-production first seen in 1964.

Since then, things haven't been quite the same. Although he has worked in the relatively classy *Hombre* (1967), *The Midnight Man* (1974), and *The Swarm* (1978) after that, he is most often seen in sick little movies playing sick big people. One of his crowning achievements in that area was *The Toolbox Murders* (1978). In it, he played the manager of an apartment building who kidnapped the one girl he considered nice, dressed her up as his dead daughter, gagged her, and bound her to a bed. All of the other female residents he murdered with items from his tool box. There were drills, hammers, saws, and even a nail-shooter.

It got to the point that Mitchell's name on the marquee almost guaranteed a gorehound delight. But *Silent Scream* was that rare instance where Mitchell played a good guy: a cop investigating the beachfront murder of a college student staying in a spooky mansion off campus. Three other students live there, landlorded over by Yvonne DeCarlo (as Mrs. Engels) and her repressed son, Mason (Brad Reardon). In addition to their friend's murder, the students also find the sound of 1950s rock music emanating from the attic.

Curiosity gets the better of pretty Scotty (Rebecca Balding), who investigates, only to be grabbed by Victoria (Barbara Steele)—the mute, homicidal, lobotomized girl living in the attic. Mrs. Engels and son show up to bind and gag Scotty in the closet next to the fresh corpse of her second friend while the truth comes out.

Mason had always thought that he was Engels' son, but in reality Victoria had tried to commit suicide after the man who got her pregnant left her at the altar. She only succeeded in giving herself the same disease Tessa Dahl had in *Happy Mother's Day, Love George*. Things were manageable until the Engels family needed money so badly that they took in lodgers.

Mason is so aghast that he is actually Victoria's son that his mind snaps. He dresses up as his late grandfather and in the best *Psycho* tradition assumes his relative's soldier personality, complete with loaded .45 automatic. In the ensuing struggle, he kills his grandmother. Horror-stricken, he shoots Victoria and then himself.

Although he splatters his own brains all over the attic, he only hits Victoria in the shoulder. She's about to chop up Scotty when her boyfriend (Steve Doubet) arrives in the nick of time. Cameron Mitchell as Lt. McGiver and Avery Schreiber as Sgt. Rusin only show up when the action's over.

All in all, *Silent Scream* was a tight, entertaining, not overly stupid effort, named for the gag in Scotty's mouth. But that was not always the case, it seems. Reports circulated that the producers and director were unsatisfied with what they first came up with. Hoping to make their names with this effort, they rallied for more money, received it, and reshot some scenes to wind up with what was finally released by American Cinema. It was this kind of support, perhaps, which wound up doing the company in.

Although this film was a success, as were their martial arts movies starring Chuck Norris (1979's *A Force of One*, 1980's *The Octagon*), they spent a great deal of money acquiring and advertising the semi-disastrous *Fade to Black* (1980), and the totally disastrous *Charlie Chan and the Curse of the Dragon Queen* (1981), among others. Although already in production on *I, the Jury* (1982), the company went out of business.

SNUFF (1976)
Produced by Who's Asking
Directed by None of Your Business
Written by What's It To Ya
Starring Kept Secret

A lousy, lousy movie—but one of the great all-time exploitation classics anyway.

"If nothing else," the *Film Journal* wrote, "*Snuff* ... confirms ... two postulates: (1) that a sucker is indeed born every minute, and (2) that if a buck is to be made by appealing to the basest possible human instincts there's always someone around willing to milk those instincts for all they're worth."

The American version of *Snuff* was the brainchild of Alan Shackleton, who should get some kind of award for "Best Exploitation Campaign." After rumors started circulating on both coasts about an Argentinean movie purportedly showing a girl actually getting murdered for the film, this exploitation entrepreneur found and bought a really rotten South American murder movie based on the Manson murders.

The film was low key, drawn out, crudely made, and really boring, but the distributor collected about five thousand dollars to liven things up at the end. He hired a crew that included a girl who looked similar to one of the actresses in the South American movie. In a sequence lasting all of four minutes, this girl is shown cleaning up on the set—supposedly unaware that she was being filmed. At that point, she is attacked by the rest of the cast, dismembered, and disemboweled.

Although this showed a lot of ingenuity, any registered gorehound would know that the sequence was totally faked, but by then the admission money had already been paid, and Shackleton had gotten what he wanted. It wasn't so much the actual film, but the little touches the distributor added that really turned this into a celebration of all that is cheap, cunning, and exploitative.

The man actually hired protesters to picket the theaters where *Snuff* was playing, which garnered a great deal of publicity and media attention. After all, the mass media were the ones who brought the existence of an Argentinean snuff film to the producer's attention—it was only fitting that they be used to promote what their news had wrought. And naturally, they went along.

To further heighten the realism, more actors were hired to portray FBI agents who would harass patrons as to why they wanted to see the film. These agents would also inquire as to who made the film, since all mention of cast or crew was purposely kept off the poster or the movie's title sequence. If FBI agents were on the scene, then obviously it had to be a real snuff film ... right?

If there's one thing most gorehounds have, it's a sense of humor. A sick sense, maybe, but a strong sense, nevertheless. The best of these films are either ones that they accept totally, or ones they can openly laugh at. Most of these people seem able to rationalize any gore-fest into a laughable state, even *Maniac*.

On the basis of a survey, many thought the film a joke. The anonymous director has gone on record saying "it's a bloodbath and should be taken as nothing else," as if a bloodbath is somehow unimportant. "(It) goes so far beyond anything ... that it must be taken 'tongue-in-cheek.'" Or, if Herschell Gordon Lewis had directed it, "tongue-ripped-out-of-mouth."

Problems arise when a viewer takes any part of these things seriously, as many haters of the genre do. If the regular viewers actually thought for a split second that anything on screen had any relation to them, they'd be unable to watch. It would be too painful.

But before anyone can do any condemning, their own closets must be cleaned and aired out. Murder movies have one important aspect that *Snuff* almost stepped beyond. They are fantasies. They are fake. Every day a majority of Americans, most of whom no doubt think of themselves as civilized, watch something far uglier, more insidious, and more graphic than exploitation films: the mass media news channels, who pretend their slanted, manufactured, subjective, biased, superficial analysis and rumor are real.

★★★ HELD OVER BY POPULAR DEMAND ★★★
Tobe Hooper

"The film you are about to see is an account of the tragedy which befell a group of five young people. In particular, Sally Hardesty and her invalid brother, Franklin. It is all the more tragic in that they were young. But had they lived very, very long lives, they could not have expected, nor would they have wished to see, as much of the mad and macabre as they were to see that day. The events of that day were to lead to the discovery of one of the most bizarre crimes in the annals of American history: *The Texas Chainsaw Massacre*."

These words are what filmgoers first saw and heard back in 1974 when Bryanston Pictures released Tobe Hooper's monumental murder movie. Its effect on the industry and whoever originally saw it in movie theaters is undiminished. It is the best of its kind ever done, and quite possibly, ever will be done. The likes of *Maniac* can go overboard on gore, but it can't hold a candle to the disturbing effect of the images in this movie. Hooper is one of the few who have successfully been able to capture the essence of insanity on film.

From the very opening shot of a wet, disintegrating corpse lashed to a gravestone monument, as a radio report chronicling the desecration of the whole graveyard crackles on the soundtrack, to the last shot of a masked, overweight madman doing a dance of death on a deserted highway, his chainsaw chattering over his head, the movie is a miraculous combination of intent, acting, and accident that results in an unequaled viewing experience.

Tobe Hooper directed, produced, wrote (with Kim Kenkel), and composed the music (with Wayne Bell) for the film, which was based on the legend of mid-western murderer Ed Gein—a man who was content to dig up dead bodies for food and used their skin for clothing until he kidnapped and murdered a young girl as well as a middle-aged woman. That led to his arrest, but his reputation grew as the years went by. Norman Bates, the lead character in *Psycho*, is said to have been based upon him. Most certainly, the lead character of *Deranged* (1974) is based upon him. But Hooper's film goes way beyond the known facts to build an entire town of terror.

Although it is less than an hour and a half, it can seem much longer, because of the risks Hooper takes. There are some long scenes that seem like exposition, but are, in fact, even more unsettling than the later episodes of flat-out destruction. After the opening shot—that long pull back from the face of the rotting corpse in order to show it tied to the cross, as it were—the radio news report continues to rattle off a series of truly gruesome crimes as the camera does a cross-fade to a close-up of a dead armadillo on its back in the road.

Sally (Marilyn Burns), her wheelchair-ridden brother Franklyn (Paul A. Partain), her boyfriend Jerry (Allen Danziger), and their friends Pam (Teri McMinn) and Kirk (William Vail), head toward the vandalized cemetery where Sally's granddad is buried. She's told by some "good old boys" that her relative's grave is all right, while Franklyn is entertained by a cackling, drinking coot who professes to know all sorts of dark secrets.

Hooper films this ominous character from ground level, and since he's lying on his back and looking up at the cripple, his head is upside down as he rants and giggles on. Once Sally gets back to their van, Franklyn decides that they should visit their grandfather's deserted farm. On the way, after a horrid stench fills the vehicle, he tells the others about the town's slaughterhouses.

Already Hooper has built a fetid foundation of unease, which is cemented when they foolishly stop to pick up a hitchhiker on the otherwise deserted, beautiful, sunlit highway. Pam thinks the hiker looks icky and tells them not to stop, but she is not heeded. The hiker (Edwin Neal) has a discoloration on his face, an epileptic manner in his movements, and a slight speech impediment.

He tells them more about the slaughterhouse legend, saying that his entire family had worked there, although some were fired for continuing to use the sledgehammer method after the air gun was introduced. He begins to get carried away with the tale until the subject is changed. He then shows them some Polaroid pictures, which are terrible, but wants two dollars for each of them. He then pulls out his pocket knife and, with great pride, shows how good it is by cutting open his own hand.

Neal's performance is exceptional. Although it could have gone the way of so many unconvincing performances in many other nut-job-centric movies, Hooper had tightened the screws so well prior to, and during, his introduction, that he comes off as legitimately disturbed. This is three hundred and sixty degrees away from something like *Silence of the Lambs* (1991) where Anthony Hopkins puts on a bravura performance that can be enjoyed, but, never for a second, believed. Neal's hitchhiker, on the other hand, comes off as genuinely crazy.

The five visitors finally manage to push him out of the van, but not before this scene encapsulates almost all the film's strengths. A palpable sense of claustrophobic heat and dread is perfectly realized, with the cast giving seemingly effortlessly realistic performances. There is a sense of being trapped that extends into any theater or home in which it is shown.

After that jarring experience, the van stops at a gas station that has no fuel, but does have another oddly intense character (Jim Siedow), who invites them in for a bite. Franklyn, especially, really likes the man's home-cured sausage. By now, the juxtaposition of men killing animals for food and the possibility of men killing other people for sustenance is clear. All that remains is to reveal the center of the dread.

Granddad's farm is the center. Pam and Kirk are desperate to cool off after Franklyn tells them about the swimming hole he used to play in. The camera follows them as they come upon another house on the wreck-strewn property. There's a strange buzzing sound coming from inside. Kirk goes in to investigate. As soon as he calls out, the buzzing stops. Just inside the door is a stairway. To its left is a sliding metal door.

Kirk approaches the partition. It slides open. The man on the other side is huge, fat, and wears a mask made out of human skin. He slams a small sledgehammer into

Kirk's skull without hesitation. Kirk's legs kick out spasmodically before Leatherface (Gunnar Hansen) drags him inside the room and slams the metal door shut.

From here on until near the finale, *The Texas Chainsaw Massacre* is as relentless, merciless, inexorable, and implacable as a sixty-ton semi running over a matchbox. The viewer can pretty much assume the worst will happen, but can only stare in awe at the brutal culminations of each attack. Remarkably, Hooper and company created constantly jolting and consistently unsettling effects with virtually no on-screen gore.

Pam comes to find Kirk. She enters a room filled with bones and barely human remains. She becomes sick. Leatherface appears to grab and carry her screaming into the butcher room where the dead Kirk lies on the table. He casually sticks the girl onto a meat-hook attached to the ceiling and continues to carve her boyfriend up—the power being driven home by the actors' behavior and reactions rather than gouting blood. Leatherface's powerful, yet apathetic, behavior is consistent with the way others kill cows in slaughterhouses.

Jerry is next. He comes to the house looking for his friends. He finds Pam in a coffin-like floor freezer. She is all blue, but horribly, not yet dead. It is she who must witness Jerry's death when Leatherface comes up behind him. Out of gas and out of friends, Sally pushes Franklyn's wheelchair around in the dark. Armed with a flashlight, he hopes to find the others and get out. Leatherface finds them instead, mutilating the helpless cripple with his chainsaw.

Sally runs, but her sense of direction is regrettable. First she finds herself in Leatherface's lair. She discovers an old couple upstairs, but once she nears, they turn out to be two nearly mummified horrors. She leaps, screaming, out an upstairs window. Badly cut and bruised, she manages to reach the gas station. Naturally, the meat-curing attendant there is in league with Leatherface.

He knocks her into the bathroom, binds her hands behind her, stuffs a cloth in her mouth, ties it in place, and puts a sack over her head. After dragging her out to his truck, he drives her back to Leatherface's place—the whole time cooing nearly incoherent things while hitting her with a broom handle.

Once he arrives, the truth comes out. The attendant is the house caretaker, while Leatherface and the hitchhiker are brothers. Their mother is dead, but their father—the best sledgehammer slaughterer ever—is still barely alive. While the attendant screams at Leatherface for almost giving them away, the hitchhiker goads and abuses the helpless girl. On the attendant's instruction, they bring down their father, cut Sally's finger, and let the old man suck on her blood. Unable to stand the terror anymore, she loses consciousness.

When she awakes, there is a moment where Hooper gives her, and much of the audience, hope that it all had been a bad dream. But then the horror comes back with all of its powerful reality as the camera pulls out. She is bound to a chair—its "arms" consisting of actual human arms—at the end of a dinner table surrounded by the Leatherface family.

They laugh and make vicious fun of her while she screams amid an offal and carcass-strewn room. There is no explaining just how convincing all of their actions are. Hooper leaves little time for the viewers to prepare for their onslaught, and the killers seem to have no motive and less remorse. By this time, Sally is a pale shadow of her former self. Her clothes are dirty and torn, her hair is a limp, streaked mop, her face seems permanently twisted into a tight mask of terror, and her eyes are mascara-streaming pockets of liquid fear.

Her captors drag her over to the ancient father and push her head over a washtub. Sticking a small sledge into dad's hands, they urge him to kill Sally the way he used to slaughter the cows. They act as if the girl should be happy that the best slaughterer in the state will do her in. But the old man is too feeble to kill her—or even knock her out. Time after time, in a scene that overcomes the amateurish old-age make-up of the dad, the hiker puts the hammer in his dad's hand and time after time, it painfully grazes her skull and drops into the tub.

Once again Sally is able to escape. She wrenches free and leaps out another window—with two brothers in hot pursuit. She makes it to the highway just as a large tanker and a truck are passing by. She manages to leap into the back of the truck while the tanker runs the hiker down. Leatherface falls and slices his leg with his own chainsaw. Sally escapes as Leatherface squeals his frustrated rage and holds his chainsaw up in the rays of the beautiful sunrise.

The Texas Chainsaw Massacre was the ultimate funhouse picture. It wormed its way underneath almost every defense and rattled the viewer. One is left in much the same state caused by a ride on a dangerous roller coaster. One can admire it for its construction, respect it for its ability to thrill, but also be glad it's over.

Apparently the creation of the film was just as grueling for the cast and crew. Because they didn't have a studio special effects department, the way they realized the brutality was fairly, well, brutal. For instance, Terry McMinn's Pam was hung on Leatherface's workshop meat-hook using a makeshift harness consisting of pantyhose that tightened and dug into her flesh. Her expression of pain and fear was reportedly real. Adding to the atmosphere was real offal, which, because of the tight budget, couldn't be replaced, so the set soon smelled of actual death.

Also horrific was the financial fate of the participants. Although the film's distributors made millions, Hooper and company allegedly made next to nothing. They had made the ultimate madhouse movie by entering a financial and creative madhouse themselves. The madhouse comparison is apt, considering Tobe Hooper's progress since 1973. His luck has been about as good as Sally's.

He did another exploitation film called *Death Trap* in 1976, with nowhere near the artistic success of *Chainsaw*. It starred Neville Brand as a southern crazy who runs the Starlight Hotel the way Norman Bates ran his *Psycho* motel. Instead of a mummified mother, Brand has a pet crocodile who chomped off his leg, and eats the blond (Roberta Collins) who Brand kills with a pitchfork. Her father comes looking for her and suffers a similar fate. A married couple with one child show up looking for a room. The man gets on the receiving end of Brand's scythe, the child is barricaded under the building, and the girl (Marilyn Burns again) is gagged and bound to an upstairs bed.

Stuart Whitman plays the sheriff who shows up to save those still alive, while Brand gets what he deserves in the belly of his pet beast. The cast may have been more professional, but the script by Alvin Fast and Mardi Rustam was definitely from hunger. Although they changed the title to *Starlight Slaughters*, then *Eaten Alive*, and then *Horror Hotel*, it didn't make anyone forget chainsaws.

Things went from bad to worse for Hooper. He started *The Dark* (1979) starring William Devane and Cathy Lee Crosby—which was about an outer space murderer—but was replaced by John Bud Cardos (1977's *Kingdom of the Spiders*) after creative differences with the producer. The same thing happened when he was set to direct *Venom* in England during 1981. Piers Haggard took over that story of a poisonous snake foiling a kidnap plot. He had made one of the greatest remorseless movies ever, and was constantly asked to then make remorseful ones.

Hooper was better represented by the projects he finally did. Richard Kobritz, the same producer who got John Carpenter to do *Someone's Watching Me*, got Hooper to direct the two-part, four-hour television version of Stephen King's seminal vampire saga, *Salem's Lot* (1979).

The television project was entertaining and relatively well done, but hardly the jaw-dropping equal of the book. Interestingly, some of the novel's best moments didn't require gore, but the TV version seemed intent on changing the work's concept in the transition.

Instead of an urbane bloodsucker who gives the small-town residents of Jerusalem's Lot power over their enemies, the CBS mini-series had a Nosferatu-like vampire (played by Reggie Nalder) who used an urbane middleman (James Mason). He is ultimately defeated by a writer and a young boy, but they must search out his victims all over the world (perhaps setting up a subsequent series that never came).

Funhouse (1981) was next on Hooper's schedule, and it seemed like a natural. It was the story of four teens who become the captives of a side-show freak at a seedy carnival. It seemed perfect for Hooper's brand of claustrophobic small-town terror. But after some crippling preproduction mistakes and some telling personality conflicts that left the crew without a solid script (or enough time to prepare one), it emerged as a meandering, mediocre movie that telegraphs and wastes all of its possibilities.

Then came *Poltergeist* (1982), the enormously successful ghost story that is more thrilling than scary. But even Hooper's participation with that is shrouded by storm clouds. Co-produced (with Frank Marshall) and co-written (with Michael Grais and Mark Victor) by Steven Spielberg, the word came out early in production that Hooper was taking directions more than giving them. Rumors continued to the effect that it was Spielberg who was really controlling the scenes, even though it would be against union rules for him to be directing *E.T.* and *Poltergeist* at the same time, in addition to producing the latter film.

It became known once the film was released that Spielberg was indeed a force on the set and that Hooper hadn't the complete freedom to bring as much as he may have wanted to the project. Even so, Spielberg had a full-page letter published in *Variety* thanking Hooper for "allowing" him to contribute on the set, commending him for a job well done, and wishing him luck on future projects.

Those future projects turned out to be things like the underrated *Lifeforce* (1985), a middling remake of *Invaders from Mars* (1986), a disappointing *Chainsaw* sequel in 1986, then lots of television work. Even so, the influence and success of *The Texas Chainsaw Massacre* can be discussed, but not argued. Although imitated and ripped off (*The Hollywood Meatcleaver Massacre*, a clever abomination by Group 1, *Hospital Massacre*—which went through *Be My Valentine or Else* and *X-Ray* as titles before being released by Golan-Globus—and *The Northfield Cemetery Massacre*, directed and produced by Will Dear and Thomas Dyke, among many others), it has never been surpassed for depravity and effectiveness.

THE UNDERTAKER AND HIS PALS (1967)
Produced and Directed by David C. Graham
Written by T.L.P. Twicegood
Starring Ray Dennis, Robert Lowery, Warrene Ott, and Marty Friedman

After all the angst of the previous pages, it is fitting that the chapter end with this charming concept, which just goes to prove how much, and what kind, of a sense of humor violence-exploiters possess. This was one of the earlier all-out gore films—made in the wake of Herschell Gordon Lewis' initial output. And like his stuff, thick layers of sick humor were evident to make the otherwise distasteful effort palatable.

This could be (and maybe was) put on a double bill with *The Corpse Grinders* without any difficulty. In some cases, the audience would be hard pressed seeing where one film ended and the other began. Robert Lowery played Mort the mortician, a swell guy who gives his clients the best send-off in town. But only their coffins go to the cemetery. Their bodies are given to the restaurant next door, Sweeny Todd-style.

This arrangement is great for both parties, since the eatery saves on meat prices, and the mortuary gives kickbacks. Complications arise when the demand for the café's unique taste exceeds the supply. It then becomes necessary for the undertaker and his pals (Ray Dennis, Warrene Ott, and Marty Friedman) to do a little foraging on their own. They keep both the diner and the funeral home in the money with a series of grisly murders—which, not surprisingly, catch up to them.

This sixty-minute curiosity would have probably passed into the language of just gorehounds if it hadn't been for one scene. After the on-screen hatchet murder of a black man, the special on the café's menu the next day reads "Dark Meat." This created a minor controversy, and gave the movie far more attention than would have originally been provided.

It just goes to show that all one needs is a little outrageousness, some savvy, and a strong case of inventive larceny to join the ranks of murder moviemakers who laughed all the way to the bank.

CHAPTER THREE
HORROR

Horror is nothing new. Some of the greatest works of the genre were done in the silent era—such classics as *Metropolis* (1926) and *The Cabinet of Dr. Caligari* (1919). When sound came around, Universal Studios became king of the monsters, giving the world *Dracula* (1931), starring Bela Lugosi, *Frankenstein* (1931), starring Boris Karloff, *The Wolfman* (1941), starring Lon Chaney, Jr., and many others.

But movies weren't alone in setting the tone for on-screen horror. For years prior to the invention of the motion picture camera, writers like Bram Stoker, Mary Shelley, Arthur Conan Doyle, H.P. Lovecraft, H.G. Wells, and many others were stirring the innermost fears of the public.

As magnificent as all this work was, it only formed the cornerstone of what was to become the exploitation horror movie market. Most of the foundation was supplied in 1947 when William M. Gaines took over his father's publishing company, Educational Comics (EC). Bill Gaines had much to live up to. His patriarch, M.C. Gaines, had been hailed as the father of comic books. But when the progeny was given control, the operation flagged.

The various adventure, cartoon, and teen love comic books he initially attempted fell on blind eyes. It was in 1950, with the appearance of editor Al Feldstein, that EC's first horror comic book was produced. The imaginations of young people everywhere were sparked by the exceptional writing, graphics, and design of those tales—not to mention their powerful and gruesome images of Kentucky-fried corpses and ax-cleaved skulls.

The various titles—*Crypt of Terror, Vault of Horror, Haunt of Fear,* and others—rarely settled into any set cliché, but a formula could be garnered in retrospect. After a punny introduction by the "Crypt Keeper" or one of the other comic book "hosts," there was usually a tale of a wronged individual who, through either an accident or murder, is killed. The wronged victim would then return from the grave to pay back his killers in kind.

That simple story was given dozens of bloodthirsty and graphic variations—all to the delight of its young audience. But in 1953, "The Man" came down hard on these publications—all but blaming them for juvenile delinquency. EC was cut down at the height of its powers, but by then it was too late. An entire generation of film hopefuls wanted to give celluloid life to the thrills the Puritans had so short-sightedly curtailed. And the film exploiters/distributors saw another way to tap a ready-made audience.

These things started as rip-offs of major studios' monster fare, but soon gained an EC-like distinction for gruesome doings in graphic detail. The sub-genre of independent, inexpensive horror films was all but borne by the England-based Hammer Studios in 1957 with *The Curse of Frankenstein*, starring Christopher Lee as the crazy-quilt, makeshift monster with what looks like a pronounced case of acne, and Peter Cushing as the supercilious Dr. Frankenstein who turns out to be far more monstrous than his creation.

Hammer's reputation was cemented the following year by the nearly seamless *Horror of Dracula*, starring Lee as the alternately erudite and blood-crazed Count, and Cushing as the best Van Helsing ever. Director Terence Fisher and scriptwriter Jimmy Sangster were never better in this remarkably taut and thrilling version of the vampire legend. Theirs was a collaboration of reasonably inexpensive quality, but the tradition of truly cheap, wonderfully dumb horror was being formulated in the States.

For the purposes of this book, the term "horror" relates to science-fiction material as well, because with such a lack of production time and budget, almost all of these sci-fi (or as the more pretentious among enthusiasts say, "SF") films were horrors anyway. Here, the greats were a bit less known.

Phil Tucker was one of the first, putting out the nearly unbelievably tacky *Robot Monster* in 1953. The most famous story from the production is that when Tucker couldn't buy an entire ape suit for his creature, a space helmet was substituted. So instead of a killer ape attack, there was this big hairy monster in a Martian helmet running around.

Ed Wood is probably the most (in)famous of the pioneering group, since it was he who made *Plan Nine from Outer Space* (1959), generally considered the worst movie ever. Coming up fast behind him, though, was the late Richard Cunha, who was hired right out of film school to make four movies for Astor Pictures during the years 1956 to 1958. In rapid succession, he ground out *She Demons* (1958) and *Missile to the Moon* (1958), among others. Incredibly, it is reported that he was amazed, shocked, and hurt over the bad reviews his work garnered. Despondent, he supposedly traveled to the Peruvian jungle and has never been seen since!

William Grefé is another of the instigators. His *Sting of Death*, seen in 1966, is special because of its plot—a man is turned into a human man-o-war who stings women to death—and its hero—a very young Neil Sadaka. The pop star went on to play the young ingénue in 1970's *Decoy for Terror*, which was a limp remake of *Color Me Blood Red* (if such a thing is possible) where a man killed women in order to pose them exactly right for his paintings.

These four men got the genre off to a suitably freakish start. Since then, the industry has never been at a want for the dreadful in thought, realization, and deed.

THE ASTRO-ZOMBIES (1969)
Produced and Directed by Ted V. Mikels

Written by Ted V. Mikels and Wayne M. Rogers

Starring Wendell Corey, John Carradine, Tom Pace, Joan Patrick, and Tura Santana

T.V. Mikels strikes again, and again and again, in this terrifically stupid science fiction story that was created specifically to make money. As such, it is a fitting start to this exploitation section.

Let it be made clear at the very outset that science fiction has not remained a favorite of exploiters. Even at the beginnings of the literary genre, it was always a showcase for the development of futuristic ideas. And if there's one thing there's a shortage of in hack horror work, it is the realization of fascinating ideas. Not only does that take thought, heaven forefend, it also takes money. Slapping fangs on a guy (or gal) is far more preferable than fitting them for an entire space suit. Hey, tin foil costs more than plastic teeth!

Take the *Astro-Zombies* ... please. It was actually the brainchild of Wayne Rogers—the Wayne Rogers who was soon to co-star on *M*A*S*H* (the television series). Although already utilizing his savvy business sense to get by, the young actor saw a way of profiting on a quickie, independent feature. Gathering together about thirty thousand bucks and T.V. Mikels (who had just finished 1966's *The Black Klansman*), Rogers executive-produced (with Kenneth Altose) and co-wrote the simple-minded combination of Frankenstein and James Bond.

This was famed 1950s TV star Wendell Corey's last performance, in which he played CIA chief Holman, who's investigating evil Professor DeMarco (the ever-dependable John Carradine). After having been fired as the head of the Astro-Space Laboratory, the doctor has holed up in a decrepit mansion with his deformed assistant Juan (Rafael Campos) to work on creating an artificial man. The law has become involved only after several murders in which the victims' vital organs were missing. But before Holman can move in, DeMarco creates his Astro-Man (Rod Wilmoth), who is perfect in every way ... except for having a brain from, as Marty Feldman put it in *Young Frankenstein* (1974), "Abby Normal."

This results in the murder of a lovely young lab assistant during one of the Astro-Man's nocturnal jaunts, so Holman manages to plant undercover operative Janine Norwalk (Joan Patrick) in her place. But she's not the only one. Foreign powers also send in a spy named Santanna, played, as luck would have it, by the awesome Tura Santana. The CIA plot pays off. The monster, now dubbed the Astro-Zombie, unsuccessfully attacks Janine, who follows it back to DeMarco's mansion.

Santanna sneaks in first, discovering that the evil prof had made a whole batch of these things, who start destroying stuff indiscriminately. Although Santanna shoots the doc, he manages to stumble over to the handy-dandy, trademarked, patent-pending master switch. And with the *Bride of Frankenstein* (1935) line "we belong dead," rattling about in everyone's brain, he expires while yanking the lever, and everything is reduced to rubble.

Film critics may have wished the switch had been pulled in the first five minutes, but Mikels and Rogers got the last laugh. Having secured a good distribution deal in Southern drive-ins, *Astro-Zombies* made three million dollars—about a hundred times its cost.

BASKET CASE (1982)
Produced by Edgar Ievins
Directed and Written by Frank Henenlotter
Starring Kevin Van Hentenryck, Terri Susan Smith, and Beverly Bonner

In medical terms, a "basket case" is an amputee of all four limbs. In psychiatric parlance, it is a patient who is no longer able to deal with anything. In semi-modern slang, it means someone somewhere between a nervous wreck and a catatonic vegetable.

In the northeastern movie community centering around New York, New Jersey, and Long Island, *Basket Case* stands as one of those great independent exploitations that is filled with more good intentions and clever invention than good ideas. Any film that starts with a dedication to Herschell Gordon Lewis can't be all good.

But the movie isn't all bad, either. In fact, the Lewis consecration is a bit of a misnomer. Anyone expecting a non-stop, brainless gore-fest is sure to be disappointed by the obvious affection and devotion the producers had lavished on their work. First, Ievins and Henenlotter spent every penny they had—and some they didn't have—then spent six months to make sure everything they needed on screen was there.

What finally appeared on screen is a morbid tale of brotherly love. Teenager Duane Bradley (Kevin Van Hentenryck) appears in New York City carrying a big wicker basket. The only place he is able to afford is a run-down fleabag hotel in the Forty-Second Street district. Taking up residence in room seven, he starts buying hamburgers, and shoving them into the basket, where something that grunts and groans scarfs the fast food down at an alarming rate.

It is not too much longer before a flashback reveals the facts. Duane was born with the mutated remains of a Siamese twin attached to his torso. Although alive, his father demanded the growth be surgically removed. The trio of doctors performing the operation had the bad luck, bad judgment, and bad taste to follow the father's orders. Belial, as the growth was named, was tied into a plastic baggie and left with the trash.

Unbeknownst to anyone, however, Belial and Duane had been linked by more than flesh. The misshapen hunk of insane skin could communicate psychically with his normal brother. On Belial's instructions, Duane rescued him from the garbage and started down the road of vengeance. Dad was the first to go, and the trail of the three surgeons led the pair to Manhattan.

Complications arise because Duane's interests begin to turn to more normal pursuits, while Belial remains dedicated to the proposition that all three surgeons should be equally dead. While the boy gets a girlfriend (Terri Susan Smith), the thing "gets" Dr. Needleman (Lloyd Pace), Dr. Kutter (Diana Browne), and various other victims, with his sharp claws and set of triple fangs where his front teeth should be.

The escalating deaths require a final confrontation between the two siblings. Although Belial is firmly convinced that his brother has forsaken him, he tries to rescue him when the subsequent fight knocks Duane out of the hotel window. Unable to hold on because of his warped shape, the two fall to their deaths together.

The director and producer had to scrimp on just about everything in order to finish the movie within their meager budget, but among the things they splurged on were the scenes of violence, and an absolutely great bunch of Belial sound effects. For such a small pile of flesh, Belial can run, jump, claw, bite, drool, screech, and throw things around like a combination of Bigfoot, the Yeti, and Jaws. His powers are shown to great effect in the original version of the film.

After lavishing such devotion on the work, the producers were delighted, at first, that Analysis—the same company that backed *Caligula* and *Maniac*—had decided to distribute their great warped hope. But they were less than overjoyed when the company decided to edit some of the gore to appease the MPAA.

The one way in which *Basket Case* separates itself from the norm may have been the makings of its initial downfall. After all, the film is a homage to all the cheap, crazy features the moviemakers had seen: pictures that had no room for integrity, resolve of purpose, and heartfelt honor. Ievins and Henenlotter were trying to recreate something slapdash with care—which was an obvious contradiction in terms.

Although the filmmakers may not have had the last laugh, at least they had the last chuckle or smirk. *Basket Case* is now venerated by many dedicated gorehounds, and it set the stage for many more, far more successful, "slapdash with care" productions.

HORROR

★★★ HELD OVER BY POPULAR DEMAND ★★★
The Exorcist

What the? Huh? What is this major studio, multi-million-dollar production doing here? Inspiring a tsunami of trash, that's what.

In 1973 an event occurred that was to both change the direction of, and legitimize, hack horror. Although the door had been cracked open with the awarding of a Best Picture Oscar to the X-rated *Midnight Cowboy* in 1969, and *Rosemary's Baby* reaped box office whirlwinds in 1968, *The Exorcist* blasted through the walls of every cinema.

While other films have touched upon the war between good and evil, that is the heart, and—if you'll excuse the expression—soul of this picture. Most would be able to view it today with interest and appreciation. But back in the early 1970s, few were prepared for the onslaught of distasteful sights and sounds that even the nastiest of exploitation efforts hadn't touched upon.

The Exorcist sounded the death knell for the independent blood baths of yore. Not only hadn't hack horror dealt with this film's issues, it couldn't come close to the power that director William Friedkin and his special effects crew achieved. Audiences suddenly discovered that the more realistic an effect was, the more visual and visceral power it packed. Why wallow in the wacko world of Wood and Lewis when a twelve-year-old girl was floating, defiling herself, and spewing pea soup with total credibility?

At the time, director Friedkin came off as a totally assured artist. He had just been awarded the Oscar for *The French Connection* (1971) and seemed intent on plastering the audience against the back walls of their cinemas with something no one had seen before.

After having helmed the Sonny and Cher movie *Good Times* (1967), the nostalgic and troubled *The Night They Raided Minsky's* (1968), and the controversial *The Boys in the Band* (1970), the ambitious filmmaker wanted to cement his reputation. William Peter Blatty's controversial novel was the perfect vehicle.

Both book and film begin in Iraq where Father Lancaster Merrin uncovers an artifact on an archeological dig. It is a statue of the demon Pazuzu, a signal of evil to come. In retrospect, Merrin's discovery seems to have given the demon a little hole in which to enter the world—a hole that is in the attic of a Georgetown, Washington D.C. home.

Divorced film actress Chris MacNeil (Ellen Burstyn) lives there with her teenage helper Sharon (Kitty Winn) and twelve-year-old daughter Regan (Linda Blair). In a charming and realistic scene where the mother and daughter communicate in the soft, abortive way many pre-teens and adults talk, Chris learns that Regan has found an "imaginary" friend in the attic while playing with a Ouija board.

The trouble starts when Regan appears in the middle of one of her mom's parties, tells an astronaut guest that he's going to die and urinates on the floor. Not a good sign. The trouble continues in earnest as the sweet girl abruptly changes into a foulmouthed banshee who screeches obscenities in a gravelly voice and punches a doctor between the legs when he tries to examine her.

MacNeil tries every rational thing to explain her daughter's change, and, in one of the most striking sequences during the first hour (of the two-hour-and-one-minute movie) Regan is given a graphic arteriography—where a needle is inserted into the carotid artery of the neck to mark the arteries of the brain for three cameras. This scene was the first to send some viewers to the loo, and let others know that the gloves were off. From here on in, it's every audience for themselves.

After having expended all the rational reasons, MacNeil finally seeks help from the Church, represented by the doubt-plagued Father Karras (Jason Miller). It is his task to decide whether the girl is actually possessed, and whether an exorcism will be required. Although those words are second nature now, they were new, exotic, and frightening to most everyone in the early 1970s.

Regan abuses herself with a cross while screaming obscenities. In uncut prints of the film, she crawls downstairs like a spider, with her head twisted a hundred and eighty degrees. Again, audiences were scandalized. When the complete head turning and bile barfing finally did arrive, viewers had mostly steeled themselves for the worst. And the worst happens. By the time Merrin shows up to perform the exorcism, Regan's room has become a madhouse of degradation and the supernatural.

Large, rended cuts cover the girl's body. At one point the words "help me" rise up like blisters on the girl's stomach. Her furniture moves by itself. The temperature lowers to freezing in the room. Regan has gained amazing strength and must be tied down. She writhes in agony as the solemn ritual continues, doing everything she can to disrupt it.

The side of light seems to be winning, so the elderly Merrin allows the doubting Karras a rest. To his horror and regret, Karras returns to find his mentor dead of an apparent heart attack and the demon about to take full possession of the innocent girl. In the startling climax, Karras accepts the demon into his own body and throws himself out the window in a "rite" of self-sacrifice. It was the one heavenly loophole remaining.

He smashes down a steep flight of stone steps—the same stairs that film director Burke Dennings (Jack MacGowran) was supposedly hurled down by the possessed Regan. Karras' friend Father Dyer (Rev. William O'Malley) finds him there, and gently, sadly, performs the last rites. The investigating cop, Lt. Kinderman (Lee J. Cobb), is left to close the case as the strangely bland Regan is driven away by her mother.

It took some time before comedians' jokes managed to dilute the effect of *The Exorcist* on the populace. Thankfully, exploitation films did much to lessen its impact and the controversy that swirled around it. Without all of the pathetic rip-offs that were made in its wake, the serious nature of the film's themes might have maintained a disturbing resonance.

Instead, hack horrorists concentrated on the exploitative aspects of the movie. Since the devil worked under no set rules, here was a perfect opportunity to pile nonsensical shock upon illogical jolt, all while blithely proclaiming that "the devil made me do it." The basic conflict of good versus evil was submerged under gallons and gallons of green pea soup.

The exploiters' cause was helped enormously by *The Exorcist II: The Heretic* (1977), which was not only one of the worst sequels of all time, but one of the dumbest mainstream movies, period. Its director, John Boorman, has always been a superb visual stylist (take a look at 1967's *Point Blank*, 1977's *Deliverance*, and 1981's *Excalibur* if you doubt), but not always a very good storyteller (check out 1970's *Leo the Last* and 1974's *Zardoz* for evidence). *The Exorcist II* was Boorman at the height of his non-communicative powers.

Idiocies abound. Father Lamont (Richard Burton) is sent to investigate the death of Father Merrin four years after the fact. He finds Regan, played by a chubbier, and far more buxom Linda Blair, in the care of pop psychologist Dr. Gene Tuskin (played by Louise Fletcher, a virtual twin of Ellen Burstyn, who was cast after she won an Oscar for her performance in 1976's *One Flew Over the Cuckoo's Nest* and "no appropriate male actor could be found").

Tuskin has a handy-dandy "thought synchronizer" that can tap a person's subconscious. The film had hardly started and already the story was leaping out the window. While Friedkin's original was rife with scientific and religious accuracy, the Boorman follow-up seemed to be made up of unsubstantiated metaphysical assumptions that were given less than no credence in their manner of presentation.

Through the futuristic (and non-existent in reality) machine, Lamont sees Merrin having his first run-in with the demon Pazuzu in deepest, darkest Africa while exorcising a native boy who could control hordes of locusts. Much to its detriment, the film came out one month after *Star Wars*, so when Merrin comes back to Lamont in a dream state, it looked like a rip-off of "The Force".

Lamont goes to see the boy, who has grown into a man played by James Earl Jones (the voice of Darth Vader). After a nearly incomprehensible series of events,

Lamont races a horde of locusts back to the site of Regan's original exorcism: the townhouse in Washington, D.C. He gets there in time to see Sharon (Kitty Winn again) burst into flames for little or no reason.

He confronts Regan, who has turned into a lecherous nymphet in a low-cut nightgown. She tries to entice him into bed as the locusts attack while the wind (not to mention the audience) howls. Ignoring the fact that the walls and floors are collapsing, Lamont embraces the girl, only to successfully punch through her chest and rip out her heart. Meanwhile, the entire block seems gripped by an earthquake.

Dr. Tuskin arrives in time to see Lamont exiting the devastation with the un-scathed, now normal Regan and says, "I understand now," (which is more than any viewer could claim). Then the priest and the girl literally walk into the sunrise. Those who weren't wondering what was going on were derisively laughing.

Although they issued extensive publicity to the contrary, Warner Brothers found their film bombing at every engagement. In desperation, they pulled every print from distribution and excised the truly ridiculous. Finally, John Boorman was called back from his home in Ireland to completely re-edit the film for its European premieres.

While all this was going down, hack horrorists weren't resting on their crosses. Almost immediately after *The Exorcist*'s success, movies featuring the words "devil" and "exorcism" in their titles started popping up like long-dormant corn kernels. Many of these were quickly distributed foreign fodder with similar content. For instance, *Beyond the Door* (1975) was one of the most notable because it actually concerned an exorcism.

Instead of an already-born child having problems, this Italian melodrama had poor, pregnant Juliet Mills (the star of television's *Nanny and the Professor*, 1970) suffering the demonized bends, as a priest, played by ex-Shakespearean actor and James Bond candidate Richard Johnson, struggled to save her. Film Ventures International was so impressed by it that they released *Beyond the Door II* in 1979, which was another of those great con jobs.

Not that it was a bad movie, it just had nothing to do with *Beyond the Door I* or an exorcism. It was actually a Mario Bava film called *Shock* made in 1977. It concerned a son's attempts to punish his mother for murdering her drug-addicted husband and burying him behind a cellar wall. He is seemingly aided in his quest by the evil spirit of his dead dad.

Equally unconnected are *The Devil's Nightmare* (1975), a European snorer where a lurid succubus wanders around an ex-Nazi's castle, and *In the Devil's Garden* (1975), a decent little British rape mystery that was subsequently retitled for a 1980 re-release as *Tower of Terror*.

When the exploiters ran out of devils, they brought in the relatives. *Exorcism's Daughter* (1974) was a Spanish movie about a woman suffering from insanity after witnessing the exorcism of her mother when but a child. Then there was *House of Exorcism* (1976), another Mario Bava picture, starring Telly Savalas, Elke Sommer, and Robert Alda (father of Alan). Now this one is a hoot. Savalas makes all manner of casual demonic speeches to the innocent Sommer while sucking on a lollipop, exactly as his famed television character Kojak did. Sommer meets a decadent Italian family and then becomes possessed by a demon who looks exactly like Savalas, except for the horns and tail. She's tied to a hospital bed, where the guilt-ridden priest played by Alda does his best to exorcise her while she levitates and ejects all manner of junk from her mouth. It is all extremely funny.

But, in spite of the crude attempts to sail to success on *The Exorcist*'s coattails, the original movie far outshines anything relatively similar to it, and remains a bold, innovative, thought-provoking, and influential film.

BILLY THE KID VS. DRACULA (1966)
Produced by Carroll Case
Directed by William Beaudine
Written by Carl Hittleman
Starring John Carradine, Chuck Courtney, Melinda Plowman, and Harry Carey, Jr.

JESSE JAMES MEETS FRANKENSTEIN'S DAUGHTER (1966)
Produced by Carroll Case
Directed by William Beaudine
Written by Carl Hittleman
Starring Narda Onyx, John Lupton, Cal Boulder, and Jim Davis

DRACULA VS. FRANKENSTEIN (1971)
Produced by Al Adamson and Samuel M. Sherman
Directed by Al Adamson
Written by William Pugsley and Samuel M. Sherman
Starring J. Carroll Naish, Lon Chaney, Jr., Russ Tamblyn, Jim Davis, Anthony Eisley, Regina Carrol, John Bloom, and Greydon Clark

FRANKENSTEIN MEETS THE SPACE MONSTER (1965)
Produced by Robert McCarty
Directed by Robert Gaffney

FOR ONE WEEK ONLY

Written by George Garret, John Rodenbeck, and R.H.W. Dillard
Starring James Karen, Nancy Marshall, and Robert Reilly

Cheaper than cheap! Dumber than dumb! All four of these ludicrous team-ups seem to be inspired by such Universal Studio classic monster fests as *House of Frankenstein* (1944), *House of Dracula* (1945), *Frankenstein Meets the Wolf Man* (1943), and even *Abbott and Costello Meet Frankenstein* (1948), which is far better than it sounds. All of these treated the various monsters with respect.

Not so the above-listed epics. Case, Beaudine, and Hittleman made their two western pastiches back-to-back—probably counting on the gimmick of cowboys to pull them through. Chuck Courtney played Billy the Kid, who was turned from a slimy, immature outlaw into a reformed, mature ranch hand ready, willing, and able to settle down with the female owner of the ranch (Melinda Plowman).

The only thing that stands in his way is Dracula (John Carradine), who has the girl under his spell, so she's telling everybody that he's her uncle. Thankfully, the local doc knows all there is to know about vampires and pulls the old mirror trick on the Count. Dracula retreats into a silver mine where the cowboys cut him off. When all their bullets don't work, somehow the doc's scalpel in the bloodsucker's heart does (what, is it made of wood?). Billy gets the girl, and the skies are not cloudy all day.

That is, until Jesse James (John Lupton) meets Frankenstein's daughter (Narda Onyx) while on the lam from the law in Mexico. A sweet Mexican girl (Estelita) directs Jesse and his men to a place where they can hide out, only to find Frankenstein's sibling in the ruins. One of Jesse's men (Cal Bolder) is hurt real bad. The woman promises to look after him while Jesse goes for medicine. And look after him she does.

She does a nifty brain transplant on him, turning him into a super-powered zombie. Jesse returns and is knocked unconscious by the creature. But before the evil woman is able to do a number on the outlaw, the sweet Mexican girl arrives with the law. They shoot down the woman and her creation before slapping the cuffs on Jesse. Realizing the error of his ways, he promises to the girl that he'll be good and he'll be back.

All is hunky-dory with the world, until Al Adamson unleashed his own monstrous talent on the monster. His film is a camp-lover's delight. Not only do Greydon Clark and Russ Tamblyn make appearances, but Forrest J. Ackerman, editor and writer of *Famous Monsters* magazine shows up as well. The rest of the cast are equally heavyweight. Veteran character actor J. Carroll Naish plays Dr. Frankenstein, who has whipped up "Groton, the Mad Zombie" (Lon Chaney, Jr.), while Dracula (Zandor Vorkov) digs up the remains of the original monster (John Bloom). Groton spends the beginning of the film ax-murdering a girl on the beach (Connie Nelson), while the Count traces the Doctor to a horror museum.

Learning that Frankenstein is working on a blood serum that will allow Dracula to walk in the sun, he promises to help bring the monster back to life. Meanwhile, the sister of the murdered beach girl (Regina Carrol) gets a writer (Anthony Eisley) to join police sergeant Martin (Jim Davis, of *Dallas* TV fame) in the hunt for the killer. They do a crackerjack job, quickly finding the museum and killing both Frankenstein and Groton.

But Dracula has his eyes on the girl, making her his slave. They retreat to a power station. The writer heroically tries to rescue the damsel, but is electrocuted for his trouble. Before the police can capture him, the Count moves on to an old, deserted church. He is just about to put the bite on the hypnotized girl when the smitten Frankenstein's monster saves the day.

The fight between the two horror stars culminates outside, as Dracula shoots electric bolts out of his fingers to fry the hapless creature. The Count is fried in return when he finds that the monster had stalled him until sunrise. When the girl snaps out of her spell, she finds the ashen remains of both vampire and zombie.

Ashen ruins are something a new Frankenstein could identify with when he meets the Space Monster. Robert Reilly plays an android astronaut created by Adam Steele (James Karen) and Karen Grant (Nancy Marshall). Upon discovering the existence of a flying saucer, the robot is damaged in a fight with a white-slaving alien named Nadir (Lou Cutell).

"He may become violent," Steele says when he learns of the damage.

"You mean," Karen gasps, "we've created a Frankenstein?"

So much for the title. Director Robert Gaffney rams his tongue into his cheek and keeps it there as the eccentric Nadir (a word meaning "the lowest point") kidnaps beach girls and loads them into his flying saucer on a conveyor belt. Naturally, the damaged android, horribly scarred on one side of his face, defeats the outer space invasion, making the world safe for blonds in bathing suits and tight dresses everywhere.

BLACULA (1972)
Produced by Joseph T. Narr
Directed by William Crain
Written by Joan Torres and Raymond Koenig
Starring William Marshall, Denise Nichols, Vonetta McGee, Gordon Pinsett, Thalmus Rasulala, Ted Harris, and Elisha Cook, Jr.

BLACKENSTEIN (1973)
Produced by Frank R. Salteri
Directed by William A. Levey
Written by Frank R. Salteri
Starring John Hart, Joe DiSue, and Ivory Stone

DR. BLACK AND MR. WHITE (1975)
Produced by Charles Walker
Directed by William Crain
Written by Larry LeBron
Starring Bernie Casey and Rosalind Cash

For every great advance in society, there are side effects. These are just three of the best. Once blaxploitation pics really began to catch on, producers seemed only interested in black versions of already existing white classics. It was rare for a movie or play to be made with an original idea showcasing black performers. It was usually the all-black version of *Hello Dolly*, or the all-black version of *Barefoot in the Park*, or even the all-black version of *The Odd Couple*.

The same went for most violence movies. *Shaft* was essentially Sam Spade. In the television series based on the trilogy of *Shaft* movies (1971's *Shaft*, 1972's *Shaft's Big Score*, 1973's *Shaft in Africa*), he was reduced to being Mannix (complete with loud tweed jackets) with black skin. It was only a matter of time before the horrorists put two and two together to get the following.

Blacula, a genius title if ever there was one, was played by notable actor William Marshall, a man known for his beautiful speaking voice. He played a victim of the original Count (Charles Macauley), who returned to his ghetto stomping grounds. Although filled with such personable stars as Denise Nichols, Thalmus Rasulala, Vonetta McGee, and Elisha Cook, Jr., the otherwise entertaining retelling of the vampire story (man bites girl, girl bites man, man sees another girl, man gets a stake in heart) is handicapped by surprisingly flat, washed-out filming, giving the stereotypical plot an embarrassingly cheap look. The film was so tacky that the screen looked sticky. The situation was rectified somewhat by a sequel, produced and written by the same people who did the first, but directed by Bob Kelljan.

In *Scream, Blacula, Scream* (1973), the tortured bloodsucker is both revived and cured of his curse by voodoo. Once more the cast is notable (including Pam Grier, Don Mitchell, Lynne Moody, and Bernie Hamilton), but the film still suffered from lack of production value. Although it contained some interesting scenes and a fair number of familiar thrills, most were relieved when *Blacula* was finally brought down (when his voodoo doll was stabbed in the heart).

But by then it was too late. Other producers had been given the idea of melding blacks with supernatural beasties. Thus was *Black Frankenstein* born. This movie appeared under both this and its more concise title during its abortive run. Its quality is cued by a note on the ad. "Warning: To People With Weak Hearts … No Doctors or Nurses In Attendance."

Joe DiSue played a Vietnam soldier who is turned into a paraplegic by an enemy mine. Thankfully, his fiancée's boss (John Hart) is Dr. Frankenstein, who decides to perform an arm and leg graft onto the hapless veteran. It is the doctor's butler who throws a wrench in the works. He wants the girl for himself, so he feeds the lad an elixir that turns him into a rampaging monster. Since the film had a ready-made monster mixture handy, it makes sense that it would also have a wide variety of women victims in various stages of undress for the monster to maul.

This movie was done so poorly that it was rejected as the obvious rip-off it was, garnering almost no attention, few bookings, and less interest. There was no *Scream, Blackenstein, Scream* to appear afterward. What did show up was a movie wonderful in its manifest racism. *Dr. Black and Mr. White* made it blatantly clear where it stood on the issue. Finding that the original title was a bit too clear, it was changed to *Dr. Black/Mr. Hyde* and finally to *The Watts Monster*. In any case, Bernie Casey played (now get this) Dr. Pride—a free-clinic physician in the ghetto. He's a real sweetheart, except for the fact that he wants to be accepted into white society. He wants to be middle-class, an average Joe Six-pack. Toward this end, he mixes up a potion that turns him into a Caucasian. Woefully, he is soon to discover that the white man is bestial at his base, so he goes on a rampage of destruction and murder.

Tragically, this great idea is rendered stupid and boring in its execution. Once more William Crain has the directorial reins, and once more he seems unable to give the motion picture any kind of depth or texture. The decent, remarkably low-key script and the acting talent of Casey (who worked through various blaxploitation efforts like 1972's *Hit Man* before graduating to such mainstream efforts as 1981's *Sharky's Machine*) failed to elevate the effort. The blaxploitmonster genre essentially died with it.

BLOOD BEACH (1981)
Produced by Sidney Beckerman
Directed and Written by Jeffrey Bloom
Starring Marianna Hill, David Huffman, John Saxon, and Burt Young

This movie was the Jerry Gross Organization's swan song. The fellow was afflicted by the same curse all his peers were: the attack of the major studios. Since they were grinding out gore with better production values (meaning lusher photography and more realistic special effects), the audience was deserting the cruddy-looking independent's output.

The ad copy for *Jaws II* (1978) was "Just when you thought it was safe to go back into the water...!" The ad copy for this movie was "Just when you thought it was safe to go back in the water … you can't get to it." And therein lies a tale of a good idea going nowhere and a long-time exploitation artist getting cut down by an ill-fated attempt to compete with the majors. When Spielberg showed a lifeguard's torn-off leg and the floating corpse of a fisherman in the original *Jaws*, he personally rang the death knell of many an exploiter.

About the only things *Blood Beach* had in common with *Jaws* were good photography and a good cast, which included exploitation perennial John Saxon (1973's *Enter the Dragon*), Burt Young (1976's *Rocky*), David Huffman, and Marianna Hill. What it didn't have was a good script. It may have had a decent idea and a workable plot, but no story.

The idea was that a monster was living beneath the beach, and sucking unsuspecting bathers down to be ingested. The script had the authorities trying to capture, or kill, the cunning creature. The story beyond that was nonexistent. It is never explained where the beast comes from, why it's here, what it's doing, and for what purpose. The picture has more inconsistencies and illogical bits, but they might have been glossed over by great gory effects, but they weren't much in evidence either. Usually a victim suddenly fell through the sand, shouted a lot, and disappeared. That was all right the first time, but it was repeated ad nauseum.

Unable to deal with it any other way, the authorities finally bomb the entire waterfront, leaving the well-worn notion that "the danger is over now … or is it?" If the film had been a hack job, the audience might not have cared, but this was a first-class job. Veteran viewers can handle either boredom or stupidity, but rarely both. This just goes to show what can happen when someone forsakes his roots. Gross and company probably saw *Tremors* in 1990 and spent the running time kicking themselves. Now that's how you make a subterranean monster movie!

THE BOOGENS (1981)
Produced by Charles E. Sellier, Jr.
Directed by James L. Conway
Written by David O'Malley, Bob Hunt, M. James Kouf, Jr., and Thomas C. Chapman

HORROR

Starring Rebecca Balding, Fred McCarren, Anne-Marie Martin, and Jeff Harlan

Now here's some folks who didn't forget their roots. This here picture is firmly entrenched in the enjoyable monster films of the 1950s—ones that are so nicely done, predictable, and so familiar that they practically exude a secure feeling. This is a perfect little post-modern Saturday matinee movie whose enjoyment requires viewers to leave their brains by the door. Although unlikely, the film makes sense and is played straight for all it's worth.

The backer and distributor of the project was Taft International, the same conglomerate that owned Quinn Martin Productions (*Barnaby Jones*, etc.) and Hanna-Barbera (*Yogi Bear*, etc.). They managed to find a movie that incorporates the blood viewers had come to expect, with a non-condescending, non-camp presentation that is still somehow ungratuitous.

The American Mining Corporation has sent out an evaluation crew to test the worth of a silver mine near Denver, although the place has been closed for sixty years since a devastating cave-in that trapped thirty men. As has become par for the course, an old man tries to warn the team about evil doings, but is ignored.

The workers reopen the mine, while two young couples take up residence in an old house nearby. All of these people are now at the mercy of small, incredibly fast, little, tentacled creatures whose faces seem to consist of two frog eyes and a mouth the size of a football. When these mouths open, they are framed by long, sharp, teeth about the size of a woman's pinky. These little beasties can not only slither and chew with the best of them, they have tentacles that can be used as long-reaching feelers and whips. Although the movie doesn't give an explanation for their existence, their purpose is made clear enough, and that's all that matters. They are protecting their turf, which is something almost every gorehound can understand.

Once the mine is reopened, they are all over the place: in tunnels crisscrossing the shafts, beneath the house, and even in the heating vents. One of the girls, played by Anne-Marie Martin, is killed during a bath. Her boyfriend, played by Jeff Harlan, gets it in the cellar. The mine workers are wiped out, and even the old man who warned them is chomped up. Rebecca Balding, no longer silent screaming, is on hand as the girlfriend of hero Mark Kinner, played by Fred McCarren.

Although originally appearing to be a secondary character, Kinner has a box of dynamite that he uses to keep the Boogens at bay after almost everyone else is done for. Finally, he manages to cause another massive cave-in that seals the cocker-spaniel-sized beasties back into their subterranean lair. Kinner and his gal leave the site sadder, wiser, lonelier, and with a bit less blood than they had coming in.

As enjoyable as *The Boogens* was, it came on the tail end of dozens of hack horror movies. Although fairly positively reviewed, it wasn't until author Stephen King gave it a rave in the pages of *Twilight Zone* magazine that most enthusiasts did a double take. The film deserves the attention. It shows the other junk just how to mount an inexpensive exploiter that is still good bloody fun.

BRAIN OF BLOOD (1971)
Produced by Al Adamson and Samuel M. Sherman
Directed by Al Adamson
Written by Joe Van Rodgers and Samuel M. Sherman
Starring Grant Williams, Kent Taylor, Reed Hadley, Regina Carrol, and Zandor Vorkov

Hack horrorists don't die—they simply film away. This was the latest in a long line of "brain" movies, which include 1958's *The Brain Eaters* (mind-stealing slugs from the earth's core), 1958's *The Brain from Planet Arous* (alien-powered psychic mind control), 1962's *The Brain that Wouldn't Die* (a girl's disembodied head controlling a Frankenstein-like monster), and the ever-wonderful 1958 *Fiend Without a Face* (killer brains that crawl around on their spinal cords like snakes).

But this was an Al Adamson production, so that meant it was wink-wink-nudge-nudge crap that both filmmaker and audience would agreed to let slide. The veteran director did his usual enjoyably abominable job here, utilizing John Bloom again as "Cor," the monstrous, deformed assistant to mad scientist Dr. Trenton (Kent Taylor, the star of television's *Boston Blackie*, who was also in *Satan's Sadists*). I suppose if he were English, he'd be "Cor Blimey (sorry)."

While Cor is out trying to find healthy young male bodies, the disciples of Middle-Eastern leader Amir (Reed Hadley, the star of television's *Racket Squad*) bring his newly dead body to Trenton. The doctor opens his skull with a laser beam, removes the brain, and puts it in a "special blood-cycling refrigerated unit" (read: fish tank), which will keep the organ alive until he can find a suitable body to use for a transplant.

The gigantic Cor is scouting for bodies while his opposite, the sadistic dwarf Dorro (Angelo Rossitto), keeps the brain supplied with blood. He does this by draining the girls he keeps chained in the doctor's subterranean dungeon. When Cor brings Trenton a body of a thief who has fallen out a window, the doctor becomes so incensed that he accidentally knocks Dorro's fresh blood supply to the floor.

Realizing he'll have to work fast to keep the brain alive, he transplants it into Cor. Meanwhile, the men, who have brought Amir to Trenton, are ambushed by a man anxious to overthrow Amir's corrupt government. The only survivor is Bob Nigserian (Grant Williams, the star of 1957's classic *The Incredible Shrinking Man*).

He goes to pick up Tracy (Regina Carrol), another Amir follower, at the airport. They return to the lab where Dorro kills one of the captive girls, but mistakenly allows the other (Vicki Volante) to escape. She stumbles around the rotting tunnels of the dungeon as Tracy tells the newly created Cor/Amir that Bob is actually the leader of the revolutionaries intent on taking over his kingdom.

The monster knocks out the doctor and Bob. Terrified of the beast's new power, Tracy hightails it out, with Cor/Amir lumbering behind. Once he awakes, the doc has Dorro stick Bob down in the dungeon while he collects his portable laser. The escaped girl jumps the dwarf and kills him with his own hypodermic needle. She and Bob go in search of Trenton, who is using the laser as a high-frequency tracking device.

But every time Trenton turns it on, the monster gets a migraine. Once Trenton catches up to the thing, he instructs it to kill Tracy. But Bob stashes the girl in a safe place, and catches up to Trenton. Although Nigserian has a gun, bullets don't hurt the Gor body, and the monster gets the better of him.

The film ends with the now recognizable Amir giving a political speech to his people on TV. In the studio, Trenton sits with the laser across his lap. He now rules the kingdom with Amir as a puppet leader. Only he knows that Amir's brain is in Bob's younger body. It is Trenton's skills as a plastic surgeon that creates the illusion of Amir's wrinkled face.

Yes, it's another happy ending from the career of Al Adamson. The story of *Brain of Blood* turned out happily as well. After a title change to *The Creature's Revenge*, the movie was sold to television, where an entirely new generation got to sample the bargain basement delights of the veteran director's work.

THE CHILD (1977)
Produced by Robert Dadashian
Directed by Robert Voskanian
Written by Ralph Lucas
Starring Richard Hanners, Laurel Barnett, Frank Janson, and Rosalie Cole

Ever since *Rosemary's Baby* (1968) racked up the green, exploiters have been hot to present little angels who are actually little devils. Seeing death and destruction behind the seemingly innocent eyes of youth is nothing new. *Bad Seed*, directed by Mervin LeRoy, was a high-water mark in odious offsprings way back in 1956. The big change that Rosemary wrought was that now the mite's maliciousness could be due to supernatural causes rather than nature or nurture.

This particular movie is just a representative of many such sagas. Although Rosemary was influential, it took *The Omen* (1976) to signal a flood of beastly babies and terrifying tots. In this variation on the theme, Rosalie Cole played Rosalie Norden, a little girl with insidious powers. After her father has the demented family gardener kill her mother, Rosalie retaliates by gaining control of the ghouls and ghosts who inhabit the nearby cemetery.

Into this wholesome atmosphere comes young and attractive governess Alicianne Del Mar (Laurel Barnett). She gets to witness the murder and consumption of her nosy neighbor and her dog, see a scarecrow come to life in order to attack her, watch the gardener get shot, and notice the father get chewed up by the child's playmates.

This is enough to unnerve even an inner city maid, but Alicianne grabs the family ax and holes up in the pump house. She knows that the ghouls are all around her, so she sinks the blade into the first thing that enters. It is Rosalie, and since she now has a hatchet in her head, the monsters lose all interest in earthly things. As they drift back into the surrounding wood, the governess wanders off into the sunset "hopelessly insane" (according to one reviewer) or "bewildered" (according to the official synopsis).

Hopelessly insane describes most of these efforts, and bewildered is what most audiences were after viewing *Cathy's Curse*, directed by Canadian Eddy Matalon. First viewed in the lower forty-eight in 1980, the movie was made in 1977 as a combination *Exorcist*, *Omen*, and *Audrey Rose* (1977). The latter part comes in when little Cathy (Randi Allen) is possessed by the spirit of her dead aunt—killed in a car crash when she was Cathy's age. The former part comes in when Cathy goes into the attic where her aunt's spirit awaits. The middle part comes with all the gore and meaningless shocks that fill the film.

The housekeeper is found, mutilated. The family dog dies from a gruesome disease. One of Cathy's playmates gets her eyes ripped up (not out, just up, the filmmakers probably couldn't afford them to be ripped all the way out). The house starts bleeding wherever Cathy's mother (Beverly Murray) goes. That much is clear. The rest is a jumbled haze as Cathy suddenly sports the rotting face of her burned relative. This make-up is representative of the film as a whole. It looks like pizza and stops at her neck. The rest of her skin is fine.

The whole affair is similar to the 1976 Spanish film *Demon Witch Child*, which concerns a girl who takes on the ancient visage of a dead devil-worshipper whenever she leads a rite or kills a victim. The cast of *The Children* (1980) don't need to resort to that sort of thing to kill their targets. The only clues to their affliction are black fingernails, out-stretched arms, and the tendency to walk like sawed-off Frankenstein monsters.

This one was the worst of all. After a busload of kids in a small town go through a radioactive cloud, they suddenly are imbued with the power to inflict deadly radiation burns with the merest touch … as well as the desire to reach out and touch someone, anyone, but particularly their own parents. It takes several corroded corpses to convince the townspeople to shoot their black-fingernailed kids on sight, but not before the dirt-cheap production has disgusted most everyone with its pitiful premise and atrocious realization. It remains one of the best advocates of planned parenthood ever.

CHILDREN SHOULDN'T PLAY WITH DEAD THINGS (1972)
Produced by Benjamin Clark and Gary Coch
Directed by Benjamin (Bob) Clark
Written by Alan Ormsby and Benjamin Clark
Starring Alan Ormsby, Anya Ormsby, Valerie Mamches, Jane Daly, and Jeffrey Gillen

This is one of the greatest loved clinkers of all time—a pleasantly pathetic picture that serves as the very definition of the hack horror movie. Made in thirty-five millimeter for under a hundred thousand dollars, the eighty-five-minute opus was a rip-off and a satire at the same time. Alan and Anya Ormsby play Alan and Anya, the married leaders of a pretentious five-person theatrical troupe. Armed with an endless array of flowery overacting and a book of the dead, Alan leads his repertory company to an island off Florida where supposedly the refuse of humanity are buried.

Continually calling his fellow actors "children," he has them dig up a crypt with the idea that he shall bring the dead to life with one of the book's rites. To the actors' surprise, arms suddenly reach out of the ground and grab them. Only after they see Alan's entertained reaction do they realize that the ghosts are really two more of the troupe's members—previously set in place as a practical joke.

After his little jest, they set about digging up a real corpse, whom he subsequently calls "Orville the Awful" (Seth Sklarey). With great anticipation, Alan performs the occult ceremony, upon the conclusion of which Orville does absolutely nothing. Disappointed but undaunted, Alan takes the corpse into a cottage where the whole bunch have a drunken bash. Full of alcoholic bravado, some of the actors stumble back to the cemetery. While laughing and unsteadily remembering Alan's ritual, two real corpse arms reach out of the ground.

Suddenly all of the bodies are transformed into all-too-lively ghouls; walking dead who live only to consume flesh. They stalk and destroy each of the performers one-by-one until only Alan is left. Orville and his friends finally surround the horrified director. As one, they fall upon him and devour him totally. Having used up all of the island's food supply, the ghouls make their way to the troupe's boat and drift off in the direction of the mainland.

The film wouldn't be complete without its "The End ... Or Is It?" fade-out. In this case, the many rampant clichés might be forgiven since it is hard to take the movie in any way but as it was intended: a campy goof on the genre. Surprisingly, Clark lived up to his promise. He next directed a film that was released as *Dead of Night* (1974), but was retitled *Deathdream*, about a dead Vietnam vet brought back to life by the prayers of his grief-stricken mother. But then he hit pay dirt with *Black Christmas* (1974), *Murder by Decree* (1979), the hugely successful *Porky's* (1982), and the beloved holiday perennial *A Christmas Story* (1983)—making him one of the most important graduates of Gorehound U.

COUNT YORGA, VAMPIRE (1970)
Produced by Michael Macready
Directed and Written by Bob Kelljan
Starring Robert Quarry, Roger Perry, Michael Murphy, Donna Anders, and Michael Macready

What can be said about a vampire movie that is highlighted by a scene in which a beautiful girl eats a cat? Just this: Bob Kelljan made his reputation with this, and a subsequent Yorga movie, which got a great deal of mileage out of a little money, and was in a small way responsible for the resurrection of the vampire movie in the early 1970s. That's actually quite a bit.

Donna Anders stars as a sweet innocent who makes the mistake of holding a séance to communicate with her dead mother—presided over by the mysterious Count Yorga (Robert Quarry). The séance fails because, one, the Count is a vampire and not a medium, and two, Donna's mom is alive and a vampire and living in Yorga's cellar. The boyfriends are a little slow on the uptake, but by the time Donna starts munching on her feline pet, they are beginning to get wise to the whole deal. Yorga has been munching on their girlfriends' throats while they are out trying to convince themselves that such a thing is possible.

Finally, they attack Yorga's house at dusk (always a genius move—why not sunrise, Einstein?), armed with crosses and wooden stakes. But their way is seriously hampered by Yorga's hulking, non-vampire assistant, Brudah (Edward Walsh). After Donna's boyfriend (Michael Murphy) is knocked back by the servant, he holds up a cross. When it is knocked aside, he then puts his forefingers together in a plus sign. It doesn't work either.

After his friends are all killed, Murphy finally gets to Yorga, and drives a broken broom handle into his heart. He grabs his girl and runs from vampire "brides" until he thinks they are safe. It is only then that his girl opens her mouth to reveal her vampire fangs (the cat eating didn't clue you?). The film ends on a freeze frame of the woman moving in for the kill.

This mixture of raw horror with modern-day surroundings proved so popular that a sequel was called for. *The Return of Count Yorga* (1971) didn't explain his resurrection, but was even nastier than its predecessor. The hero was played by Roger Perry, and the vampire was still ably embodied by Robert Quarry, but the damsel-in-distress was played by Mariette Hartley, who was to capture America's heart as James Garner's mate in a long-running series of Polaroid camera commercials.

This time Kelljan really milked the formula. Yorga shows up in a small town and decimates an orphanage. On the side of good are a girl, another sweet-faced girl who's mute, Perry, and two likeable (but stolid) cops. On the side of evil are Yorga, his new brides, and a blank-faced little boy orphan who's as rotten as they come. Once more Yorga does his thing until the heroes can't afford to do anything but attack.

Their theorizing is constantly upset by the actions of the seemingly hypnotized boy who not only can waltz around in sunlight, but plant knives into the chests of anyone who gets too close to the truth—like the mute girl. Once more the men attack Yorga's place, although Perry hasn't completely convinced the cops of the vampire's supernatural origins. They become believers when faced with the vampire brides who take all their bullets and keep coming. One of them is done in by the women, but the other gets another blade in the chest, courtesy of the little boy.

It looks bad for our hero as he is thrown to the brides by Yorga. The Count then whisks Hartley up to the balcony of his mansion in order to deliver the coup de grace. Just before his molars sink in, Perry sinks a wood-handled ax deep into his back. His heart pierced by the wood, he topples over the balcony edge to die on the stones below. Hartley is deliriously happy to see her beau, but can't help wondering how he survived the attack. The answer is, of course, that he hadn't. This movie ends with a freeze frame of Perry doing the pointy-toothed, vampiric honors to his lady love.

No further Yorga film was forthcoming, but Quarry returned as a vampire in 1972's ludicrous *Deathmaster*, directed by ex-actor Ray Danton. Danton did much to further the cause of hack horror himself. After starring in *The Rise and Fall of*

Legs Diamond (1960), *The George Raft Story* (1961)—where the tall, handsome actor played the short, rough Raft—and *The Longest Day* (1962), he began appearing in foreign films like *The Spy Who Went into Hell* (1965) and *Secret Agent Super Dragon* (1966).

Forsaking acting for directing, he helmed *Crypt of the Dead* (1973) and the closest he got to a masterwork, *Psychic Killer* (1975), starring Jim Hutton. *The Deathmaster* was one of his first behind-the-camera assignments, and it's a shame to say it looks it. Cheesiness aside, this film is one of the hack delights, as is almost everything utilizing hippie mystique. Hollywood has never been able to handle hippies, and almost all of its attempts are ludicrous at best or hysterically funny at worst.

Deathmaster was somewhere between two extremes. The philosophical script by R.L. Grove (supposedly with a minor assist by *Prophet* author Kahlil Gibran) takes up the first half of the film, as a commune of love children is invaded by a bearded, robed man who talks of everlasting life. The kids think that it is all just so groovy and far-out that some even harbor the thought that this could be the son of you-know-who back for the second you-know-what.

Actually, it is a Yorga clone named Khorda who has hit upon a great new con in order to feed himself. Leading the hippies to a cave like the Pied Piper leading rats to a cliff, he feeds them drugs and takes them to an adjoining crypt for a severe bleeding. After most of the commune has fallen victim to his wiles, some start getting suspicious, and band together to fight back. Luckily for them, Khorda has a whole fishbowl full of leeches, which the long-haired hero (Bill Ewing) uses to distract him. That diversion consists of throwing the fishbowl on Khorda's head.

While he's screaming and trying to get the buggers off, the head hippie lets him have it in the chest. The poor guy did it all for love, only to have his bitten girlfriend—as well as all the rest of Khorda's victims—disintegrate upon the Deathmaster's demise. Bummer, man.

THE DEMON LOVER (1976)

Produced, Directed, and Written by Donald G. Jackson and Jerry Younkins
Starring Christmas Robbins, Val Mayerik, Gunnar Hansen, Sonny Bell, and Linda Conrad

This Wolf Lore Cinema Limited Production was a merry, mangled in-joke. As described by the makers, the picture "includes tremendous visual excitement with police action, karate, occult black magic, sex, rock 'n' roll, the youth movement, and good comedy. [It] ... sparks comparisons to *American Graffiti*, *Last House on the Left*, *The Exorcist*, *The Omen*, and *The Texas Chainsaw Massacre*." Well, you can't fault them for ambition, or chutzpah.

It begins with the murder of Pamela Kirby (Kyra Nash). In a flashback, we see her unwilling to participate in the occult ceremony of Laval Blessing (Christmas Robbins), which precipitates a wholesale takeover of the coven by Damian Kaluta (Val Mayerick).

Angered and alone, Laval calls upon "The Spirit," who appears in the form of a beautiful girl. Together they plot the deaths of Laval's treacherous followers.

Kirby is the first to go. After two kids find her body, police detective Tom Frazetta (Tom Hutton) is called in to investigate. He first questions Elaine Ormsby (Linda Conrad), who is next to die along with friend Janis Romero (Kathy Stewart). Officer Lester Gould (Sonny Bell) goes over some clues with Frazetta before he questions Professor Peckinpah (Gunnar Hansen) about the occult world. While he's getting educated, the cops get a tip to locate Laval Blessing. That interrogation gains nothing except the madman's reaffirmed intent to wipe out the surviving coven members.

Alex Redondo (Phil Foreman) finds his girlfriend Sally Jones (Carol Lasowski) stuck to a tree trunk with a pitchfork. Paul, Garrett, and Charles Wrightson (Ron Hiveley, Michael McGivern, and David Howard) find Susan (Susan Bullen) and Jane (Jan Porter) dead as well. The guys head out to get Blessing as Damian picks up their angry psychic vibrations. As soon as the boys enter Laval's house, his supernatural power forces them to kill each other. Damian bursts in with a gun, but a demon appears and chokes the man into submission. Frazetta arrives right afterward, but Blessing steps out of his protective magic circle to order the demon to kill the cop. The demon kills Blessing instead and disappears before the amazed eyes of the detective.

The Demon Lover is pretty poor, but the crew deserves a round of applause for its in-jokes. Almost every one of the characters is named in honor of an artist. Val Mayerick, a well-known comic artist in his own rite (sic) played Damian Kaluta, who's named after renowned painter Mike Kaluta. Tom Frazetta is named for Frank Frazetta (artist of *Conan* book covers); Lester Gould is for Chester Gould (creator of *Dick Tracy*); Sally Jones could be for Jeff Jones (creator of *Idyll* in *Heavy Metal* magazine); Paul Foster is for Alex Foster (famed *Flash Gordon* comic strip artist); Susan Ackerman is for super-fan Forrest J. Ackerman; Charles Wrightson is for Bernie Wrightson (*Swamp Thing* artist); Jane Corben for Richard Corben (creator of *Den* in *Heavy Metal*); Garret Adams for Neal Adams (revolutionary comic artist who changed the look of Batman); Janis Romero is for director George Romero; Pamela Kirby is for Jack Kirby (*Fantastic Four* artist); and "The Spirit" (played "by herself" according to the credits) is probably for Will Eisner's great comic character of the same name.

This picture also marked Gunnar Hansen's return to film after playing Leatherface in *The Texas Chainsaw Massacre*. With all this mirth and talent behind it, *The Demon Lover* had its heart in the right place. Too bad the same could not be said of the camera.

FLESH FEAST (1971)
Produced by Brad F. Grinter and Veronica Lake
Directed by Brad F. Grinter
Written by Thomas Casey
Starring Veronica Lake, Phil Philbin, Heather Hughes, Yanka Mann, and Chris Martell

In the early 1970s, some Miami filmmakers worked up a script about a mad male scientist who discovered a distasteful way to rejuvenate dead bodies. They were going to film it around the Jacksonville, Florida, area when they discovered that Veronica Lake, the beloved actress who had starred in such major studio classics as *Sullivan's Travels* (1942) and *This Gun For Hire* (1942) was waitressing—waitressing!—in a diner nearby. They changed the leading role to a woman and convinced the actress to appear.

So it was that *Flesh Feast* was Veronica Lake's last movie. In it she played Dr. Elaine Frederick, a scientist who supports her experiments by renting out rooms in her mansion-cum-laboratory to nurses. Her first clients are a bunch of South American revolutionaries. They want her to give new youth to their leader with her process. Her process is to eliminate aged skin and tissue with a specially developed breed of maggot.

Unbeknownst to the doctor, one of her tenants is an undercover policewoman on the trail of the South Americans who had killed an overtly curious reporter. But she is as helpless as the other lodgers when the nurses are held captive on the occasion of Frederick's operation. Dr. Elaine straps her patient to the table, only to discover it is Adolf Hitler.

Unluckily for the dictator, his men are not very good researchers. Although they found out about Frederick's process, they hadn't learned that her mother had been tortured and murdered by the Nazis during the war. Oops. As revenge, Dr. Elaine unleashes all her flesh-eating maggots, who completely consume Adolph.

Sadly, this film is terrible, and made even worse when the moviemakers trumped it up as a Veronica Lake "comeback" picture. Afterward, the once-famous actress moved to England and wrote her memoirs before dying of hepatitis in 1973. Her final film received an even more obscure death.

GRAVE OF THE VAMPIRE (1973)
Produced by Daniel Cady
Directed by John Hayes
Written by David Chase
Starring Michael Pataki, Kitty Vallacher, and William Smith

Some films play like a dream. Some play like a glorified home movie. Some play like a nightmare. A rare few play like a fascinating fever dream. This film, a.k.a. *Seed of Terror*, is one of the latter, no doubt largely due to the script by David Chase, based on his novel *The Still Life* ... the David Chase who later created *The Sopranos*. Whether by accident or intent, this is one of the great blood-sucking pictures coming in the wake of Count Yorga. It is perverse, interesting, and exciting in concept and presentation.

It starts in a graveyard with a denizen of the undead rising from a long sleep. With clothes stolen from a more recent corpse, the starving and extremely thirsty vampire goes in search of sustenance. It turns out that this vampire doesn't just hunger for blood. Once he comes upon a couple necking (all puns intended) in the backseat of their car, he breaks the boy's neck atop a gravestone and drags the hysterical girl into an open grave to rape her.

The scene is made even more effective by the you-are-there eyewitness photography style and the frenetic performances of Michael Pataki as the vampire and Kitty Vallacher as his victim. She is completely believable while screeching and clawing at the ground in desperation, while he manages to convey immense power and savage bestiality despite his short stature. But, then again, Pataki was an actor's actor. Featured in more than a hundred and fifty TV shows and movies, he played a good guy (1975's *The Bat People*), a bad guy ("Korax" in a 1967 episode of *Star Trek* and "Karnas" in a 1988 episode of *Star Trek the Next Generation*), and everything in between (1985's *Rocky IV*, 1988's *Halloween 4*, even the voice of "George Liquor" on *Ren & Stimpy*).

The girl is not made a vampire. Instead, she's made pregnant, and stubbornly insists on giving birth to the hell-spawn, while a handsome, obviously heroic, police detective investigates the crime. Again, the filmmakers throw a *Psycho*-like curve by having the desperate vampire smash the supposed hero's skull in a crypt before the movie is even half-over. After the harried, tattered vampire escapes from the police dragnet and disappears, his female victim—teetering on the edge of sanity herself—raises her pale, newborn baby.

An especially arresting scene occurs when it refuses to take milk, so she feeds it with her own blood from her cut breast. With such nourishment, the vampire child grows up to become a muscular giant played by the great William Smith. Since he is half-human, he does not require as much blood as his dad, and can even hazard sunlight in very small doses. Deeply in love with his mother, he vows to bring her despoiler, his own father, to justice. He traces the vampire down until he finds him at a university. Utilizing the knowledge of his eternal life, the elder bloodsucker had become a professor.

The movie slows down while the two men circle each other, but it can be forgiven thanks to the rip-roaring climax and finale, where father and son go at each other tooth and nail. Pataki's civilized veneer is stripped away as he battles his son all over a dormitory. And this isn't just one of those "I-punch-you-you-punch-me" fake fights, either. This is a biting, kicking, scratching, "smash-your-head-repeatedly-against-the-wall," *Darker than Amber*-style free-for-all; it culminates with Smith wrapping a chain around Pataki's throat and dragging him to death. Still smashing his father's limp figure against the floor, Smith reverts to his natural state as well. The movie ends with a close-up of the son's anguished face and his telltale fangs.

Pataki had a way of appearing in seemingly ludicrous films, and imbuing a legitimacy that would not have been apparent otherwise. He slipped on the fangs again in 1979 for *Dracula's Dog*. As dumb as that sounds, it made a certain entertaining sense as written by Frank Ray Perilli and directed by Albert Band. One night a vampire got so thirsty that he sucked on a Doberman pinscher. Naturally, the pooch grew fangs and became a slave to the Count. Oscar-winning José Ferrer played the protagonist here, who is justifiably confused when he tries to figure out who left the animal-like marks on victims' throats—the human beast or the canine sidekick? Ultimately, it makes little difference since Frank Ray Perilli was no David Chase.

HORROR HIGH (1974)
Produced by Tom Moore
Directed by Larry Stouffer
Written by Jake Fowler
Starring Pat Cardi, Rosie Holotik, John Niland, Austin Stocker, and Joye Hash

By now the plot is comfortably familiar. A nice but geeky kid is brow-beaten by his school peers. He is teased by younger kids, abused by the older kids, rejected by those his age, and ignored by girls. Through a variety of organic and supernatural means, the doofus is changed into a rampaging beast who takes revenge on those who had scorned him.

Probably the ultimate statement of this theme came in *Carrie* (1976), director Brian DePalma's adaptation (from a script by Lawrence D. Cohen) of Stephen King's novel. That movie was not only the high point of this theme, but probably DePalma at the height of his powers. Having made several anti-establishment comedies (1968's *Greetings* and 1970's *Hi Mom*) and a couple of murder mysteries (1968's *Murder A La Mod* and 1973's *Sisters*), his subsequent films, with rare exception, have grown increasingly more derivative and less story-oriented. For him, the style always seems to be more important than the substance.

In most hack horror cases, sadly, the budget dictates both the content and style. In *Horror High*, originally called *Twisted Brain*, Pat Cardi plays the school jerk, Vernon, who gets hold of a mixture that turns him into a mass student murderer. This flick harks back to the fun films of producer Herman Cohen, such as 1957's *I Was a Teenage Werewolf* and *I Was a Teenage Frankenstein*. Unfortunately, hark as it might, it couldn't hold a candle to those earlier films' entertainment value.

THE INCREDIBLY STRANGE CREATURES (1965)
Produced and Directed by Ray Dennis Steckler
Written by Gene Pollock and Robert Silliphant
Starring Cash Flagg (Ray Dennis Steckler)

This curiosity, originally produced in 1963, about a guy hypnotized by a zombie-making gypsy who murders women to serve as mates for the gypsy's mutilated boyfriends whom she keeps in her back room(!), is really just an excuse to discuss a myriad of "Incredible" films. Actually, when Hollywood Star Distributing acquired this film, which had also been called *Teenage Psycho Meets Bloody Mary*, they took one look at the hack horror-comedy-musical and hit upon the title that was to give the film long-lasting fame. In 1966, it was released for a third time under the title *The Incredibly Strange Creatures Who Stopped Living and Became Mixed Up Zombies*. Let's hear it for bravado and ingenuity.

Let's also hear it for William Sachs, who returns to these pages with another "incredible" idea that doesn't quite hack it on screen. That is 1978's *The Incredible Melting Man*. Alex Rebar starred as astronaut Steve West, the first man on Saturn. He comes back in one piece but brings along an organism that causes his skin to melt. His doctor (Burr DeBenning) is confused, his commanding officer (Myron Healey) is stonewalling, and the local sheriff (Michael Aldredge) is perplexed, but the audience is probably infuriated by seeing what could have been a riveting science-fiction thriller turned into just another nonsensical "monster on the loose" melodrama.

It is especially unfortunate since the leading character had been designed by future Oscar-winning special effects make-up man Rick Baker in four distinct eroding phases—phases that were lost when Rebar was reluctant to suffer the many hours of make-up, and the footage was used out of original sequence (Nigel Kneale did it far better in the 1955 Quatermass adventure *The Creeping Unknown*, a.k.a. *The Quatermass Xperiment*).

More incredible stuff comes with 1970's *The Incredible Two-Headed Transplant*, starring Bruce Dern as a weasely, t-shirted, squinty-eyed scientist who is perfecting a method to graft heads in the laboratory of his Spanish-ranch-style home. He lives with a pretty young wife, played by Pat Priest (a veteran of *The Munsters* television show), a gay assistant, and a hulking, slow-witted groundskeeper (John Bloom).

Invading this peaceful property is a psychotic criminal who has already terrorized the backwoods community. He kills the groundskeeper's kindly brother and ties everyone up except the bathing-suit-clad wife, who he takes along with him. Escaping their bonds, the scientist and his assistant give chase. They rescue the woman and blast the wide-eyed, giggling, maniacal crook in the chest with a shotgun. Then the scientist gets a great idea. Why not test his grafting process on the sociopath and the groundskeeper? What could possibly go wrong?

Actually it works just great … except for occasional migraines that instigate the murders of lovers and motorcycle gang members. Finally, the patient wife decides to blow the whistle, only to get bound and gagged in the lab, then stuffed in the bedroom by her loving hubby, who then tries to track down his rampaging creation.

Onto the scene comes the doc's fellow medico and the wife's good friend (Casey Kasem, the long-time host of *America's Top Ten* and voice of *Scooby-Doo's* Shaggy, in one of his few live action movie roles). Wearing a ridiculously puffed-sleeve and wide-collared shirt, he rescues the wife and alerts the cops to the predicament. It all ends badly for the doctor and the beast, proving once and for all that two heads are not better than one.

But American International didn't feel that way. Less than a year later they unleashed *The Thing with Two Heads*. Produced by Wes Bishop, directed by Lee Frost, and written by the two along with James Gordon White, this was more of the same trash, only instead of two unknowns sharing the same torso, Ray Milland and Rosey Grier's skulls were resting on the same shoulders.

Also along for the ridiculous ride were Don Marshall, Roger Perry, and the buxom Kathy Baumann. She was about the only thing worth watching (beside special effects make-up artist Rick Baker's two-headed gorilla suit that high-lighted the opening half-hour). The beast was racist scientist Milland's "crowning achievement"—which trashes a supermarket before recapture.

Naturally, after that, he is certain that his grafting process will work, despite the fact that the host body needs a month to adjust to the extra head, but then doesn't require the original head anymore. Since he is cancer-ridden, the tyrannical scientist instructs his assistants to use him as the ultimate guinea pig. Only after the operation does he discover that the only body available was that of a big black convict sentenced to the electric chair. The sight of award-winning actor Milland emoting while unconvincingly attached to football star Grier's now even-more ample torso is a cause for raucous, derisive celebration.

After a career spanning more than fifty years, and starring in such classics as *Beau Geste* (1939), *The Uninvited* (1944), *The Lost Weekend* (1945), and *Dial M for Murder* (1954), Milland refused to go quietly into disuse, instead opting to elevate the likes of *Panic in the Year Zero* (1962), *Premature Burial* (1962), *X: The Man with the X-Ray Eyes* (1963), and *Frogs* (1972) before being embraced full-time by television. Perhaps his career is the most incredible thing of all.

★★★ HELD OVER BY POPULAR DEMAND ★★★
Larry Cohen & William Girdler

These are two filmmakers whose careers aligned in subject matter and appreciation until one took off on a series of cerebral subjects, and the other's life was cut short in a freak accident. Both men started gaining notice while making blaxploitation pictures, both men moved into hack horror work, both men's films warranted serious study, and both men suffered life-changing setbacks.

Girdler was originally the more prolific of the two, grinding out *Zebra Killer*, *Asylum of Satan*, *Sheba Baby,* and *Abby* for General Film, Studio I, and American International in 1975 and 1976. Only one was straight horror ("Love Slaves of Satan Tortured to Blood Dripping Death!"), while the others were blaxploitation with notable twists.

Zebra, was, in no small way, based on a real-life series of murders in San Francisco (which also inspired 1971's *Dirty Harry*, and 2007's *Zodiac*). *Sheba* was a Pam Grier vehicle in which she played a Second City private eye who comes home to protect her father in Louisville, Kentucky. The white mob boss has sent his black heat with a bomb to lean on the old man and let Sheba know she isn't wanted. The next day they get serious by gunning her dad down. She then gets funky with a .44 Magnum. She sees to it that the white kingpin gets the point with a harpoon in the back. As strenuous as all that was, it was nothing compared to what Girdler put his

Abby actors through.

This was the black version of *The Exorcist*, but instead of a possessed white pre-teen, it is pretty, black Abby (Carol Speed) who is possessed by the Algerian god of evil, Esu. She wipes out various men while her minister husband (Terry Carter) calls her father (William Marshall)—who just happens to have been the one to unleash Esu in the first place. He takes a plane back from Nigeria and corners the demonized Abby in a bar. With booze and blood flying everywhere, they wrest the demon from her soul. As far as Warner Brothers was concerned, however, imitation is not the sincerest form of flattery. They sued *Abby* and won.

Writer/producer/director Larry Cohen had started his black action films in the early 1970s, culminating in *Hell Up in Harlem* (1974), a sequel to his previous year's *Black Caesar*. Both starred blaxploitation icon Fred Williamson as Harlem's underworld king. Relative morality and heroics are beside the point. Everybody is bad here, and they all have guns.

The white mob wants to wipe out the black mob, the corrupt government wants to keep getting payoffs, and the black mob are busy keeping their heads above the ocean of blood. The New York district attorney puts a price on Williamson's head and everybody is out to collect, including Black Caesar's own bodyguard. He beats up most of the white syndicate, chokes his own men, and blasts the D.A., all in an action-packed, hand-held, zooming, ninety-six minutes.

From then on, the two filmmakers parted conceptual company. Girdler had discovered a successful formula in the woods after directing a rip-off of *Jaws* that should have been called *Paws*. Instead, it was titled *Grizzly* (1976), and that's just what the script by Harvey Flaxman and David Sheldon was. The plot was just like the shark story except for more gore. Instead of Robert Shaw, there was Christopher George as an intrepid park ranger. Instead of Richard Dreyfuss, there was Richard Jaekel as an eccentric naturalist. Instead of Roy Scheider, there was Andrew Prine as a fellow ranger. And instead of Murray Hamilton, there was Joe Dorsey as a supervisor who worries more about profits than campers.

While he keeps the park open, a fifteen-foot tall, two-ton grizzly bear starts decimating all the female campers it can find. A pretty park scout played by Vicki Johnson is kind enough to skinny dip so he can have some flesh without all those clothes in the way, and Jaekel allows him to decapitate his horse. Finally, after a child is maimed and his mother killed, the supervisor allows George and Prine to go a-hunting in their rocket-shooting copter. But this is a beast who can knock down a watchtower with his bare (bear) paws. He pulls the helicopter down too, leaving the two rangers to fight him mano a bearo.

So successful was this man-against-nature effort—sparked by a great poster painted by Neal Adams—that producer Edward L. Montoro and director Girdler repeated the formula with a vengeance the following year. Armed with a new script by Girdler and Eleanor Norton, they took Christopher George and Richard Jaekel, added George's wife Lynda Day, hired Leslie Nielsen, Michael Ansara, Ruth Roman, Paul Mantee, Jon Cedar, and Andrew Stevens, among others, and moved them all up into the California mountains for *Day of the Animals*.

The real villains here are not wild beasts, but aerosol cans. They've so depleted the ozone layer that all of the beasties residing five thousand feet above the water line are acting mighty aggressive. Four couples become victims of everything from vultures to tarantulas. In between there's a wildcat, wolf, German shepherd, eagle, rattlesnake, and, for old times sake, a bear.

Fight as they might, almost no one survives this camping trip as the environmental message is made clear. It's not nice to fool Mother Nature. That is, unless, you're a director eager to make his mark on the industry.

Day of the Animals did well enough that Girdler could pick and choose his next project. He found it on an airport bookstore rack: *The Manitou* by Graham Masterton. The director got his friends and associates—several from the prior picture—together, and set to work. He and Jon Cedar co-wrote the script. They sold the idea to Melvin G. Gordy. He put together an eleven-hundred-page prospectus for the film in order to get additional funding. A three-million-dollar budget was collected, as well as a cast that included Tony Curtis, Susan Strasberg, Burgess Meredith, Jeanette Nolan, Ann Sothern and Girdler vets Cedar, Mantee, and Ansara.

The film starts beautifully. Karen Tandy (Strasberg) is a girl with a problem. She has a lump on her back, which is growing. Harry Erskine (Curtis) is a man with a problem. He was making a fine living off bilking old ladies with a fortune-telling scam until ex-love Tandy came back into his life. His involvement with the girl begins to take over. Tandy says strange things in her sleep. An elderly client starts speaking Native American, does a ceremonial dance, and then floats down the hallway to fall to her death down the stairs.

Meanwhile, the lump just keeps getting bigger. Tandy's doctors make a terrible mistake of X-raying the lump, which mutates the creature inside, and then double their troubles when they try to cut the lump off. First the operating surgeon cuts his own hand, and then the surgical laser goes wild.

Erskine visits fellow psychics Amelia Crusoe (Stevens) and Mrs. Karmann (Southern) to have an investigating séance. Rising out of the table top is the head of "Misquamacus"—a four-hundred-year-old medicine man. Upon the suggestion of a specialist, Dr. Snow (Meredith), Erskine quickly gets in touch with a modern-day medicine man (Ansara), who explains that the evil spirit is being reincarnated on Tandy's back. Well, duh. They rush to save her while Misquamacus begins to make mincemeat of the hospital.

And that's where the film falls apart. The subsequent action requires a multitude of special effects that Girdler just didn't have the money for. The best scene is the climactic birth of the midget monster from the huge bubble on Strasberg's back (that's the best scene, mind you). From there, it's humans versus Misquamacus as he magically transforms the hospital floor from an Arctic wasteland to a level hanging in the cosmos.

Just when it seems as if the monster will triumph, Erskine realizes that all things have spirits—or as the native Americans put it, a "manitou." He uses the manitou of the hospital's computer as an energy source and the power of love as a channeler. Misquamacus is blasted into nothingness by bolts shooting out of Tandy's hands. But by then, the movie has collapsed into nonsense, but it did make for a mediocre light show. All ends happily for Tandy and Erskine, as well as author Masterton, who wrote a sequel.

That never made it to film. Girdler was all set to start his next project when he died at the age of thirty in a helicopter crash while scouting locations for his next film.

While Girdler was starting *Sheba, Baby*, Larry Cohen had already finished his most heartfelt film to date. It was a tale of business corruption and the love parents have for their children. "There's only one thing wrong with the Davis' baby," said a 1975 ad, "It's Alive." But that was the second of two ad campaigns. The first was a miasma of incorrect images that turned off everyone and relegated the intrepid film to failure.

It was only after positive critical response that the distributor, Warner Brothers, was inspired to try again. With a clever and subtle poster, featuring the above legend and a picture of an old-fashioned wicker baby carriage with a blood-stained claw hanging out—the inexpensively produced horror film made a million dollars in its first week of re-release and went on to profit by ten times that amount.

Because of an ill-produced pill, Frank (John Ryan) and Lenore (Sharon Farrell) Davis' second child is a fanged, clawed monstrosity that kills almost everyone in the delivery room. It slaughters a variety of others in town until it psychically finds its way "home." In the meantime, the family has been beset by callous news reporters, all eager to exploit their tragedy. The last straw comes when their housekeeper tries to pump the nearly insane mother for information that she can sell to a tabloid.

The father dedicates himself to personally killing the monstrous child—an off-spring he cannot believe himself responsible for. He loses his job, he sends his other boy away, and he watches as his wife slowly falls to pieces. Finally the cops and

Frank have cornered the creature in the Los Angeles sewers. The father goes in first, but cannot bring himself to shoot the crying monster baby.

He realizes that the creature was as confused and frightened as its victims, and it responds to his father's warm overtures with calm happiness. He takes the child outside, trying to protect it from the bloodthirsty authorities and the pill manufacturer (who is intent on destroying any evidence of his company's duplicity). Unable to shield the baby beast, Frank is forced to hurl it at the pill representative, whose throat is ripped out. The film ends with the family together, while a report comes over the radio that another beastly baby has been born in Seattle.

The sequel, *It Lives Again*, arrived in 1978. Unfortunately, the novelty had worn off. Again distributed by Warner Brothers and again written, directed, and produced by Cohen, it stars Frederic Forrest and Kathleen Lloyd as the new parents of a beast baby who are sheltered by the returning Frank Davis, again portrayed by John Ryan.

After a baby shower, Davis tells the expectant mother that the government is now able to locate and abort the epidemic of monster children. Davis is now consumed with saving other people's offspring since he was unable to save his own. He is allied with a millionaire (Eddie Constantine) and has, as helpers, other beast-baby parents and assorted fanatics.

Hijacking the ambulance taking Lloyd to the hospital, they safely deliver her monster and put it in a nursery with "Adam and Eve," two other creatures they have been able to save. But they can't teach a young monster new tricks. The trio get loose and wreak havoc until they're found and exterminated.

Although clever, Cohen had inflated his terror tale into a science-fiction epic that his budget couldn't support. One person who especially felt the strain was babymaker Rick Baker, who built the beasts for both films. Having only enough money to build a doll for the first, it was Baker himself who had to lie on his back in the muddy sewers to give the thing motion for the finale. And it was his then-wife, Elaine, who had fangs attached to her mouth for chewing close-ups.

In the sequel, Baker repeated these cost-saving techniques, but also built a full-scale baby suit that could be worn by a small actor in an oversized set. After making the trio of dolls with more detail, he visited the set, only to discover that the babies had been made to crawl by being pulled across the floor with a string. "We did it other times and it looked fine," Baker remembered Cohen telling him.

For the veteran filmmaker, it seems, the idea is everything—the actual realization of the idea is somewhat secondary. As long as the point gets across, Cohen is content. Between his two beastly baby tales, he had made another audacious science-fiction horror tome that turned out to be far more controversial than anyone seemed to want. It was originally called *God Told Me To* (1976).

"God told me to," is what a sniper tells police detective Peter Nicholas (Tony Lo Bianco), before leaping to his death. It is the same excuse a man who stabbed shoppers, and a patrolman who fired into a parade crowd, gave before they, too, died. Nicholas discovers the one thing the trio had in common was association with hippie Bernard Phillips (Richard Lynch). He tries to question Bernard's mother, only to have the woman attack him and kill herself after uttering the same four words.

Things go from creepy to crazy as the autopsy reveals that the woman was a virgin. Digging some more, the cop finds out that the woman had reported being kidnapped by a flying saucer in 1951. Nine months later, Bernard was born without gender. More modem-day "God told me to" slayings follow, until Nicholas is under attack from Bernard's followers. Undaunted, he tracks his leads until he comes face-to-face with Bernard, who actually glows with an ethereal light. As much as the man tries to kill the cop, he is unsuccessful.

Following that clue to its natural conclusion, Nicholas—a foster child—finds his real mother (Sylvia Sidney). She had been made pregnant by an other-worldly phenomenon at the 1939 World's Fair. Flushed with newly found psychic power, the cop forces a drug pusher to kill his bodyguards and himself. He then confronts Bernard a second time. The younger alien half-breed admits to his God-like control and tells his unearthly brethren that only together can they make a perfect species—the second coming. Disgusted, Nicholas attacks Bernard, and the entire building bursts into flames. The stronger cop escapes, while the younger man dies in the conflagration. Arrested for the hippie's murder, the press asks him why. You can guess what four words he says.

Besides the sacrilegious content, the movie is sparked by good performances, especially that of Lo Bianco. But again, the work falters from Cohen's seeming lack of concern in execution. New World Pictures took *God Told Me To* out of distribution for a re-edit and a retitling, then put it back into circulation as *Demon* ("Conceived in a Hell Beyond Our Galaxy ... Destined to Rule Our World! Warning: This Film Contains Scenes of Violence and Intense Horror").

After suffering bad reviews on *The Private Files of J. Edgar Hoover* (1979), starring Broderick Crawford, Cohen started work on *Full Moon High* (1981), a werewolf comedy starring Adam Arkin. It would spend some time on the shelf before it was finally released by Filmways. All the negative notices seemed to have caught up with Cohen. Without any previous fanfare, *Variety* ran a rave review in mid-1982 for *The Winged Serpent*, a Larco production. But when it was released as the retitled *Q*, it turned out to be a fun mess with negligible suspense. Larry Cohen had struck again.

And he would keep on striking. *The Stuff* (1985) was another great idea—a food additive with a mind, and world-domineering plan, of its own—but it was, once again, hobbled in execution. Do you see a pattern emerging here? *It's Alive 3: Island of the Alive* arrived in 1987, as did *A Return to Salem's Lot*. Cohen tried a few more stabs at remaining consistent all the way through an entire project, then finally seemed to accept that where he most excelled, and what he most enjoyed, was being an idea man.

As of this writing, he is still grinding them out, his ideas resulting in such major features as *Phone Booth* (2002) and *Cellular* (2004). And as long as he does so, it, and his work, will be alive.

MARK OF THE DEVIL (1972)
Produced by Hallmark Releasing
Directed by Michael Armstrong
Written by Sergio Cassner
Starring Herbert Lom, Udo Kier, Reggie Nalder, Gaby Fuchs, and Ingeborg Schoener

The company that promoted *Last House on the Left* to glory struck marketing gold again with this simple, yet supremely sadistic story of early American witch trials. In a mere ninety minutes there are about fifteen major torture sequences, some with comely young women (one of whom, Herschell Gordon Lewis be praised, has her tongue torn out). Or, roughly speaking, one about every six minutes.

The "hero" of the work is a young Baron (Udo Kier). who is a soldier out to stop an old Baron who has been commissioned by the church to hunt down witches and garner confessions any way he sees fit. And he sees fit with everything from thumbscrews, the rack, a bed of nails, foot brandings, sole whipping, and even needles to the eye.

"Be happy," a young girl suggests to the young Baron.

"You mustn't say such things," Kier replies.

The superstar of the proceedings is Hallmark, again, since it was they who came up with the stark, highly visible ad campaign. It utilized the wide-eyed and wide-mouthed damsel about to lose her tongue, along with the printed offering of a "stomach distress bag" to each and every customer. Like most of the hack horror that succeeds, Hallmark delivered on its stomach-turning promise. The film, meanwhile, had to live up to its ads' promise, and *Mark of the Devil* made it with flying colors—mostly red.

NIGHT OF A THOUSAND CATS (1974)
Produced by Zachary Mars
Directed by Renee Cardona
Starring Anjanette Comer, Hugo Stiglitz, Christa Linder, and Gerardo Zepeda

Yes, this is it. This is what the world had been waiting for. The only movie worse than *Night of the Lepus* (1972). That was the MGM movie (based on a book by Russell Braddon and directed by William F. Claxton) starring Stuart Whitman and Janet Leigh featuring cute, furry bunnies on miniature sets, made to almost look threatening by slow motion filming, loud soundtrack noises, and having the ends of their sweet little buck-toothies painted blood red. Every time those lovable little fellows with their wriggling noses and fluffy tails appear, audiences were more inclined to sigh "awwwww," than scream. And gorehounds were more willing to laugh than look up "Lepus" (Latin for rabbit).

Which brings the subject back to cats. Felines can be ominous, but to make them look that way on film is difficult. Poe managed to infuse some fright into *The Black Cat*, but the directors of *Eye of the Cat* (1969) and *Because of the Cats* (1973) found that only their adorability translated to celluloid. Better that the felines remain hissing witnesses to ignominy, or suddenly-appearing red herrings who make girls scream, then be relieved just prior to their attack by the real villain.

But *Night of a Thousand Cats* was a different breed entirely. A real laugh-fest, as well as a snoozer, it was made in Spain by some folk who realized that one American actor in the cast made an American distribution sale easier. So Mars and Cardona hired Anjanette Comer (1965's *The Loved One*, 1970's *Rabbit Run*) to follow up her crackerjack job in 1973's *The Baby*, a nasty piece of business about a family who bilks welfare with a normal adult they purposely made retarded. Comer plays a seemingly sweet social worker who, after nearly getting murdered, kills the family in order to make "the baby" a companion to her own forcibly retarded adult.

After that, this production was a step up. It's about a guy who starves a "thousand" cats. When they're at the point of death, he feeds them human flesh. Before long he has an army of cannibal cats. Then he subjugates an entire island and takes his pick of the prettiest women. If anyone gets in his way or tries to stop him, he sics the cats on them.

This, of course, was the best part. It is completely obvious that the actors to be "eaten" are smeared with cat food. They dubbed in savage cat noises and the actors scream and writhe in mock pain while all the cats are doing is calmly licking them. Whenever one wanders away disinterested, it is thrown back onto the intended victim from off screen.

The film's dry kitty litter wit extended to the poster by Trans-International Films. At the very bottom were two notes. The first was: "Bring your cat with you and get one free ticket!" The second was: "Burial Insurance. If you die from fright or nausea during the performance, we will give you a nice but simple funeral free of charge." In small print below that it concluded:

"Casket Optional, on West Coast Only."

★★★ HELD OVER BY POPULAR DEMAND ★★★
George A. Romero

Herschell Gordon Lewis may have started it, but George Romero initially gave it respectability and integrity. He originally showed all of the hack horrorists that there could be more to shoot for than just gratuitous blood and guts. He showed that exploitation could have wit, intelligence, and meaning while still raking in the big bucks.

He started by directing, filming, and co-writing a ninety-minute black and white horror movie called *Night of the Living Dead* (1968). It wasn't so much that he wanted to make it—he needed to. After college he had opened a small commercial company in Pittsburgh called Latent Image. It made industrials and ads while Romero tried to sell various movie scripts. He found that the only things distributors seemed interested in were horror films.

Still unable to find substantial backing, but secure enough to give it a shot, he found ten people to put up six hundred dollars each, so the new production facility was named Image Ten. One of its members, John Russo, helped Romero develop a full-fledged screenplay from a trilogy of short stories that the director had conceived.

The trilogy concerned the slow and painful takeover of the world by the living dead. It was meant to be a basic allegory of every transference of power that ever has —and probably ever will—occurred. That was the between-the-lines theme. The actual lines concerned twelve hours of abject terror where six people are trapped in a house surrounded by unreasoning ghouls who exist only to eat them.

Over a period of seven months, utilizing local Pennsylvania talent and a sixteen-millimeter camera, Romero shot his cult classic epic for less than a hundred and fifteen thousand dollars. Once the initial six thousand had run out, Romero had enough film to convince more wealthy backers to support the project. When it was finally completed, the usual hack horror distributors didn't want to touch it. Continental Films took it on, but then proceeded to violate their contract with

Romero up, down, and sideways. But by the time Image Ten won in court, Continental was no more. Surprisingly, the Walter Reade Organization—which had its own chain of theaters—picked up the pieces.

They distributed an accurate, disturbing, gruesome preview of coming attraction trailer and then unleashed the movie in their prestigious theaters. In spite of the preview, many thought that the film was going to be just another "Saturday Matinee" filler and dropped off their kiddies for a fun time on the weekend. They were certain that the Walter Reade Organization wouldn't do anything to hurt them. They were enraged when they returned two hours later to find their children throwing up in the bathroom or stumbling around, blank-eyed, like the living dead themselves.

Night of the Living Dead had received its first infamous notoriety. What many couldn't completely understand was why the apparently amateurish film—with performances that ranged from fair to abysmal—was so effective. Romero managed to turn every exploitation preconception upside down while still maintaining a sense of claustrophobic, inescapable horror. His movie was the first to tread in the landscape of true nightmare. In the film, as in dreams, things are not perfect—scenes are ragged, sounds change, and the image isn't always clear.

But one thing is clear from the outset. The dead are coming to life with the sole purpose of turning the living into the living dead. Johnny and his sister Barbara (Russell Streiner and Judith O'Dea) discover that much when visiting the grave of their father. A strange man appears from over the hill and marches right at them. Johnny makes a joke about how strange the man is acting, but the joke is on him when the man unswervingly attacks them without pause.

Johnny is killed when he hits his head on a stone, and Barbara rushes back to the car. There is no safety there, either, as the zombie smashes the window with a rock. Barbara flees again, this time to an old house. She hesitantly walks up the stairs, only to find a partly consumed corpse.

Already, there are similarities to movies that had come before and movies that have been made since. *The Texas Chainsaw Massacre* has a similar opening, while Barbara ascending the staircase seems to have its roots in a similar scene from *Psycho*. But from there, *Night of the Living Dead* takes on a unique character of its own.

Not counting the corpse, Barbara is not alone in the house. Her screams bring Ben (Duane Jones), a black man who has escaped inside from more of the living dead. The two barricade the windows and doors as the rest of the occupants make themselves known. There's Tom and Judy (Keith Wayne and Judith Ridley), a young couple, as well as Harry and Helen Cooper (Karl Hardman, who is also a co-producer on the film, and Marilyn Eastman), who are nursing their little daughter

Karen (Kyra Schon), who was bitten by one of the ghouls.

Things continue to go haywire. Instead of swallowing the death of her brother and accepting the insanity that is going on all around her (like any good heroine would), Barbara regresses inside herself. She becomes a near-catatonic drone. Instead of forgetting their differences and banding together, Ben and Harry bicker endlessly about who should be boss. Harry is a self-important, self-righteous clod, while Ben is assured and forthright, so the group sides with the black man ... much to their infinite regret.

A television report spells the situation out. A Venus space probe has brought back a spore that is making the dead live, kill, and eat. Everyone they kill and don't consume will become one of them. The only way to destroy them is to shoot them in the head. The authorities are roaming the country, doing their best, and they suggest the living attempt to reach fallout shelters.

Ben knows there is a truck outside, but he also knows that it is low on fuel. The needed fuel is in some tanks a few hundred yards away. Ben, Tom, and Judy make it to the truck and the truck makes it to the tanks, but the torches they used to protect themselves from the horde of zombies ignite the gas. Ben escapes, but the young couple is caught in the subsequent explosion.

The "hero" gets back to the house as the living dead gleefully surround the bonfire and make dinner of the lovers' remains. The terrified Harry tries to keep him from getting inside. All along he has been saying that they should barricade themselves into the cellar, but Ben has maintained that the upstairs is the safest. Their argument finally results in a fistfight, which Ben easily wins. Ben gets a rifle and starts mobilizing the survivors to defend the house from an all-out attack. Harry tries to get the gun away from him, but is shot.

Arms punch through the wooden barricades to clutch at Ben, as Harry stumbles down into the basement. Frightened that the sight of her father will scare their daughter, Helen runs into the cellar to see her chewed-on husband. Karen then falls upon her with a trowel, using it as a knife to stab her mother repeatedly. The end comes for the delirious Barbara when her dead brother gets in. Now a zombie himself, he makes quick work of his sibling.

Ben races for the basement, dodges an attacking Karen, and locks the mob outside. To be on the safe side, he puts a bullet in the Coopers' brains. He remains there, safe, until morning—together with the corpse of the overbearing man who had the key to all their survival in the first place. If they had only listened to him instead of Ben, they might have lived. Instead, the man they wrongfully followed made it, after wasting all of their lives.

He pays an ironic price for his stubbornness. By morning the police have cleared most of the area. They march in, shooting the living dead in their collective heads. Tired and relieved, Ben shows himself. A sheriff sees him and shoots him right between the eyes.

The critical reaction was, to put it mildly, extreme. The usually perceptive *Variety* called it an "unrelieved orgy of sadism," and labeled it "repellant," "distasteful," "brutal," "disgusting," and "nauseous." And they were just getting started.

"Director George A. Romero appears incapable of contriving a single graceful set-up ... photography is abysmally lit ... the processing seems to have been done on twenty-year old Army stock ... and the sound has the 'echo in an empty room' quality of most unprofessional low budget efforts. John Russo's screenplay is a model of verbal banality and suggests a total antipathy for his characters ... if not for all mankind. On no level is the unrelieved grossness of *Night of the Living Dead* disguised by a feeble attempt at art or significance."

Yes, but other than that, how did you like the play, Mrs. Lincoln?

Vincent Canby in *The New York Times* was a bit more philosophical. "The dialogue and background music seem ... recorded in an empty swimming pool, and the wobbly camera seems to have a fetishist's interest in hands—clutched, wrung, scratched, severed, and finally, in the ultimate consumption, eaten like pizza."

But once gorehounds discovered it, they ate the movie up like pizza. Slowly but surely, other critics came around to Romero's way of thinking. The positive reaction was so clear that distributors were clamoring for more of the same. Only Romero didn't want to give it to them. He saw an opportunity to get his other films made.

First out of the Pittsburgh chute was a light romantic comedy called *There's Always Vanilla*, then came the supernatural drama *Jack's Wife* (1971). Jack Harris took this low-key movie about a woman dabbling in witchcraft, radically re-edited it, and shoved it into theaters under the title *Hungry Wives*. Suffice it to say that neither of these films went any place people would like to go.

To avoid the uncaring masses, Romero finally returned to the unremitting horror he had instigated four years earlier. With a budget supplied by Lee Hessel, Romero worked up *The Crazies* (1973), a movie that seemed to have its roots in *The Andromeda Strain* (1971).

While the latter dealt with a top notch government team of scientists working toward isolating and destroying a deadly alien virus with millions of dollars' worth of specialized equipment, the former had an ultimately deadly virus accidentally released by the government, who then work harder to cover it up than to cure it.

Romero incorporated all sorts of touches that seem to be uniquely his. The virus (with the code name "Trixie") makes people go nuts. That created a wide range of reactions—some harmless, some funny, some deadly. The film centered on a man who hadn't yet been affected, trying desperately to get his family through the soldiers cordoning off the town.

As he tries to escape, a harried scientist tries desperately to create an antidote for the germ. But true to governmental incompetence, his makeshift lab is housed in the school where all the captured crazies are kept. No sooner has he solved the problem than a mob of crazies break through security and knock him over a stairway banister to his death. The secret of the antidote dies with him.

In a recognizably Romero-esque finale, the escaping man is cut off from freedom by a gang of his own friends, who have since gone bonkers. His wife is killed, and then the soldiers move in to finish him off. The final irony is that while the military declares the cordon a success, the germ has broken out in another town. The movie ends with the officer in charge being air-lifted to his new assignment.

The title was pointlessly changed to *Code Name: Trixie* for a 1973 re-release, but it was changed back soon afterward. Romero, in the meantime, had met Richard Rubenstein, with whom he created Laurel Entertainment, Inc. They fashioned a strong monetary foundation by doing sports films, and then produced *Martin* in 1976. It is a modern-day vampire psychodrama that is seen both as Romero's most-accomplished, and least-accomplished, film.

John Amplas starred as a troubled (which is putting it mildly) teenager who feels the need to murder, rape, and then drink the blood of female victims. He does this by injecting them with sodium pentathol, and then slitting their wrists. The movie starts with the boy doing just that to a pretty girl in a train compartment, and then debarking at a Pennsylvania steel town to meet his guardian—his elder cousin Cuda (Lincoln Maazel).

All around him things are dying, and Martin goes along by living out his vampiric fantasy. He is not a supernatural being, but his guardian comes to believe he is. After his one normal sexual relationship with a despondent divorcee, she slits her own wrists. It is for this death—the one for which he was not responsible—that Cuda pounds a wooden stake through Martin's heart.

Just as the old man has exorcized the human demon in the young murderer, Martin seemed to exorcize Romero's fascination with the steel towns he grew up in. An enjoyable undercurrent in the film was all of the Pittsburgh-oriented satire, loneliness, and frustration the aimless residents felt. After it was released by Libra Films in 1977 as *Martin the Blood Lover*, Romero was finally ready to take on the second installment of his Living Dead series.

The original short story was all but jettisoned to give the movie a modern appeal. The initial idea was to have the *Night of the Living Dead* house become the focal point for all the movies. The second film was to take place six months after the first ended, and the third was to occur fifteen years after that. But upon recalling how zombie-like patrons look in huge shopping malls, Romero knew he had the location for *Dawn of the Dead* (1978).

The new film opens with a television report about just how widespread the horror has become. A SWAT-like team of heavily armed people raid a housing project to blow open living dead heads. Forced into a shopping center, they spend a part of the remaining two-hour-and-seven-minute movie creating a "normal" home for themselves in the barricaded mall, and another part fighting for their lives when unsavory types intrude.

Ironically, it is not the living dead who ultimately invade the oasis of tranquil consumerism the team creates in the stores, it is a human, though beastly, motorcycle gang who want to use the place as a headquarters. The SWAT team practically joins in with the living dead to fight the bikers, who gleefully trash everything the team had worked so hard to maintain.

The film climaxes in an orgy of death that rivals the devastation with which the movie opened. In the 1968 black and white movie, Romero used Bosco (a chocolate-flavored syrup) for blood. In 1979, he had Tom Savini pouring on the red stuff by the bucket full. The violence in *Dawn* came fast and graphic. No amount of chopping, splattering, or chewing was shied away from. Everything was so extreme and so sharply done that there was no time for questions.

At the very end of the movie, when only two SWAT members survive (Ken Foree and Gaylen Ross); Romero gives a hint that the living dead are developing intelligence. That laid the way open for *Day of the Dead* (1985), which was supposed to be the concluding chapter of the series. In the early 1980s, Romero conceived it as taking place in a Florida retirement home where the now socially-functioning dead are being controlled by the more cunning living. The question is how to keep the dead fed … a question that has the elderly residents literally fighting for the remainder of their lives against both zombies and the weasels who would feed them to the living dead.

But that audacious vision was not to be. After realizing *Knightriders* (1981), his modern-day motorcycle take on *Camelot*, and slumming with Stephen King for *Creepshow* (1982), a campy EC Comic *Tales from the Crypt* variant, the *Day of the Dead* that reached screens in 1985 was a bunker-contained tale of soldiers trying to survive while their Code-Name-Trixie-type scientists attempted to either cure or train the zombies that had overridden the planet.

But essentially, Romero had shown others the way, then sat back as zombie king emeritus while his students out-mastered the master. Italy's *Zombi 2* (1979),

Sam Raimi's *Evil Dead* series (1981, 1987, 1992), Peter Jackson's *Dead Alive* a.k.a. *Braindead* (1992), Japan's *Versus* (2000), *28 Days Later* (2002), *Shaun of the Dead* (2004), *Zombieland* (2009) and even the *Dawn of the Dead* non-Romero remake (2004) are better than Romero's own three follow-ups (2005's *Land of the Dead*, 2007's *Diary of the Dead*, and 2010's *Survival of the Dead*).

But one thing is for certain. Without Romero, and his ground-breaking, critic-baiting work, none of those others would probably have been made. That still makes him king of the dead, and long may he reign.

PARASITE (1982)
Produced and Directed by Charles Band
Written by Alan Alder, Michael Shoob, and Frank Levering
Starring Robert Glaudini, Demi Moore, Luca Bercovici, Cherie Currie, and Vivian Blaine

This is probably the best 3-D movie and the worst hack horror film of its era. The 3-D technique was something new to him, but producer-director Band had been involved with hack horror films for years. The son of *Grave of the Vampire* maker Albert Band, Charles started doing his own films in 1977 with the subtly titled *Mansion of the Doomed*, directed by the ever-great Michael Pataki.

One "good" idea followed another, as Band produced one mediocre movie after the other. In cinema, there are "time-users," "time-consumers," and "time-wasters." Band was stuck squarely in the middle. He had some fun ideas but not much skill in making them pay off. There was 1977's *Crash* (not to be confused with the 2004 Oscar winner), starring Sue Lyon, José Ferrer, John Ericson, and in another cameo, John Carradine.

After Lyon brings home a supernatural relic from a "swap and shop" tag sale, its spirit possesses anything with wheels, including cripple Ferrer's wheelchair and the family auto. Since Ferrer lost the use of his legs in a car accident for which he blames Lyon, he tries to kill her while the possessed vehicle tries to kill him (this was no better than 1977's *The Car*, Universal's laughable effort about the "devil's limo" starring "Mr. Barbra Streisand" James Brolin).

Band went from running over José Ferrer to destroying earth in the aptly titled *End of the World* (1977). Before the planet actually explodes on screen in a ball of dirt and liquid, the audience must wade through eighty-one minutes of tired and tiring cross-plotting featuring an alien race who disguise themselves as priests and nuns. The world suffers this cataclysmic fate because the aliens decided, à la *The Day the Earth Stood Still* (1951 and 2008) that we had contaminated the universe.

Band continued to contaminate theaters with *Laserblast* (1978), the simple story of what can happen when a nerd stumbles across a pendant and ray gun that turn him into a blue-skinned executioner. Its short length was taken up with rampant ray gun destruction before two model-animated aliens put the boy out of our misery.

Band had quickly gained a reputation as an interesting hack horrorist on the basis of his movies' concepts and minor touches that made them bearable. Although the films were acknowledged cheapies, there always seemed to be something extra that showed where Band's heart lay. And he certainly didn't give up easy. Next on his hit parade was *Tourist Trap* (1979), a memorable sickie that combined *Carrie*, *Last House on the Left*, *Texas Chainsaw Massacre*, and *Charlie's Angels*.

Chuck Connors, TV's *Rifleman*, starred as the psychic, and psychotic, owner of a dusty desert "museum"—a road-side attraction—which lures three lovelies and their boyfriends to their deaths. Not only does Connors kill them with his strangling strength and an ax, but the mannequins that fill his house are brought to life with his mental powers. He covers some victims with plastic goo to make them mannequins as well.

The high point came when Tanya Roberts—soon to be a Charlie's Angel on the television show (1980), the new cinema *Sheena Queen of the Jungle* (1984) and James Bond girl in, arguably, the worst 007 film *A View to a Kill* (1985)—gets a knife in the back of the head that was thrown by a dummy.

Band hardly looked back. He was already producing *The Day Time Ended* (1980). Jim Davis (TV's *Dallas*) and Chris Mitchum (son of Robert) starred in the eager effort directed by the cool John Bud Cardos, who began in the Hal Roach *Our Gang* comedies, worked his way up to being an animal wrangler in Alfred Hitchcock's *The Birds*, co-starred in *Satan's Sadists*, stunted on the likes of *The Incredible Two-Headed Transplant*, and served on the second-unit for *The Wild Bunch* (1969) before making it to the director's chair.

After helming the fun but flawed *The Kingdom of the Spiders* (1977) and *The Dark* (1979), he led this film about a family living on a dimensional "fault line." Their home is bombarded by other-worldly occurrences until they decide to brave whatever the universe has in store for them, together. All Band's movies could be sloppy, arbitrary, and makeshift, but they had a certain vitality that kept most people from running out of the theater.

Parasite—one of the first movies Band personally directed—had the added "dimension" of fine 3-D effects supplied by the Stereovision company. Many prior 3-D movies required two cameras filming in perfect synchronization. Chris Condon's process needed only one camera, but glasses were still required to receive the effect (someone should invent prescription 3-D glasses for wealthy myopics who love bad movies). And some effects they were. It all hinged on a plot that had a renegade scientist running away from the all-powerful Zyrex Corporation in the near future.

He's running away because the company wants something he has in a thermos and his stomach. A group of seedy, futuristic bikers also want what the doctor has, thinking it must be worth a lot of money. As soon as they open the thermos, however, the title character leaps onto one of the gang's chests and starts munching away. The Parasite (nicknamed Perry by the crew) is essentially a giant booger with teeth. It is what one might come up with if one crossed a slug, a stingray, and a piranha. It completely empties the biker of his internal organs and then works its way through a female member of the gang.

Complicating matters is the baby booger in the doctor's stomach. He has to get rid of that before he can save the world from his other creation. Further messing up his mind is the Zyrex "hit-doc"—a corporate assassin with a PhD, assigned to kill the renegade and bring the Parasite back alive. The good doc (Robert Glaudini) battles the bikers, the hired gun, and the monster as glass seems to fly out into the theater and, in the most memorable moment, a pipe rammed into a bad guy's torso drips blood onto the audience' heads.

The central scene shows just how effective the 3-D is. Actress Vivian Blaine is combing her hair and doing her make-up while the Parasite climbs up the wall, then slithers across the room's ceiling. The camera looks up at it as grey sludge from its body drips down. The drops seem certain to splatter into the viewers' faces. The drops then dot the top of Blaine's fingers. She looks up and opens her mouth to scream. The Parasite goes right into her mouth. She looks at the audience. Her head explodes, and the monster shoots right out at you.

The Parasite is finally "destroyed" after latching onto the face of the hit man. The doctor and his girlfriend (Demi Moore) douse both creature and human killer with gasoline and set them aflame. Everything blows up at the end, but, as the black smoke swirls toward the sky, the viewers recall that the doc has said that even the Parasite's molecules would be enough to give rise to a horde of the things. The immediate danger is over, but the worst is yet to come. The End…?

In spite of some clever touches—like fuel costing forty dollars a gallon in the projected future—*Parasite* was received with the same critical responses Band's other films garnered. *Film Journal* called it "below average" and "strictly one-dimensional." The *Gore Gazette* put it in terms consistent with its content. "An annoying exercise in tedium containing … the most repellant … dialogue heard since Al Adamson's *Dracula Vs. Frankenstein*."

But almost everyone agreed with the film's executive producer, Irwin Yablans.

After viewing a rough cut, he was reported to have turned to the young hack horror veteran and complimented, "I think you've hit a new low."

And Band kept hitting as many lows as the medium would allow him. He has produced nearly two hundred and fifty films (and probably more by the time you read this)—for theaters, television, direct-to-video, and direct to DVD—with no signs of stopping. He had three films (*Demonic Toys 2*, *Puppet Master: Axis of Evil*, and *Killjoy 3*) set for release in 2010 alone. Bank, I'd like you to meet laughing Charles Band. Laughing Charles Band, Bank.

★★★ HELD OVER BY POPULAR DEMAND ★★★
David Cronenberg

The man who might have inspired Charles Band to scale the heights of low taste is this Canadian, whose films have set new standards for gore and the orifices that gore can come from. It is not surprising, therefore, that the first major film from a man now considered one of Canada's greatest film directors, was based on an idea that was originally going to be a sex film.

Cronenberg first called it *Orgy of the Blood Parasites*. European theaters advertised it as *The Parasite Murders*. Its Canadian title was *Shivers*. In the lower forty-eight we knew it as *They Came from Within* (1976). A parasite by any other name would smell as sickly. While most filmmakers start small and build their way up, Cronenberg's career seems to chart from the opposite direction. Although his films became more polished and professional as the years went on, nothing could match the visceral punch and abhorrent theme of this, his first major effort, following smaller films and Canadian TV assignments.

A mad scientist has developed a leech-like creature from a combination of an aphrodisiac and a venereal disease. It gets loose in the pristine, almost sterile environment of the residential "Starliner Towers—Just Twelve Minutes From Downtown Montreal." These things are particularly offensive-looking little "bugs" (as Cronenberg called them) whose purpose is not to eat human interiors—à la Band's 3-D Parasite—but to reawaken one's libido. What then could have become a sex comedy was transformed into pure horror by Cronenberg's concentration on how the parasites spread, rather than what fun they cause.

They start small, content to leap onto people when they least expect it. Then the transitions become a bit bolder. One appears through the drain of a bathtub and takes the opportunity to slither between the legs of the apartment building's resident lesbian (Barbara Steele). She transmits it in a kiss to Forsythe (Lynn Lowry, who also starred in *The Crazies*). The audience can see Steele's neck bulge as the bug moves up her throat and then Lowry's neck bulge as it goes down. But the most aggressive attack occurs upon the body of Nicholas Tudor (Alan Migicovsky).

At first his body cannot handle the slugs. Sickened, he runs to the balcony where he retches one of the critters up. It smashes down onto the clear plastic umbrella of an old lady below. Later, he comes to enjoy them, cooing as they move around his torso, beneath his skin. His wife is horrified to find one slithering out of his mouth.

She calls in Dr. Linsky (Joe Silver), who stares in amazement as the parasites break out from under Tudor's skin and then leap onto the doctor's face. He crashes about the apartment, screaming in pain, as the bugs try to burrow into him. He tries to rip them off using pliers, but they won't budge. His face is a blood-painted wreck by the time Tudor pulls them off and stuffs them back in his mouth.

This sort of logical extremism is part and parcel of *They Came from Within* and the director's on-going approach. The effects were created by special effects make-up artist Joe Blasco, who was once Lawrence Welk's make-up man. It was he who devised a system of balloon-like bladders beneath fake skin to create the lesbian neck and Tudor torso images. This was the same technique that the dean of American make-up men, Dick Smith, would use in *Altered States* (1980); Rob Bottin would use in *The Howling* (1981); and Rick Baker would use in *An American Werewolf in London* (1981).

The movie exists to detail the parasites' eventual triumph. The nominal hero of the piece is Dr. St. Luc (Paul Hampton), who is trapped by dozens of infected sex fiends in the swimming pool area. They drag him into their orgy and then merrily bundle into cars for the twelve-minute drive to Montreal. The message is clear. Cronenberg's and Band's parasites are going to spread until they meet someplace in the middle.

Cronenberg got more than his share of fireworks when the film was released, as did his producer, Ivan Reitman. The critical establishment made a run for the bathroom almost as one. That was nothing new to Reitman. Years before he had made a hack horror film called *Cannibal Girls* (1973), starring *Second City* comedy actors Eugene Levy and Andrea Martin. This film came complete with an unnecessary "Warning Bell: When It Rings, Close Your Eyes If You're Squeamish." He quickly learned the errors of his ways, finding his greatest success in comedy—producing, writing, and/or directing 1978's *Animal House*, 1979's *Meatballs*, 1981's *Stripes*, and 1984's *Ghostbusters* (right after producing the abortive *Ilsa the Tigress of Siberia*).

Canadian audiences vindicated him and Cronenberg by pushing the account books into the black, but the American version—somewhat abridged by its U.S.

distributors, American International—received only spotty distribution. Still, whatever American saw it, remembered it. While his producer tried his hand at comedy, Cronenberg replaced him with John Dunning and kept making horror.

Shivers' success led to *Rabid* (1977), the director's second contribution to the "cinema of the extreme." It served as X-rated actress Marilyn Chambers' first "mainstream" movie, and Americans' first real taste of what Cronenberg cooked up. Chambers played Rose, an innocent girl whose only crime is to be a victim of a motorcycle accident. She is taken to a nearby plastic surgeon (demented doctor Dan Keloid) who tests a new surgical device on her.

This unauthorized testing results in an organic syringe that lives in Rose's underarm. Whenever she gets close enough to be serious, the thing can pop out and suck blood from her victims. It isn't what the vampiric growth takes that causes trouble, but what it leaves: a rabies-like disease that can change a normal Joe into a goo-drooling demonoid.

Her first victim is fellow patient Lloyd Walsh (J. Roger Periard), who winds up attacking a taxi driver and dies in the subsequent crash. The night after her first attack, Rose wanders out of the hospital to a nearby farm, where she ravishes the owner. He starts spitting out yellow foam at a diner and must be forcibly subdued. Her third victim is the doctor who caused the problem in the first place. He later goes wacko in the operating room and starts biting all the medicos.

Rose's rabies not only forces yellow ooze to slop out of your eyes, but also makes you want to bite the ones you love. And if you can't be with the ones you love, honey, bite the ones you're with. The disease starts spreading all over town. The government steps in with martial law and Rose's boyfriend (Frank Moore) steps in to help. But Rose cannot believe that she is to blame for all the horror. Frightened and desperate, she takes another man, sucks his blood with her arm syringe, and waits to see if he becomes rabid. She calls her boyfriend with the news just as her victim changes. The boy listens as Rose is thrown from the building's window.

Rabid's final image is Rose's corpse being swept up with all the other human garbage. New World took on the American distribution this time, utilizing an impressive poster that pictured a bathing-suit clad girl frozen to death in a hospital refrigerator. Her open-eyed look of blue-skinned death brought gorehounds out by the bucketload. They lapped up *Rabid* (a.k.a. *Rage*) the same way the on-screen villains drooled colored Bromo-Seltzer.

Cronenberg made pictures gorehounds loved because he made them with the same artistic vision and dramatic skill that he would make with any movie—whether it was comedy or drama. He established often-outrageous ideas, then followed them through with unpitying logic and humanity.

HORROR

Cronenberg's second film was a greater success than his first, putting him in the enviable position of being the most successful director in Canada. Those in the Great White North had a different method of film production than the rest of the world—the Canadian Film Development Corporation (CFDC), which allows some directors easier access to budget money. Being in the catbird seat, Cronenberg pretty much got what he wanted.

What he wanted next was a car crash picture starring the venerable William Smith and Claudia Jennings, called *Fast Company* (1979). Sadly, it went almost nowhere, not even getting American distribution. But he made up for that by making *The Brood* (1979)—his most personal film to that time, and what many consider his finest hack horror achievement.

The magnificent Oliver Reed starred as Dr. Raglan, the head of the Somafree Institute of Psychoplasmics, where he taught his patients to manifest their inner anger as sores on their skin. He keeps Frank Carveth (Art Hindle) away from his insane wife Nola (Samantha Eggar), but demands that the Carveths' five-year-old daughter Candy (Cindy Hinds) visit once a week.

After finding bruises on the little girl's back, Frank decides that he must discredit Raglan in order to keep complete custody of the girl. He greatly fears that Candy will become a victim of child abuse just as Nola had been at the hands of her own mother (Nuala Fitzgerald). While he is investigating the Institute, Nola's mother is killed by a tiny figure in a red raincoat (looking similar to the murdering demon in director Nicholas Roeg's exceptional 1973 *Don't Look Now*).

Nola's estranged father arrives in Toronto for his ex-wife's funeral. He stays in his ex-wife's house. Under his ex-wife's bed is a tiny figure who kills the man as well. Frank rushes in, and the little thing almost kills him too, but suddenly expires. The autopsy reveals that the creature had a metabolism that simply ran out of power. It also has no gender or navel, so it couldn't have been conceived in the traditional manner.

The next to die is Candy's teacher (Susan Hogan). By now it has been established that whomever Nola hates is attacked by these little buggers. Nola hated the teacher because she is babysitting Candy when the mother calls. Nola assumed the woman was carrying on with her ex-husband so a pair of tiny, white-faced creatures kill her the next day and take Candy away with them.

Raglan has emptied the Institute of every patient except Nola. Frank breaks in that very night, only to be confronted by the gun-carrying doctor. He explains that the Brood are the manifestation—the children—of Nola's powerful rage. He realizes that there will be no controlling her, or them, unless something is done quickly. He promises to rescue Candy if Frank will divert Nola with loving lies.

Raglan gets as far as the Brood's room when Nola sees through the charade and gets mad. The Brood instantly attack and kill the doctor before he is able to free Candy from their clutches. Nola takes a moment to give birth to another child of rage—which hangs off her body in its own clear sack; a perverted version of pregnancy somewhat similar to *The Manitou*.

Nola bites the sack open and cleans the baby with her tongue. She tells her ex-husband that she would rather Candy die than stay with him. He strangles his ex-wife while the Brood jumps the child. The newly "born" Brood member is crushed between the Carveths' struggling bodies just before Nola dies. The rest of the Brood die with her. The father takes his crying daughter away from the Institute.

The Brood script came after some trying times in Cronenberg's personal life. He had a difficult custody battle for his own daughter, and the death of his father affected him deeply. Sadly, he felt the need to mar the otherwise satisfying ending with a close-up of Candy's arm—displaying the same welts that became her mother's Brood. The End...? Again.

Once *The Brood* was out of his system, Cronenberg returned to the project he had promised the CFDC before the killer children tale swept him away. It was a vision of powerful psychics battling a computerized corporation. It was *Scanners* (1981). Since the company was expecting this story before *The Brood*, the money was collected and the production scheduled far faster than anticipated. This caused filming to start without a finished script. Although he had more money than ever before and a fairly strong cast, Cronenberg was reeling under the strain of filming what had already been written, and trying to fit it into what was yet to be written or filmed. Doing this all out of sequence was like trying to juggle four balls with one eye and one arm.

What wound up rescuing the film from total confusion was Cronenberg's striking visual sense. The film had barely begun when the scene that turned out to be the centerpiece of the publicity campaign took place. After explaining that "Scanners" were men with incredible mental powers, a scanner played by Louis Del Grande attempts an example by reading the mind of an audience member, without knowing that the man he picked is Revok (Michael Ironside), an immensely powerful leader of renegade Scanners.

It only takes seconds before the rest of the corporate audience watching the presentation realizes that something is seriously amiss. Revok is sneering while Del Grande is shaking uncontrollably. A few moments later his head explodes.

The head explosion was soon abused in films like *Maniac* and *The Prowler*, among others, but Cronenberg hit the gorehounds where they lived with that one. It hardly mattered that the rest of the film didn't have his usual panache. Between the head detonation and the stunning climax, hack horror vets had as much as they could handle.

The imposing Patrick McGoohan plays Dr. Ruth, the head of the Consec Corporation, which wants to control the world's supply of Scanners. His lackeys are intent on the same goal, but not for altruistic reasons. They want to use the telepaths as weapons. Revok sees all normal people as inferior and wants to become leader of the world. Caught in the middle of it is Vale (Stephen Lack), who just wants to settle down with fellow Scanner Kim (Jennifer O'Neill) and make little scannees.

In order to do that, he must defeat Consec and Revok. He accomplishes the former by psychically overloading their massive computer through a phone line, causing the whole place to blow up. He does the latter after learning that he and Revok are brothers, and that the late Dr. Ruth—killed by his right-hand man—was their father.

Forget the coincidences that came out of left field. It is all just trappings for the psychic shootout the brothers have—a telepathic duel that makes their bodies do the strangest things. Make-up master Dick Smith was hired after the principal photography to work the mental wonders, and he all but saved the picture. Veins grow thick with blood, and squirt. Flesh rips off faces, revealing pulpy red bone and muscle. Hands sprout flames, and, in the final breath-holding moment, Vale's glowing eyes explode.

As comparatively realistic and well-delineated as that scene was, the finale remains perplexing. Kim enters the dueling room to find an unrecognizably burned corpse. She hears Vale's voice calling from behind a chair. When it is pushed around, it is Revok's unharmed body sitting there. For a split second there is a fear that Cronenberg had slipped in another surprise sad ending, but then Vale's voice makes it clear that he had somehow taken over his evil brother's mind. It doesn't make sense, but can be forgiven considering the rushed circumstances and what Cronenberg managed to get on-screen.

Although *Scanners* may be Cronenberg's weakest film structurally, it made a big enough splash to bring him to the attention of Universal Studios. This major distributed his next film *Videodrome* (1982), which was conceived as Cronenberg's magnum opus. But as soon as the powers-that-were took a look at his tale of "venereal horror" where a man's torso sprouts a vagina-like videotape slot, the censorship machetes started flying.

The finished film is a nearly incomprehensible mess whose one redeeming facet was to push Cronenberg out of exploitation films. While always dancing with the genre he obviously loves, his subsequent, mainstream movies (1983's *The Dead Zone*, 1986's *The Fly*, 1988's *Dead Ringers*) moved from existential explorations

(1991's *Naked Lunch*, 1996's *Crash*, 1999's *eXistenZ*) to lean, mean, crime thrillers (2005's *A History of Violence*, 2007's *Eastern Promises*).

As Cronenberg has forced the genre open with his bold concepts and even bolder visualizations, the industry has caught up with him. The majors have been prepared for his visions by the inferior variations on his work by far less talented people. But no one has been able—or willing—to match his patented screen combination of perverted science, perverted sex, and perverted violence. It is always exciting to see what he perverts next.

SHOCK WAVES (1977)
Produced by Reuben Trane
Directed by Ken Weiderhorn
Written by John Harrison and Ken Weiderhorn
Starring Brooke Adams, Peter Cushing, Fred Buch, and John Carradine

Weiderhorn took nearly everyone by surprise with this tight and atmospheric piece originally called *Death Corps*. Although he utilized many of the well-worn devices that seem like clichés in other films, he used them well enough to distinguish himself and his work. The revered Peter Cushing stars as an old scientist who has marooned himself on a Pacific island. Bitter, with a long facial scar, he is trying to come to terms with the fact that he created a team of superhuman Nazi soldiers who could breathe underwater.

Their Achilles heel, however, was their eyes. If ever they took off their dark goggles, the sun's rays would burn straight through their brains. Thankfully for the Allies in WWII, their submarine was sunk on its first mission. Unthankfully for a group of vacationing young folk who stumble onto Cushing's isle, they're not dead yet. It's open season on vacationers, as well as their creator and an old sea salt (Carradine).

The only survivor is played by Brooke Adams (a year before she broke through to movie stardom in *Days of Heaven*). The film opens in her hospital room with her soundtrack narration as she is writing her experience in a notebook. The twist at the end is the camera shows that what she was actually writing was gibberish—having been driven nuts by the ordeal.

Luckily, Weiderhorn did not go nuts making the film. He was one of several then-new directors who were trying to do more than just "break even" in terms of story and visualization. Another such hopeful, Don Coscarelli, wrote, produced, directed, photographed, and edited *Phantasm* (1980), a child's garden of imaginative gore. Telling it all from a kid's point of view, he managed to capture the elusive feeling of a particularly tragic fairy tale—the kind Grimm told that were very grim indeed. Highlights included a chopped-off finger that bled yellow gook and then gained a mind of its own, and a labyrinthine mortuary guarded by a flying metal ball that sprouted hooks and a brain-scrambling drill.

Frank LaLoggia is another inventive filmmaker who made three short subjects before graduating to *Fear No Evil* (1981)—a movie that did the likes of *The Omen* one better by actually detailing a fight between good and evil (rather than evil simply knocking off innocent bystanders one after another). Filming in and around Rochester, New York, LaLoggia filled his ultimately moralistic story with interesting fantasy touches, cleverly utilizing optical, as well as make-up, effects. It was the tale of three archangels reborn as human beings, intent on finding and destroying the human incarnation of Lucifer. Both this and Coscarelli's film show more imagination, invention, and promise than most of the major studios' hack horrors put together.

Their fates were telling. Ken Weiderhorn's promise was damaged by the Warner Communications' release of his *Eyes of a Stranger* (1981), starring Lauren Tewes (*The Love Boat*) as a television reporter who tracks down a savage rapist-murderer. Originally produced by Georgetown Productions before they released *Friday the 13th*, it was the success of the latter film that convinced them to hire Tom Savini to add gruesome inserts to the originally bloodless Tewes movie. Weiderhorn went on to make the likes of *Meatballs II* (1984) and *Return of the Living Dead Part II* (1988) before moving into television.

Coscarelli made lightning strike thrice, first with *The Beastmaster* in 1982, then with *Bubba Ho-tep* (2002), his amusing story of Elvis alive and well in a retirement home fighting a mummy. LaLoggia made only two more promising films: the evocative ghost story *Lady in White* (1988), and *Mother* (1996), a tale of maternal menace starring Diane Ladd and Olympia Dukakis.

SQUIRM (1976)
Produced by George Manasse
Directed and Written by Jeff Lieberman
Starring Don Scardino, Patricia Pearcy, R.A. Dow, Jean Sullivan, and Peter MacLean

A violent storm batters the tiny southern town of Fly Creek, Georgia. A power line is accidentally cut and pumps millions of volts into the sodden ground. This causes millions of "bloodworms"—the kind which move only at night—to wriggle from their subterranean lairs and start attacking humans.

The town's one hope is the visiting New York nerd played by Don Scardino, who discovers the wrath of the fishbait first. Discovering it second is actor R.A. Dow, portraying the redneck beau of the pretty Georgia peach (Patricia Pearcy) who invited the Manhattan man down in the first place.

Feeling threatened, he invites the girl out for some fishing. Just as he's about to show the girl how he feels, the worms burrow right into his face, wriggling up under his skin as she screams and runs into the woods. Besides the unique monsters, Lieberman's movie differentiates itself from the norm by having the macho-hero type become a villain and the, if you'll pardon the expression, bookworm becoming the hero.

As night approaches and the power lines are still zapping the dirt, the worms mass for an all-out obliteration of the town. *Squirm* sets itself apart again by pulling all the stops out at the climax. While many directors would have a few hundred worms carpeting the floor, Lieberman pictures tens of thousands of the slimy things. An entire wall made up of worms falls out of a bathroom door, and the house is filled by a mass of worms more than six feet thick!

But other than the excellent miniature photography to create close-ups of the bloodworms, and the sight of the beasties wriggling through a gore-encrusted skeleton that used to be a woman, the film falters at the conclusion. Characters who had no hope of survival are saved by crawling into a trunk, and climbing up a tree, when it was shown earlier that the worms could have circumvented the obstructions quite easily.

Even though the worms kill the girl's mother, the wounded redneck keeps the girl captive and lures the nerd to the attic. Their fight continues down the stairs until the nerd manages to throw the redneck into the worm ocean below. Although it looks like he drowned, the man manages to hold on until he slithers (like a worm) up the stairs and bites the nerd's leg (again like the worms) as he's escaping out a window. The nerd bashes his romantic rival with a flashlight and holds out with the girl until daybreak when the power lines are repaired and the worms go home … making for a finale that whimpers rather than bangs.

Lieberman's follow-up was just as original. Young people who had taken a certain hallucinogen called *Blue Sunshine* in college grew up to go completely bald and totally crazy. Zalman King starred in the 1977 movie, as a man who must trace blue sunshine to its source in order to solve the mystery before its side effects reach him too. Lieberman wove a political cover-up plot into the proceedings as well. The blue sunshine pusher is now running for government office and doesn't want his past to catch up with him. What does catch up with everybody are bald psychotics with butcher knives.

Lieberman's name and fame were cemented with gorehounds, but there was a surprising lack of product over the next few years. His following feature was the rarely seen *Just Before Dawn* (1982), a fairly traditional murder movie based on a supernatural script called *The Last Ritual*. Lieberman originally wanted his new film to be a cross between *Deliverance* (1972) and *Lord of the Flies* (1963) as five young campers fight for their lives against a pair of twin, inbred, mountain men with really big knives.

What resulted was a familiar "slasher loose in the woods" fest featuring the cameo performance of George Kennedy as a horse-riding park ranger. The only truly effective Lieberman touch came at the end after all but two of the kids are killed. In another personality switch reminiscent of *Squirm*, the good-looking guy (Gregg Henry) folds up in the face of the killer while the sweet innocent (Deborah Benson) fights the hulking brute on his own terms.

One mountain man survived after the park ranger shot the first. Bursting into their campsite, the killer slices into the "hero's" leg with his serrated machete, and then grabs the girl in a crushing bear hug. He soundlessly laughs up at her as she is being crushed to death. Seeing his open mouth, the girl slams her fist into it, pushing her fingers into his windpipe. She suffocates him to death with her arm deep in his throat.

It was a nice twist on the traditional, and a good end to an otherwise all too usual film. Lieberman pretty much left movies behind after that and moved on to television work.

WEREWOLVES ON WHEELS (1971)
Produced by Paul Lewis
Directed by Michael Levesque
Written by David M. Kaufman and Michael Levesque
Starring Stephen Oliver, Severn Darden, Billy Gray, and Barry McGuire

Of all the classic monsters, the werewolf seems to be one of the most fascinating and least successful. There is probably something to the fact that the werewolf represents the savage part of human nature. There's probably something else to the fact that many contradicting legends have grown up around it. And there's probably something to the fact that werewolf movies require extra cost in make-up and stuntwork.

One of John Landis' favorite lines in his *American Werewolf* comes after the leading character muses that a silver bullet is needed to kill him. His living dead friend tells him to get serious. Landis was maintaining that the concept of a silver bullet was ridiculous … after carefully establishing that a man turned into a wolf on the night of a full moon and must be killed in order for his living dead victims to rest in peace. After all that, what's so ridiculous about a silver bullet? Besides, consider the source. It was a living dead who said it. It might have been smarter, and more honestly funny, if the leading character had pointed that out.

While Landis and Joe Dante (1981's *The Howling*) directed their entertaining werewolf stories, hack horrorists have been attempting the legend for years. This combination of *Wolfman* and *Easy Rider* (1969) starred Stephen Oliver as the leader of the cutely-named Devil's Advocates motorcycle gang who gets in trouble because his "mama" (D.J. Anderson) is just too attractive to a coven of satanistic monks.

After a black magic ritual interrupted by the angry gang, Adam, the gang leader, is bitten by his "old lady." From then on, the other members of the gang are mangled by night. Only Tarot (Deuce Berry) has the supernatural knowledge necessary to save the day. Adam challenges him to a fight and stacks the odds in his favor by turning into a wolfman.

To back him up, his old lady turns into a wolf-woman. Tarot quickly leads the surviving gang members in a torching. Setting both ablaze with logs from the campfire, Adam goes flaming away on his motorcycle before crashing to his death. Not leaving well enough alone, Tarot then leads the group to take revenge on the monks. But any outfit that could change a motorcycle mama into a werewolf in one sitting is more than Tarot can handle. The Devil's Advocates become just that at the fade-out … in hell.

Not only was the motorcycle atmosphere different in this opus, but the presence of a female werewolf set it apart as well. Although different, it was not unique. There was also *Legend of the Wolfwoman* (1976), a creaky foreign clinker starring Anne Borel as a nice blond who grows fuzz and fangs almost every night. It told the supposedly true story of a woman who killed her sister's husband and others before being institutionalized in 1968.

Her problem was the certainty that she was a reincarnation of a werewolf that had died a century before. She has nightmares about the bestial murder of a man who turns out to look exactly like her brother-in-law. Sure enough, she soon sprouts carpeting across her naked form and kills him out in the garden. She is nearly saved by the young man who falls in love with her, but he is murdered by a trio who rape her. Her bestial nature reborn, she slaughters the three and dances in a ring of fire in the forest until the authorities find her.

As unconvincingly produced as that was, it couldn't hold a candle to *The Werewolf Vs. the Vampire Woman* (1971), another Spanish film starring Paul Naschy. Two doctors make the mistake of removing the silver bullet from the heart of a dead werewolf. Like his brethren the vampire—who is reborn if the stake is pulled from his heart—this wolfman kills the curious men and escapes.

His simple life of murdering the populace is complicated when a girl accidentally drops some blood on the skull of a long-dead vampiress. That method, apparently, will also do the resurrection trick. The two monsters murder people at cross-purposes until the finale, when they decide that the Spanish countryside isn't big enough for the two of them.

American theaters were big enough for two more home-grown werewolf exploiters. *The Boy Who Cried Werewolf* (1973) starred Kerwin Matthews (1958's *The 7th Voyage of Sinbad*) as a lycanthrope who made life hard for a little boy who can't convince anyone of his existence. And 1975's *The Werewolf of Washington* (a.k.a. *Werewolf at Midnight*) starring Dean Stockwell and Clifton James, had an ambitious wolfman who managed to sink his claws into the President. Insert your own political joke here.

THE WORM EATERS (1977)
Produced by Ted V. Mikels
Directed and Written by Herb Robins
Starring Herb Robins, Barry Hostetler, Lindsay Armstrong Black, and Joseph Sackett

This part started with T.V. Mikels, so it's fitting that it should end with him as well. The industry hadn't heard much from the exploiter since *The Doll Squad*, but this little curiosity caught everyone's eye. Termed a "laff riot," it is Herb Robins' baby. In addition to writing and directing, Herb starred in this story of worms versus humanity.

Hermann Umgar is the name of the old man who lives near a forest lake. He eats with, sleeps with, talks to, and tends thousands of worms who live in an old water tower. All is peachy in the town of Melnick, California, until Mayor Sunny Melnick hatches a plan to re-zone the lake and build condominiums.

That destroys Umgar's long-range happiness—and his short-term happiness is marred with the arrival of a wealthy family on vacation. The father is a doof, the mother is a banshee, and the two beautiful daughters are spoiled silly. All the young girls want is hot dogs, and all the older woman wants is "eggs with no goo in them!"

Although miserable, Umgar hatches a plan to have all his worms eat the community's crops so the town will be bankrupt and therefore unable to level the beautiful forest. Before he can implement his decision, however, three strange-looking human-shaped things surround his bed late one night. They reveal themselves to be the Champion Bass Fishing Club men who disappeared months before.

They tell him that they are now worm-men (after having eaten some bass caught with Umgar's worms). They live under the red tide in the lake and demand worm-women to mate with. Umgar strikes a bargain. If they will eat the crops, he will get them mates. His first victim is a waitress who sucks up some Umgar worms he snuck into her spaghetti. He sticks worms inside hot dogs, thereby capturing the two rich daughters. He gets their mother as well by slipping a worm into her favorite cream-filled dessert. He keeps all four in a specially built cage.

He is content and assured that the crops are as good as gone when he hears a radio report that the Mayor will start working on the condominiums immediately. Enraged, he races into town and starts dropping worms into hamburgers, fried chicken, ice cream, chocolate malts, chewing tobacco, and tequila (of course).

The entire town is turning wormy as the Mayor grabs his gun and goes after Umgar. He meets up with the caged worm-women instead, and is consumed by them. All is right in Umgar's world until a fish hook sinks into his neck, and he is reeled out to the lake by the worm-men. They force feed him his own worms and then raid the town to rape and pillage women in their beds, their kitchens, and their showers.

Alone and wormy, Umgar slithers through the woods to consume all the crops by himself. Only, when he gets to the highway, he is splattered against a truck's windshield in what the distributors call "one of the most horrifying messes ever seen on film."

Quite a fitting finale for the movie … and the world of exploitation films.

POSTFACE

The exploitation film is dead … long live the exploitation film.

The golden age of the independently-produced exploitation film wasn't really about the films themselves—it was an unwritten, unspoken pact between the audience and, mostly, the distributor. It was the latter's job to get the former into the theater, and the former's task to find what entertainment they could.

It was like Charlie Brown and that damn football Lucy would hold for him to kick every autumn for fifty years. Every year he would somehow convince himself that Lucy wouldn't pull the pigskin away at the last second … but every year she would, sending Charlie flying up, only to crash back down. But the next year, there she'd be with the football again … and there he'd be, too.

We were Charlie Brown, and the exploitation filmmakers were Lucy. And just like Charlie, we probably came to appreciate the pattern … even revel in it. We had somehow learned by osmosis that these films represented freedom. Even making a terrible full-length feature requires ridiculous effort, and the makers suffer the creative death of a thousand duck bites, sometimes every exhausting day. But even the worst of them were somehow better, and more vindicating, than the hundreds of soulless, pandering, cynical junk-heaps the major studios were grinding out.

But that's all over now … yet it isn't. Small, independent, films (mostly horror) are still taking audiences by hundred-million-dollar surprise (1999's *The Blair Witch Project* and 2007's *Paranormal Activity* being just two), but no one's really being tricked into seeing them anymore. Misleading ad campaigns are all the purview of the major studios now, who have learned their lessons quite well, and are using them to push romantic comedies.

Besides, making a film is easier than ever, and the medium for them to be seen is pervasive. You can see exploitation films, of any length, or genre, on your TV, PC, phone, or similar device via the Web anytime. But the real problem for the future of exploitation films is a matter of content and style.

You want sex, drugs, and rock 'n' roll? Check out MTV/VH1's increasingly demoralizing "date" and "subculture" shows. You want violence? Check out any of CBS' *CSI* shows, Fox's *Bones* and *House*, or even on Cartoon Network's *Adult Swim*. You want horror? Vampires, zombies, werewolves, oh my, are all over movies and TV. At least three major filmmakers—Danny DeVito, Sam Raimi, and Joel Silver—had their own low-budget gore mini-studios.

When one episode of the fifteen-minute *Tim and Eric's Awesome Show, Great Job* (also on *Adult Swim*) out-grosses-out John Waters' entire oeuvre, what possible chance does the classic tradition of crummy exploitation films have? You want to know just how toothless the once-scandalous exploitation films in this book have become? In the time it took to rewrite and republish this book, a bunch of them have been shown, without a cut, on the prestigious Turner Classic Movies cable channel. But that's just as well. To be honest, most of the movies made during this convulsive era were far better to read or hear about than actually see (you're welcome).

But make no mistake. Then as now, the exploitation film will never die. Because it calls attention to the lies we all live. Lies of civility, hypocrisy, insincerity, insecurity, pretense, duplicity, greed, fear, desire, and stupidity. Russ Meyer laughed at it, Herschell Gordon Lewis tore at it, Wes Craven screamed at it, Tobe Hooper tortured it, George Romero savaged it, and John Waters threw up on it.

Long may many continue to do the same.

Ric Meyers
January 2011

Index

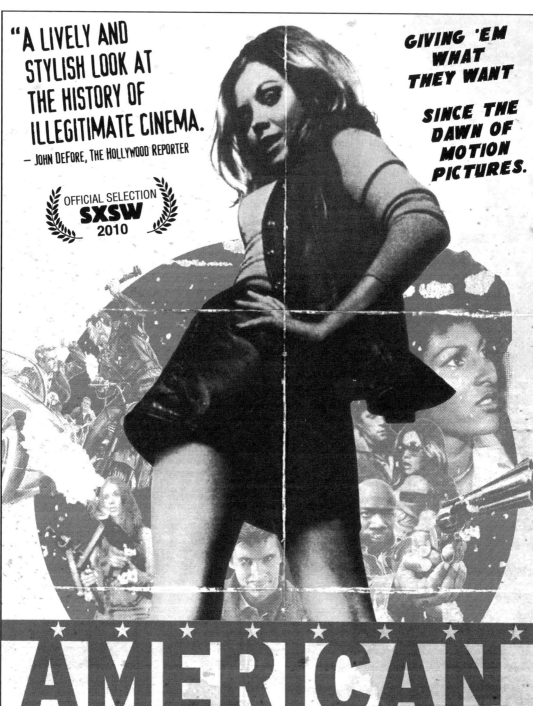

Made in the USA
Charleston, SC
05 November 2011